Natural Cooking
the Old-Fashioned Way

The Autograph Collector
Marijuana: 101 Things You Should Know
Free for Housewives
Complete Gypsy Fortune Teller
Complete Book of Voodoo
How to Go to High School or College by Mail
What Your Handwriting Reveals
What Your Child's Handwriting Reveals
Telling Fortunes with Cards
Free for Teens
Voodoo Secrets from A to Z
Natural Baking the Old-Fashioned Way
Lost Secrets of Astrology
Your Future—Your Fortune

Natural Cooking the Old-Fashioned Way

Robert W. Pelton

South Brunswick and New York: A. S. Barnes and Company
London: Thomas Yoseloff Ltd

© 1975 by A. S. Barnes and Co., Inc.

A. S. Barnes and Co., Inc.
Cranbury, New Jersey 08512

Thomas Yoseloff Ltd
108 New Bond Street
London W1Y OQX, England

Library of Congress Cataloging in Publication Data

Pelton, Robert W.   1934–
    Natural cooking the old-fashioned way.

    1. Cookery. I. Title.
TX715.P39   641.5   73-112
ISBN 0-498-01274-3

PRINTED IN THE UNITED STATES OF AMERICA

Dedicated to

some of the earlier members of my family
—the Peltons, Mitchells, Collisters, Northrups, Daniels, and Tylers;

and especially to

Barnabus Horton of Leichestershire, England,
who came to America on the ship *Swallow*
some time between 1633 and 1638 with his
wife Mary and two children, Joseph and Ben-
jamin. They landed at Hampton, Massachusetts, and were Puritans;

and also to

my Great-Great-Grandmother Huldah
(Radike) Horton, one of the finest and most
famous horsewomen of her day. She rode with
Lafayette in a parade in his honor in Newburgh, New York, in 1824. The French general and friend of the young country was
making his second and last visit.

Contents

Preface 9

A Note on Natural Ingredients 11

English Equivalent Measures 17

1. Soup-Making the Natural Way 19
2. Old-Fashioned Fish Cookery 34
3. Vegetable Preparation the Natural Way 52
4. Old-Fashioned Beef Cookery 68
5. Veal Cookery the Natural Way 84
6. Old-Fashioned Lamb Cookery 96
7. Pork Cookery the Natural Way 103
8. Old-Fashioned Poultry Cookery 116
9. Egg Cookery the Natural Way 131
10. Old-Fashioned Fried Cakes and Fritters 140
11. Salad-Making the Natural Way 148
12. Old-Fashioned Puddings and Sauces 156
13. Fish and Meat Sauces the Natural Way 169
14. Old-Fashioned Beverages 179
15. Sandwich-Making the Natural Way 186
16. Old-Fashioned Ice Cream 193
17. Dessert-Making the Natural Way 200

7

18. Old-Fashioned Preservatives and Jellies   209
19. Catsup, Mustard, and Vinegar the Natural Way   218
20. Old-Fashioned Pickling   227
21. Homemade Candy-Making the Natural Way   237
22. Old-Fashioned Miscellaneous Recipes of Importance 244
Index   253

Preface

The start of many serious human ills occurs at the average table with the consumption of unwholesome food. Prevention is certainly better than cure. Special attention, therefore, must always be given to the proper preparation of more healthful, as well as palatable, meals.

The knowledge concerning proper food and diet has been advanced increasingly in recent years. In these days of enlightenment, many people are taking up the sound idea of natural cooking and of eating only chemically free, pure foods. They are putting natural cookery into practical everyday use. It is fast becoming more apparent that uncontaminated unadulterated foods are essential to our well being.

Great progress has been made toward understanding the body and the basic laws governing it. As man unfolds spiritually, he comes to question more seriously the rightness of chemically treated, impure foods, as part of his daily fare.

Natural Cooking the Old-Fashioned Way is a book designed for the average person—of average means, desires, and resources. The economics of the kitchen are certainly not below the dignity of anyone who honestly wishes to make the most of opportunity without extravagance.

Every recipe given herein was a favorite in days gone by.

Many were carefully treasured for years and handed down through the family over a number of generations. They were used by my great-grandmothers Pelton, Mitchell, Shaw, Collister, and those earlier relatives who came before them— the Hortons, Northrups, and Daniels, to name but a few. Other recipes are classics in the historical sense for they were known to be the favorites of, or inventions of, notable families from the distant past. Each recipe is completely concocted with natural and unadulterated ingredients. All are appetizing and healthful.

Tainted, commercial frozen and canned foods, so widespread in today's supermarkets, can in no way be compared to natural foods for palatability or nutritional value. They are loaded with unnatural preservatives and numerous chemical additives. The distinct superiority of natural foods is widely recognized. The advantages of this type of diet are no longer a matter of experimentation. The prevalence of disease and sickness is leading thousands of thinking people to turn in this direction.

Good natural food cookery is not the result of accident or a form of good luck. There is a reason in every process. A simple course in psychology certainly does not make one a psychologist. Nor will a collection of choice natural recipes automatically make a top notch cook. One must be willing to try—to engage in the real "doing." Theory alone will not suffice. But experience, which practice only can give, is of the utmost importance.

Natural Cooking the Old-Fashioned Way contains, as the title suggests, only natural food preparation methods—cooking with nothing except pure, unadulterated foods. These foods are those that *do not* contain dangerous chemical preservatives, synthetic flavorings, and artificial color additives. All who will give natural cooking a fair trial will find a wholesome diet of these foods both pleasing and more healthful.

A Note on Natural Ingredients

Each ingredient called for in these healthful old-time recipes is listed in its most commonly used form for convenience of understanding. Nevertheless, every ingredient should be pure, chemical-free, and without unnatural preservatives. Every item is relatively easy to procure. Many can now be obtained in regular supermarkets—often in a special section reserved for natural foods. Others are readily found in any good health food or natural food store. They are also available through mail-order outlets. An excellent guide to natural food sources is available for $1.00 from: Rodale Press, 33 East Minor Street, Emmaus, Pa. 18049.

Commercial Item   *Natural Counterpart*

Baking powder   Use only those brands containing no
                   aluminum compounds
                            or
                   Substitute 2 egg whites for every tea-
                   spoon of baking powder called for.

11

Baking soda	Many people prefer using baking powder instead. Baking soda is generally avoided because it is believed to destroy B vitamins in other foods. If baking powder is substituted use 2 teaspoons for every 1/2 teaspoon baking soda
	or
	Substitute 1 or 2 tablespoons yeast.
Brown sugar	Natural brown sugar or honey
Butter	Raw or natural butter. Some people prefer natural margarine over any kind of butter. See *Margarine*.
Cheese	Natural cheese made from raw milk. Any cheese without chemical additives. Any cheese not labeled "processed."
Chocolate	Pure chocolate or substitute carob powder. Carob is wholesome and readily digested. It is richer than chocolate in protein and lower in starch and fat. Carob is stronger in flavor. Use less when substituting in recipes.
Coconut	Unsweetened coconut, freshly grated.
Cooking oil[1]	Any nonhydrogenated liquid vegetable oils. Cold-pressed oils are higher in essential fatty acids. They are free of all preservatives. Try:
	Cold-pressed corn oil
	Cold-pressed olive oil
	Cold-pressed sesame oil
	Cold-pressed soy oil
	Pure safflower oil (an all purpose oil)

---

1. Preservatives are usually added to prevent rancidity.

Cornmeal (degermed)[2]	Coarse ground cornmeal or whole corn kernels. Can be ground at home. Contains the germ of the kernel.
Corn starch	Arrowroot starch is preferred.
Cottage cheese	Natural cottage cheese. (Recipes can be found in Chapter 22.)
Eggs[3]	Eggs produced by laying hens raised with a rooster. Such eggs are called "fertile" and contain important enzymes as well as hormones.
Fish[4]	Deep-sea fish and so-called bottom fish are the only kinds considered to be safe for eating. Or those fish caught in out of the way mountain streams and lakes.
Flour[5] also called *wheat flour*	Unbleached flour. Contains no foreign preservatives or bleaches. Has not been chemically treated in any manner. *Note:* seal in plastic bags or jars to preserve its freshness. Can also be frozen.
Fruit	Organic fruits or those organically grown. Fruit grown without chemical fertilizers or sprays. Use fresh fruit or pure home-canned varieties.

2. Refined to a point where it has little nutritional value. Made from sterile hybrid corn.
3. Eggs are usually sprayed with disinfectant.
4. Generally toxic because of pollution of the coastal areas, lakes, and rivers.
5. Overrefined wheat product. Contains chemical bleaches.

Honey	Unfiltered, unblended, uncooked honey. It has more minerals and enzymes.
Macaroni and spaghetti[6]	Soy macaroni and spaghetti. Unbleached wheat macaroni and spaghetti. Sesame macaroni and spaghetti.
Margarine	Natural margarine. Any good margarine made without chemical additives. One of the best is made from soybean extracts. Some people like to use corn germ oil as a substitute in recipes.
Meat[7]	Naturally fed meats. From animals not injected with chemicals. Called organically grown or organic meat. *Note:* Sweetbreads, liver, kidney, tongue, and heart are the richest in B vitamins.
Milk[8]	Raw milk, preferably from a certified dairy herd. If unavailable, fortify regular milk with powdered milk.
Molasses	Unsulphured molasses. Blackstrap molasses is one of the best to use. It contains valuable minerals and B vitamins. Has a strong flavor.
Oats	Old-fashioned rolled oats, unhulled oats, oat groats, or steel-cut oats. Never use commercially processed oatmeal. Rolled oats are simply the flattened whole oat kernels.

6. Commercial products made with bleached flour, often containing chemical preservatives.

7. Avoid prepackaged meats and prepared luncheon meats. Luncheon meats contain questionable ingredients and are heavily saturated with chemical additives.

8. Pasteurized milk has reduced calcium. Enzymes and hormones are destroyed in processing. Preservatives are often added to the milk.

Peanut butter	Nonhydrogenated peanut butter.
Poultry	Poultry (chickens, turkeys, etc.) that have not been injected with antibiotics.[9] And those raised on natural feed. Known as organically grown poultry.
Rice	Natural brown rice tastes better and it is much more nutritional. Wild rice, or as a final choice, "converted" rice.
Salad oil	See *Cooking oil*.
Salt	Sea salt or unrefined salt. Contains important trace elements lacking in most diets. Sea salt does not contain chemicals as does ordinary table salt.
Shortening[10]	Pure safflower shortening.
Spices and herbs	Use commercial dried herbs and spices. They are generally pure. Fresh herbs may be home grown (in a garden or pots).
Starch	Arrowroot starch is generally preferred over corn starch.
Sugar	Natural or raw sugar. Honey is often substituted for sugar in a recipe. If it is, use only 2/3 the amount of sugar called for.
Vanilla or other flavorings	Use only extracts. All extracts must be pure according to federal law.

9. California recently passed legislation forbidding this practice.
10. Often contains chemical additives. Carefully check label.

Vegetables[11]	Organic vegetables or those organically grown. Vegetables grown without chemical fertilizers or sprays. Use fresh vegetables or pure home-canned varieties.
Wheat flour	See *Flour*.

---

11. Frozen or canned commercial vegetables contain chemical preservatives or other unsavory additives.

English Equivalent Measures

	American	English
1 cup of breadcrumbs (fresh)	1½ oz.	3 oz.
1 cup of flour or other powdered grains	4 oz.	5 oz.
1 cup of sugar	7 oz.	8 oz.
1 cup of icing sugar	4½ oz.	5 oz.
1 cup of butter or other fats	8 oz.	8 oz.
1 cup of raisins, etc.	5 oz.	6 oz.
1 cup of grated cheese	4 oz.	4 oz.
1 cup of syrup, etc.	12 oz.	14 oz.

1 English pint	20 fluid ounces
1 American pint	16 fluid ounces
1 American cup	8 fluid ounces
8 American tablespoons	4 fluid ounces
1 American tablespoon	½ fluid ounce
3 American teaspoons	½ fluid ounce
1 English tablespoon	⅔ to 1 fluid ounce (approx.)
1 English tablespoon	4 teaspoons

The American measuring tablespoon holds ¼ oz. flour

17

1
Soup-Making the Natural Way

Points on Making Old-Time Natural Soups

Colonel Ben Thurston, a veteran New England tavern owner of the early 1800s and friend of my Great-great-grandmother Horton, used to brag that he always gave his guests a good soup to start dinner with. In his estimation, this saved a good deal later in the bill of fare.

Berdan's Sharpshooters were Swiss riflemen of note who saw service during the winter of 1861 and 1862 in Washington. These men were praised for their robust health. Captain Trepp, their commander, himself a veteran Swiss soldier, said it was because they all knew how to make a good soup, which our Yankee soldiers knew nothing about.

Soups were an important addition to every table in early America, and there were certain rules to be followed for making a better-than-average soup. My great-great-grandmother never allowed the water into which meat was put to boil for 1/2 hour or more. She heated it slowly so the juices from the meat could be properly extracted. But once

19

the water did reach the boiling point, she simmered it until the soup was finished.

For a good natural soup of average richness, 1 quart (4 cups) of water to 1 pound of meat is about right. Of course the less water used the richer the soup will be. And soft water, as a rule, makes much better soup than does hard water.

Different vegetables require different amounts of time for proper cooking. Notice must be taken of this fact before the vegetables are put into the soup stock. Onions may be put in with the meat. Carrots and celery are never put in until the soup has boiled for at least 3 hours. Turnips are put in about a 1/2 hour before the soup is done.

Great-Grandmother Mitchell's Old-Fashioned Soup Stocks

NOTES ON OLD-TIME NATURAL SOUP STOCKS

Natural soup stock can be made with meat procured especially for this purpose, or as it so often was in the old days, from trimmings and leftovers. Every early American kitchen had a "catch all." One or two large bowls, or deep earthen dishes—provided they were clean and did not leak—best answered the purpose. Today a sealed plastic bag or container will suffice.

Recycle all of your scraps. After breakfast or dinner, do not throw away the remnants of steaks or roasts on the platters. Look them over carefully. Put aside any pieces that can be used again. Then put in all the bones, trimmings, gristle, fat, and such, especially the platter gravy, into the "catch all." If you have just one bone from a steak or chop, and if it isn't burned, it is well worth saving. Most butchers will *give* you chicken feet and various bones, often free for the asking. If you have boiled a fresh tongue, fowl, leg of lamb, etc., save the water for making soup.

MAKING OLD-FASHIONED NATURAL MEAT STOCK

As a rule, use beef, for *brown stock*. Take off all of the fat. Cut the meat in small pieces. Crack the larger bones. Soup bones are inexpensive (sometimes free) and available in the markets. Marrow bones should also be cracked and the marrow taken out. It is the best kind of fat for soup stocks. The best bones for making good stock are shoulder, ribs, back, etc.

In adding the remnants of cooked meat, care should be taken to remove the burned or smoked parts, and the stuffing, if there is any. Put the meat, bones, etc., into cold water in a tightly covered kettle. Let it all soak for 1 hour. Then simmer, but do not boil, for several hours. It is not essential that the "scum" is removed, if the ingredients are clean and unspoiled at the start. Scum due to any other cause than dirt is the very material we are seeking. The fat may be skimmed off when the stock has cooled.

Seasoning for old-time soup stock is generally 1 teaspoon salt, 1/2 teaspoon white or black pepper, 2 allspice corns, a little celery seed or flakes, and such dried herbs as are fancied—sage, savory, thyme, marjoram, and bay leaves. These herbs can be varied to suit any taste. It is unwise to use vegetables for flavoring the stock. After the basic stock is made it can be flavored for each specific type of soup as desired.

When the meat has simmered until all the juice is drawn out, strain the stock. If the water has boiled away more than half, the stock may be diluted when used as the basis for any type soup.

WHITE STOCK

White soup stock is made from veal or fowl. Any seasoning that would discolor it should be avoided. Milk or cream is often used to enrich it. Young veal bones or any good marrow bones are excellent. Chicken feet or backs are wonderful for making old-fashioned white stock. Chicken feet, when available, are usually given away free. Backs are very inexpensive. Almost any kind of delicious natural soup can be made from a basic brown stock or a basic white stock.

A great number of people will not use most herbs found in the usual soup recipes. Nor are they absolute essentials. The herbs are relatively easy to obtain, but some are rather expensive. And the delicate results attained by using them are not fully appreciated by the average palate. So the fact that herbs are specified in a recipe need not prevent usage. Try it without the herbs if you do not have them on hand.

Making Delicious Old-Fashioned Natural Soups

MARTHA WASHINGTON'S WHITE ALMOND SOUP

4 pounds veal knuckle	1 tablespoon butter
1 onion, sliced	1 1/2 tablespoons corn
2 celery stalks, cut up	starch
1 sprig of parsley	1 cup cream
1 tablespoon salt	1/2 cup blanched almonds
6 peppercorns	finely pounded

This was a much-loved old recipe originating with the young nation's *first* First Lady. Cut the veal knuckles into small pieces. Break or saw the bones into small pieces. Put into a large soup kettle with 3 quarts cold water. Simmer for 4 hours. Add the vegetables and seasoning. Let it all simmer for 1 more hour. Strain. When cool, skim off the grease and put on the stove to heat again. Cream together the butter and corn starch. Add this to the boiling soup. Cook for 10 minutes and then take off the fire. Stir in the cream. Salt and pepper to taste. Add the almonds and serve immediately.

GREAT-GREAT-GRANDMOTHER HORTON'S CALF'S-HEAD SOUP

1 calf's head	1 piece celery root
1 tablespoon salt	1 teaspoon marjoram or
6 whole cloves	thyme
6 peppercorns	1 teaspoon pepper
6 allspice	2 cups brown stock
1 cinnamon stick	2 tablespoons butter
2 small onions	2 tablespoons flour
1 carrot	3 eggs, hard-boiled
1 turnip	1 egg, well beaten

Slowly boil the calf's head, dressed with the skin on, in 4 quarts water and the salt. When done, let it cool. Cut the face meat into small pieces and chop it very fine. Set this aside for later making meatballs. Now add the cloves, peppercorns, allspice, cinnamon, and vegetables to the soup. Simmer until it is reduced to 2 quarts of liquid. Strain and let cool. Then skim off the grease and put the soup on to boil. Season with the marjoram or thyme and pepper. Salt to taste. Blend the butter and flour. Add it to the brown stock as a thickener. Stir this into the soup.

Take the hardened yolks from the boiled eggs, or simply cut the whole eggs into 1/4-inch slices. Then make meatballs from the meat previously set aside. Season the meat highly and add the beaten egg to moisten the meat. The meatballs should be about the size of a hickory nut. Sprinkle them with flour. Brown some butter in a frying pan. Fry the meatballs until browned. Put the meatballs and egg balls or slices into the tureen.[1] Pour the soup over this and serve while very hot. *Note:* A glass of wine is sometimes added to this soup for additional flavor.

POTATO POT SOUP OF COLONIAL DAYS

1 slice bacon
beef leftovers
1 onion, sliced

1 bay leaf
sprig of parsley
2 large potatoes, diced

Cut the bacon slice into small pieces and put it in a frying pan. Add the beef scraps and onion. Stir until everything has browned nicely. Put these ingredients into a soup kettle with 6 cups cold water. Add the bay leaf and parsley. Simmer gently for 1 hour. Strain. Add the potatoes. Boil for 10 minutes. Season with salt and pepper to taste. Serve while hot.

GREAT-GRANDMOTHER SHAW'S OXTAIL SOUP

2 oxtails
1 onion, cut fine
4 cloves
4 peppercorns

1 tablespoon Bouquet
Garni[2]
1 tablespoon salt

Oxtails can be readily purchased in any market. Wash

---

1. Table bowl
2. Thyme, bay leaves, and parsley blended and tied in a piece of cheesecloth.

them carefully and cut up at the joints. Brown with the
onion in hot beef drippings. Then put into a kettle containing 4 quarts cold water. Add all the spices. Simmer
slowly until the meat separates from the bones. Skim off
the grease and then strain the soup. Serve while hot. *Note:*
Numerous vegetables can be cooked in this soup if desired.
Some of the oxtail pieces should be served with the soup.

GREAT-GRANDMOTHER MITCHELL'S MOCK TURTLE SOUP

2 cups black beans
6 slices salt pork
1 onion, sliced
1 pound lean beef
2 carrots, sliced

2 turnips, sliced
12 cloves
2 hard-boiled eggs, sliced
1 lemon, sliced

Soak the beans overnight. The next morning fry the salt
pork and onion until both are browned. Cut the beef into
small pieces. Put these into a kettle with 5 quarts cold
water. Now put in the pork and onion. Simmer slowly for
3 hours. Add the vegetables and cloves. Simmer for another
hour. Then strain and return to the stove. Take the eggs
and lemon and place them in a tureen. Season the soup to
taste with salt and pepper. Pour it over the eggs and lemon.
Note: Many old-timers added a small glass of wine to this
soup.

REVOLUTIONARY PERIOD POOR MAN'S SOUP

4 tablespoons beef
    drippings
1/4 cup butter

3 cups potatoes, sliced
1 head white cabbage,
    shredded

This was a common soup prepared by soldiers in the field during the Revolutionary War. It was considered a necessary evil, and, although it tastes quite good, was disliked by many of Washington's veterans. Put the drippings, butter, and potatoes into a kettle containing 4 quarts boiling water. Boil for 1 hour. Then put the torn cabbage leaves in the soup and allow it to boil for 10 more minutes. Season to taste with salt and pepper, and serve while hot.

GREAT-AUNT SHIRLEY'S
PUREE OF GREEN PEA SOUP

1 slice salt pork	1 bay leaf
1 onion, sliced	1 teaspoon pepper
1 carrot, sliced	4 cups chicken stock
1 celery stalk, cut up	2 cups young peas
3 sprigs of parsley	1/2 cup cream
1 sprig of thyme	1 tablespoon butter
2 whole cloves	

Put the salt pork in a pot over the fire. Fry to a light brown. Add all the vegetables and spices. Fry together until the vegetables turn a delicate brown. Then drain off the surplus grease. Add the chicken stock and peas. Let the soup simmer for 1 hour. Remove it from the stove and strain. Now blend in the cream—heated to scalding—and the butter. Serve with little square croutons of fried bread.

EARLY AMERICAN CHICKEN SOUP SUPREME

1/2 cup bread or cracker crumbs[3]	1 cup roast chicken, finely chopped[4]
1 cup cream	3 egg yolks
2 cups strong chicken stock	1 teaspoon salt
	1/2 teaspoon pepper

---

3. Many excellent recipes for old-time homemade breads and crackers can be found in *Natural Baking the Old-Fashioned Way*, by the same author.

4. Recipe in Chapter 8

Soak the crumbs in the cream. Put the chicken stock in a kettle and bring to a boil. Add the pieces of chicken. Drop the egg yolks carefully into a pot of boiling water (*not the stock*). Leave until they are hard. Then remove the yolks and rub them to a powder. Add to the soup with the soaked crumbs and cream, salt and pepper. Simmer for 10 minutes. Serve while very hot.

GREAT-AUNT DORIS MARIE'S DUCHESS DELIGHT SOUP

2 slices carrot	1/4 cup flour
2 slices onion	1 teaspoon salt
blade of mace	pinch of pepper
4 cups white stock	2 cups milk, hot
1/4 cup butter	1/2 cup mild cheese, grated

Put a little butter in a cast iron skillet and sauté the carrot and onion. Reduce the heat and cover the pan. Allow to briefly steam. Add these vegetables and the mace to the stock. Cook for 15 minutes. Strain through a collander. Blend the butter and flour together. Put into the soup to thicken it. Add the salt, pepper, hot milk, and cheese. Stir well and serve while hot.

REAL OLD-FASHIONED CREAMED RICE SOUP

3/4 cup brown rice	1 celery stalk, cut up
8 cups chicken stock	2 cups milk
1 onion, chopped	2 cups cream

Wash the rice and put it in the chicken stock. Add the onion and celery. Bring to a boil and then let simmer for 2 hours. When finished, strain through a sieve. Put the milk and cream in a saucepan and bring it to a boil. Stir this into the stock. Season to taste with salt and pepper. *Note:* A double amount of milk can be used if cream is unavailable. In such cases, simply add a little butter to enrich the soup.

GREAT-GREAT-GRANDMOTHER HORTON'S CUCUMBER SOUP

3 cups cucumbers,
   sliced
4 cups chicken stock
1 slice of onion

1/4 cup butter
1/4 cup flour
2 cups milk, hot

Parboil the cucumber slices for 10 minutes. Put the stock in a kettle and let simmer. Drain the cucumber slices and add them to the chicken stock. Put in the onion. Cook until the cucumbers and onion are soft. Rub through a sieve. Mix the butter and flour together. Add to the soup to thicken it. Season with salt and pepper to taste, then stir in the hot milk. Strain and serve while hot.

BEEF TEA OF COLONIAL DAYS

"Beef tea" is one type of old-fashioned bouillon that is considered extremely nutritious. And it was commonly used in days long past as a remedy for numerous illnesses. This method secures all the juice from meat better than if the meat is simply boiled in water. Here is how they made it in the old days: Cut lean beef into small pieces. Put into a jar or "tin" with a tight cover. Place the jar or "tin" in a kettle of cold water. Bring it to a boil. Continue cooking the meat until all juice has been extracted.

UNCLE ALBERT'S FAVORITE BEAN SOUP

4 cups black beans   pinch of parsley
1 pound shin beef   1 small onion, quartered
1 bay leaf

Soak the beans overnight in 2 quarts water. In the morning, add the shin beef and simmer for 3 hours. Then flavor with the bay leaf, parsley, and onion. Simmer for another hour. Then take out the beans. Press them through a sieve. Put them back into the liquor. Season with salt and pepper to taste. *Note:* Thorough cooking and fine straining are the secrets of good bean soup. A little lemon juice may be added if desired. Serve while steaming hot.

OLD-TIME CONSOMMÉ RECIPE
OF GRANDMOTHER COLLISTER

This very old recipe for homemade consommé is delightful. Consommé is simply the brown meat stock that has been clarified (made clear) after the fat has been skimmed off. It is served as a good broth or in cups as a tasty drink. Thoroughly blend the shell and white of an egg with 4 cups cold stock. Add 1/2 teaspoon celery seed, the rind and juice of 1 lemon, salt and pepper. Boil together for 10 minutes. Strain through a fine sieve. Heat to boiling once again before serving. *Note:* Wine or more lemon juice may be added to suit taste.

GRANDMOTHER PELTON'S
SPECIAL ROYAL CONSOMMÉ CUSTARD

This is the previous consommé made into a special custard for adding to soups. The consommé custard is made as follows: Take 2 eggs and beat for several minutes. Add a little salt and 5 tablespoons cold consomme. Beat again for 3 minutes. Put this into a buttered dish and set it in a pan of warm water. Cover with a piece of buttered paper. Place the pan in a moderate oven (350 degrees) and bake for 30 minutes. It is done when the custard will not adhere to a knife. Chill and then cut into small cubes. The cubes are placed in the soup after it has been poured into the tureen.

EARLY NEW ENGLAND CORNED BEEF SOUP

An extremely tasty soup dish can be made from the pot liquor in which corned beef[5] has been boiled. Or if the flavor of vegetables is not objectionable, the liquor in which an old-fashioned New England boiled dinner[6] has been cooked may be suitably used. To most old-timers, however, the plain corned beef liquor was preferable. And it was also often used as a basic stock for making split pea, bean, and many other delicious vegetable soups. To make regular corned beef soup, first remove the grease from the liquor. Then add 4 cups of stewed and strained tomatoes. Season highly with tomato catsup[7] and boil for 30 minutes. Serve while hot.

COUSIN ELIZABETH'S OLD-TIME GIBLET SOUP

Slice up 1 large onion, a turnip and a carrot. Put into a frying pan with enough butter to fry. When they begin to brown, sift in 1 tablespoon flour. Add the giblets taken from 6 chickens. Brown them all nicely. Dump all of this from the frying pan into a large kettle containing 1 1/2

---

5. Recipe in Chapter 4
6. Recipe in Chapter 22
7. Recipe in Chapter 19

gallons water. Chicken stock may be used if it is available. Let this simmer for 4 hours. Season with salt and pepper to taste. Pour over the yolks of hard-boiled eggs in a tureen.

MULLIGATAWNY SOUP
OF THE CIVIL WAR PERIOD

Cut up a whole chicken and put it in a large kettle containing 2 cups of good white stock.[8] Season with the following:

1/2 teaspoon curry powder   2 whole cloves
pinch of mace   1 sprig of parsley

Now slice 2 onions, 1 carrot, 1 stalk celery and 1 large apple. Put these in a frying pan with a little butter and let them brown. Add them to the soup. Boil for 1/2 hour. Then add 1 cup stewed tomatoes. Let this simmer for another 1/2 hour. Just before serving, stir in 1/2 cup cream. *Note:* If coconuts are available, use coconut milk with the juice of 1 lemon instead of the cream. It's a treat you won't soon forget.

GREAT-GREAT-GRANDMOTHER DANIELS'
SPLIT PEA SOUP

4 cups dried split peas   1 tablespoon rice flour
1 pound lean salt pork

Soak the dried split peas overnight. If the soup is to be used for a late dinner, they may be put to soak in the morning. After proper soaking, put them into a kettle containing 4 quarts cold water. Add the salt pork and bring

---

8. Recipe included herein

to a boil. Let it simmer for 3 full hours, or until the liquid
has reduced in half. Then strain it through a colander. Rub
the peas through as much as possible. Season to taste with
celery flakes, salt and pepper. Thicken with the rice flour
mixed with cold water. Simmer for 10 minutes longer. Serve
in a tureen with strips of crisped bread. *Note:* The crisped
bread is prepared by thickly buttering thin slices of bread.
Set them in a moderate oven (350 degrees) until crisp.
They can then be cut in narrow strips and scattered on top
of the soup.

OLD CHARLESTON CHICKEN BROTH WITH RICE

Take a large chicken, remove the skin, and cut the meat
up in very small pieces. Crack all the bones. Put in a large
soup kettle. Add 4 cups cold water for every pound of
chicken. Season to taste with salt and pepper. Heat slowly
and allow to simmer until the meat is in shreds. Strain off
the liquor and skim off the grease from the top. Add 1 cup
of well-washed brown rice to the liquor. Bring to a boil
and cook until the rice is nice and tender.

In the meantime, remove all the meat from the chicken
bones. Cut it up in small pieces. These are then added to
the broth, with 1/2 cup cream, just before serving. *Note:*
A small pinch of curry powder, or a leaf of fresh mint,
makes an agreeable seasoning.

JULIA D. GRANT'S CREAM OF CELERY SOUP

This is a delicious old-time soup that was popular in
General Grant's household. It requires white broth or stock
made from veal or chicken. Cook plenty of celery stalks in
this white stock. When tender, rub through a sieve. Thicken
stock with flour mixed smoothly in cold milk. Add butter

to suit and stir the soup well. *Note:* Mrs. Grant always added 1 teaspoon honey to her celery soup in order to give it a distinctive touch.

OLD-TIME RHODE ISLAND LOBSTER SOUP

Take the meat from 1 large lobster and chop it finely. Crush 3 crackers,[9] and put them into a pot with the lobster. Add 2 tablespoons butter and salt and pepper to taste. Blend well and then stir in 2 cups boiling milk. Let the mixture come to a boil. Serve immediately. *Note:* If the lobster is fresh this soup is difficult to beat. Vegetables were often added in the old days. The choice of which ones to use was left up to the individual cook.

9. Many excellent recipes for old-time homemade crackers can be found in *Natural Baking the Old-Fashioned Way*, by the same author.

2

Old-Fashioned Fish Cookery

Fish of some sort may be had almost anywhere in the country today but it hasn't always been this way. Before the days of cold storage and refrigerated railway cars, salt-water or "sea fish" could not be obtained away from the seaport or coastal areas of the nation. With the radical changes that took place in the 1800s, raw oysters could be found on bills of fare all the way across the continent, and almost as fresh as in Baltimore or Providence.

Fish, when fresh and properly cooked, is a luxury. There are few foods, however, of which the average housewife knows so little, or so often fails. Even the little fish of our freshwater streams and ponds may be so presented and garnished to make most acceptable dishes. And our shad, salmon, brook trout, lake trout, pickerel, and bass are among the best freshwater fish.

There is no fish that needs to "hang" or "ripen" (age) to improve its edibleness. Great-grandmother Mitchell, herself an old country girl, said that "the sooner it reaches the fire after it leaves the water the better it is." In this respect, fish differs from every other known meat unless there is a foundation for the 1850 fad that a broiled chicken is best if killed and served within 15 minutes. The old-timers believed a white-meated fish was more readily digested than one of dark meat. This is because its oil is concentrated in its liver, instead of being spread through the whole body.

GREAT-GRANDMOTHER MITCHELL'S FISH POINTERS

It is not easy to cook fish properly, unless one knows how. In broiling fish, a special skill is required to thoroughly cook the fish and not break it up. Fish should be well cooked. Underdone fish is, in great-grandmother's words, "an abomination," although cured fish may be eaten raw.

The strong "fish taste," which can be offensive, generally comes from the skin. If that is taken off, much of the rank flavor can be avoided. A mackerel and a bluefish are especially strong in flavor among saltwater fish, and a black bass and a trout among freshwater fish. It is easy to skin a fish. And for chowders this was always done in the good old days. It was usually done with boiled fish also. But for baking, the skin was always left on.

According to old timers, the freshness of a fish is determined by the gills. These should be red and lively in color. The flesh should be firm and elastic also.

Lemon is almost universally an adjunct of fish dishes. It has always been used to tone down or cut the fishy taste.

Sliced cucumbers were another old-fashioned accompaniment of fish.

My great-grandmother boiled a fish by beginning with cold water. She put in 4 tablespoons of salt to a gallon. The fish was boiled about 10 minutes to the pound. But if the fish were large, the boiling time was 6 minutes per pound. At any rate, it should be well done. Great-grandmother never left the fish in the water after it was done cooking. If not ready to serve, it was placed where it would drain.

The ordinary catfish was made more palatable by putting

it in running water several hours before killing. Any fresh-water fish with a brackish taste was sweetened by soaking in salt water.

EARLY NEW ENGLAND PILOT BOAT FRY

The old-time New England fishing boat pilots had every facility for securing the freshest of saltwater fish. And in 1853, one of them told my great-grandfather's father-in-law, David Horton, the secrets of fresh fish cookery. He said: "the only way to fry fish is to have pork fat enough to sub-merge the fish, and fry the pieces as you would doughnuts. They must not be allowed to stick to the frying pan, and be broken up. In other words, the slices are to be boiled in very hot pork fat, until a nice brown."

OLD SOUTHERN OYSTER FRICASSEE

1 cup butter	pepper to suit
2 quarts oysters	1 tablespoon flour
1 cup cream	3 egg yolks, well beaten

Melt the butter in a frying pan. Put in the oysters and let them come to a boil. Add the cream, pepper, and the flour (mixed smoothly in a little cold milk). Let this boil gently until the oysters are done. Remove from the stove and stir in the beaten egg yolks. Pour over a platter of toasted crackers. Serve while very hot.

MARTHA WASHINGTON'S BEST FISH CHOWDER

This very old recipe was handed down by my Great-great-grandmother Horton's aunt. She claimed the words are those of Martha Washington: "In a deep chowder kettle fry thoroughly four or five pieces of pork cut very thin. Take about six pounds of haddock, cut into thick pieces, and about one dozen and a half potatoes, sliced not too thin. After the pork is fried take it out, and into the same kettle put the fish, potatoes, and a little chopped onion in alternate layers. The onion may, of course, be omitted by those who don't like it. Cover with boiling water and let it boil until the potatoes are quite soft. Then add one pint of milk, a very small piece of butter, a tablespoon of thickening (flour), and pepper and salt to taste. Just before serving, cut the pork into small pieces, or dice, and add to the rest. Pour into the tureen and add four or five Boston chowder crackers."

A mild criticism was made on the above recipe by my Great-great-grandmother Horton. She notes that it would be an improvement to "slice the onion and fry it brown in the pork fat." And she adds that "almost any fish can be used for a chowder, although fresh cod and haddock are the favorites of David and my family."

MARTHA WASHINGTON'S CLAM CHOWDER

Martha Washington liked her clam chowder to be made in the same manner as the above fish chowder. One pint (2 cups) of clams were chopped up and added in place of the fish. And 1 cup of home-canned tomatoes was also added. This was said to be George's favorite kind of chowder.

OLD NEW ORLEANS CREAMED OYSTERS

1 tablespoon flour	salt to taste
2 cups cream	pepper to taste

Mix the flour with a little of the cold cream until it becomes a smooth paste. Put the rest of the cream in a saucepan and bring it to a boil. Then stir in the flour and let it all cook for 10 minutes, but take care not to burn. Let 1 quart of oysters come to a boil in their own liquor. Then strain and add the hot oysters to the cream. Season with salt and pepper to taste. *Note:* Many old southerners added a flavoring of onion and mace to the cream.

GREAT-AUNT RUTH'S FRIED OYSTERS

Select only large oysters. Wash them in their own liquor. Shake them free from the liquid. Dip the oysters in fine cracker crumbs that have been well seasoned with salt and pepper. Place so that each oyster will touch the bottom in a hot frying pan with equal parts of butter and lard (just enough to cover the bottom of the pan). When the oysters are puffed and brown on one side, turn each one separately with a thin knife. Add more butter and lard, as it is needed, to keep the oysters and crumbs from sticking and burning. Serve very hot, garnished with thin slices of lemon.

SPECAL OLDEN-DAY BROILED HALIBUT

Take 1 slice of halibut cut from the tail end of the fish— but not the extreme end. Lay a few slices of onion and a bit of bay leaf in a shallow baking pan. After the fish has been wiped with a clean damp cloth, spread 1 side with butter. Lay onion on the buttered side. Sprinkle with salt and place it in the broiling oven. Watch it carefully. If necessary, turn the fish without breaking. When nearly done, spread it with a mixture of melted butter thickened with bread crumbs. Then let it brown nicely. Serve on a warm platter and garnish with parsley. *Note:* If the flavor of onion is distasteful it can be omitted.

GREAT-GRANDMOTHER SHAW'S ESCALLOPED OYSTERS

Most old-time cooks prepared a dish of escalloped oysters by placing the cracker crumbs and oysters in layers. But my Great-grandmother Shaw, who was noted for this dish, always blended the ingredients together. She first buttered a baking dish and sprinkled it with coarse cracker crumbs. Then the oysters were soaked in melted butter. Each oyster was rolled in cracker crumbs, seasoned with salt and pepper, and placed in the baking dish. A little sherry was sprinkled over each layer. When the dish was full, a layer of crumbs was sprinkled over the top. The dish was put in a moderate oven (350 degrees) and baked until browned on top. *Note:* If you prefer not to use sherry as above, add cream to this dish instead.

EARLY AMERICAN OYSTER PIE

1 quart oysters
4 cups milk
10 large oyster crackers, rolled fine

salt to taste
pepper to taste
1 tablespoon butter, well rounded

Stir all of the above ingredients together. Pour into a well-buttered baking dish lined with a thick puff paste.[1] Cover with an upper puff-paste crust and bake for 3/4 hour in a slow oven (300 degrees).

GENERAL LEE'S FAVORITE FISH TIMBALES

1/2 cup cream

1 tablespoon lemon juice

---

1. Puff paste recipes can be found in *Natural Baking the Old-Fashioned Way,* by the same author.

2 tablespoons stale	few drops onion juice
bread crumbs	1 cup boiled salmon, cold[2]
pinch of salt	1 teaspoon parsley, minced
pinch of pepper	3 egg yolks, well beaten

Put the cream into a saucepan with the bread crumbs. Add the salt, pepper, lemon juice, parsley and onion juice. When this is hot add the cold salmon and mash it fine. Bring to a boil and pour the mixture over the well-beaten egg yolks. Stir lightly and fill well-buttered cups 2/3 full. Set them in a pan of boiling water. Bake in a moderate oven (350 degrees) for about 15 minutes, or until firm. Serve with Hollandaise sauce.[3] *Note:* Of course the cups can be omitted and the salmon mixture can be baked in a well-buttered baking pan or dish. Some old-timers liked it better with fine bread crumbs sprinkled all over the top before baking.

BROILED OYSTERS IN EARLY AMERICA

My Great-great-grandmother Horton felt that only large oysters were really good to broil. Take the oysters from the liquor and dry them with a napkin. Dip in melted butter and put them into the broiler. Let the surplus liquor drip off as they cook. Broil on both sides. When done, butter well, and serve on buttered toast with pieces of lemon.

EARLY NEW ENGLAND PLAIN LOBSTER

The lobster is the most popular and most valuable of our shell fish. The meat is delicious, even without any accom-

---

2. Recipe included herein
3. Recipe in Chapter 13

paniment. To relish it most highly one should be on a New England harbor pilot boat with an appetite born of the salt air and with the lobsters just taken from some fisherman's "lobster pot," and boiled on the cook's fire in seawater.

My Great-grandfather Elias said: "As soon as they are cool enough to handle the repast is ready. Not even salt or pepper, or any such thing is needed to create a relish."

If you can secure live lobsters, you can be sure they are fresh by boiling them yourself. Few people bought ready-cooked lobsters in the old days. The live lobster should be put head first into a pot of boiling water. This instantly kills it. If good clean seawater is not available, add 4 tablespoons salt to a gallon of fresh water. Many people season plain boiled lobster with vinegar,[4] salt and pepper. The most delightful morsels of meat are found in the complication of small bones that form the junction of the claws with the body.

In early times the "fish man" would crack the claws and shell if asked. This was a good idea as it was rather difficult to do in the kitchen. It need not be suggested that a stale lobster is worse than disagreeable. It is dangerous. The value of a lobster, according to my great-grandmother, is determined by its solidity. She always said that "light lobsters are not desirable."

UNRIVALED OLD-FASHIONED ESCALLOPED LOBSTER

Pound lobster meat in a mortar moistened with a little butter. Season with salt and red pepper to taste. Put the pounded meat back into the empty shells. Cover with bread crumbs and bake in a moderate oven (350 degrees) until nicely browned. Serve while hot with a good fish sauce.[5]

4. Recipes in Chapter 19
5. Recipes in Chapter 13

COUSIN ELIZABETH'S
OLD-TIME LOBSTER A LA NEWBURG

1 cup cream	pinch of red pepper
1 tablespoon butter	1 large lobster, boiled
1 tablespoon flour	Juice of 1/2 lemon
2 egg yolks	1/4 cup sherry wine
pinch of salt	

Make a smooth mixture of the cream, butter, flour, egg yolks, salt and pepper. Put the lobster meat, cut in small pieces the size of a filbert, in a double boiler. When hot, add the cream mixture. Allow it to come just to a boil. Then stir in the lemon juice and wine. More wine may be added to suit the taste. This dish must be served very hot. It makes a delightful treat for the chafing dish. *Note:* Oysters, fresh fish, sweetbreads, or scallops are delicious when served with this old-fashioned cream blend.

GRANDMOTHER'S FINEST LOBSTER CUTLETS

This is a very old recipe that is quite easy to prepare. Pound the meat of 6 large lobsters until it is fine and then season to taste with salt, red pepper, nutmeg and mace. Blend 12 well-beaten egg yolks with 6 stiffly beaten egg whites. Stir in 6 teaspoons of anchovy paste. Blend all together well and then roll out on a dusting of flour. The finished sheet should be about 1 1/2 inches thick. Cut into cutlets and brush over with a beaten egg. Sprinkle heavily with bread crumbs. Fry in butter until browned. Serve while hot.

OLDEN-DAY OYSTER PURSES

This is an old English recipe my Great-grandmother-Mitchell dearly loved. She obtained it from her mother. It is really a classic for both taste and appearance. Take 36 large, fat oysters, season to taste with salt and red pepper, and lay in a sieve to drain. Put the oyster juice in a saucepan. Stew the liquor down to half its original quantity and thicken with 1 tablespoon butter rolled in flour. Let it cool and then dip each oyster in the sauce until it is well coated. Roll out a sheet of puff paste until it is 1/8-inch thick. Cut into round pieces large enough to cover an oyster. Lay 1 oyster on each piece of puff paste. Gather the dough up with floured fingers. Pass a thin strip of dough around it twice, and tie. Flatten the bottom so as to give a baglike shape. Deep fry in hot grease. Drain well on brown paper and serve while still hot.

GENERAL GRANT'S FAVORITE CREAMED FISH DISH

2 cups milk	pepper to taste
1 tablespoon flour	1 tablespoon butter
fish to suit	1 egg, well beaten
salt to taste	pinch of paprika

Take 1 cup of the milk and blend with flour. Bring other cup milk to a boil and stir the first into it. When thick and smooth, add the meat of any cold fish (picked free from skin and bones). Season to taste with salt and pepper. Stir in the butter and let simmer for 5 minutes. Add the beaten egg to the mixture 1 minute before taking it from the stove. Then stir in a pinch of paprika and serve while hot.

GREAT-GREAT-GRANDMOTHER NORTHRUP'S BAKED FISH

Great-great-grandmother Northrup always claimed that "fish is better if baked in an agate pan." Place the fish, after it has been washed and cleaned, in the baking pan. Put very little water in the pan to prevent burning. Score the top of the fish, and place little pieces of butter or salt pork in the cuts. Season with salt, and then dredge (sprinkle) lightly with flour. Baste the fish, while it bakes, with the pan juices and melted butter. It is to be baked in a moderate oven (350 degrees) until the flesh is firm and white. *Note:* Baked fish was often stuffed in the old days. A favorite stuffing was made of cracker crumbs soaked in milk or cream, and seasoned with salt, pepper, butter, and sage.

EARLY AMERICAN BOILED FISH

The same old-time rule applied to boiled fish as to baked fish—it was considered much better if boiled in an agate kettle. Thoroughly wash and clean the fish to be boiled. Dredge (sprinkle) with salt and tie it in a thin cloth. Plunge the bag into boiling water, to which 1 tablespoon vinegar[6] has been added. Boil a fish weighing 4 pounds for at least 25 minutes. Serve with drawn butter sauce or egg sauce.[7]

GREAT-GREAT-GRANDMOTHER HORTON'S FRIED FISH

Wash the pieces of fish to be fried. Partly dry them by draining on a towel. Then dredge (sprinkle) with flour. My great-great-grandmother sometimes liked to use corn-meal, but she said flour makes a smoother crust when fried. Fry the fish in a mixture of half butter and half lard. Take care in turning the pieces to keep them whole. If the pan in which the fish is frying is kept covered, the flesh of the fish will be much whiter and juicier. *Note:* In the

6. Recipes in Chapter 19
7. Recipes in Chapter 13

old days, many people preferred to fry salt pork until it was crisp. This furnished the fat in which the fish was fried. The pieces of salt pork were then served with the fish. The slices should not be too thick and they must be thoroughly cooked.

GREAT-AUNT DORIS MARIE'S FISH AU GRATIN

Thoroughly wash the fish and remove the skin and bones. Cut into small pieces. Season with salt and pepper. Place a layer of the fish in a well-buttered baking dish. Pour over enough brown sauce[8] to moisten. Add another layer of fish and sauce. Continue until the baking dish is full. Then cover it with bread crumbs soaked in melted butter. Bake for 1/2 hour in a moderate oven (350 degrees). *Note:* Leftover baked or boiled fish may be utilized in this manner. And grated cheese on top adds to its toothsomeness. Cheese seems to go with fish as naturally as lemon juice.

SARAH POLK'S RECIPE FOR BROILED SHAD

Sarah Polk, wife of President James Polk (1845–1849), gives these directions for the broiling of a shad, one of her husband's most relished dishes: "Split the shad down the back, lay it open, clean, remove the back bone and as many of the fine bones as possible, and wipe dry. Brush all over with oil or melted butter. Lay it on a greased broiler, and cook over coals, flesh side first until brown; then turn and cook the skin side until crisp. Meanwhile have prepared one large tablespoonful buttered cream with one level teaspoonful salt, one saltspoonful (1/8 teaspoon) pepper or paprika, one tablespoonful lemon juice or walnut catsup and one tablespoonful minced parsley, and when the fish

8. Recipes in Chapter 13

is on the platter spread this over the surface and make several incisions that it may penetrate the fish. Garnish with lemon points and parsley, and serve very hot."

OLD NEW ORLEANS COURT BOUILLON

An old New Orleans negro cook furnished my Great-grandmother Mitchell with this concoction. Fry any good fish steak, such as halibut, in a little butter and lard until not quite done. Take the fish out of the frying pan and set aside. Then add the following to the grease in the frying pan:

2 tablespoons flour
1 tablespoon Worcester-
 shire sauce[9]
pinch of cloves

1/2 onion, minced
pinch of mace
pinch of thyme

In another pan stew 4 large tomatoes until thoroughly done. Pass them through a sieve and add to the sauce in the frying pan. Blend everything smoothly together. Put in the fish and let it all stew together for 3 minutes. Serve hot.

GREAT-GRANDMOTHER SHAW'S
TIPS ON BROOK TROUT

My Great-grandmother Shaw claimed that the best brook trout "comes from a quick mountain stream, and will not exceed four ounces in weight." She felt a cultivated brook trout was very indifferent eating. To cook brook trout, she first thoroughly cleaned them. They were then washed inside and out, and rolled in fine cornmeal. Great-grandmother

9. Recipes in Chapter 13

fried her trout only in hot pork fat, which she said was much better than lard or butter. They are to be fried until crisp and served hot.

REVOLUTIONARY PERIOD SALT-FISH DINNER

Correctly prepared this dish is a luxury. The first essential is real codfish, and you cannot be sure of this unless you know what real codfish is. According to an old, old family recipe: "If you take the 'boneless' article, or the 'shredded' article, or any other prepared fish, you don't know what you are getting—cod, haddock, hake, or pollock. If the fish is too dry, put it down cellar a day or two and it will absorb moisture enough to enable you to pick it up. Then let it simmer slowly at least two hours, but do not actively boil, and change the water occasionally. Fry dices of good salt pork until they are crisp, and leave them in the fat, or a part of it. Boil new beets, and new potatoes, and let those who eat mix the ingredients to their liking. If you like it at all, you are apt to like it exceedingly."

GREAT-AUNT CAROL ANN'S BAKED DEVILED FISH

1 cup milk	dash of pepper
1 cup stale bread crumbs, fine	1/4 teaspoon paprika
	1 teaspoon salt
1 tablespoon parsley, chopped	1 teaspoon onion juice
	2 cups cooked fish,
3 hard-boiled eggs, chopped	flaked and boned

Put the milk in a saucepan and scald it. Add the bread crumbs and stir over the fire for a moment. Then take it from stove and stir in the parsley, eggs, pepper, paprika, salt, and onion juice. Blend well and then add the fish. Pour into small baked tartlet shells[10] for individual servings. Cover each pie with fried bread crumbs. Bake in a quick oven (about 400 degrees) until the tops have browned. This will serve 8 people.

MACARONI WITH CODFISH—
A LINCOLN FAVORITE

Soak 1/2 pound of codfish overnight. Then drain and break it in small flakes, removing any skin and bones. Steam it until tender. On a platter arrange a layer of boiled macaroni, then a layer of the fish. Add slices of hard-boiled egg. Then add another layer of the macaroni and fish. Set this over a steamer while preparing the sauce as follows:

1 tablespoon butter	1/4 teaspoon pepper
1 tablespoon flour	1 cup milk
1/4 teaspoon salt	

Put the butter, flour, salt and pepper in a saucepan and stir over the fire until thoroughly blended. Then add the milk and continue stirring until it is smooth and thick. Pour this over the fish and macaroni on the platter. Sprinkle with finely chopped parsley and serve.

GREAT-GREAT-GRANDMOTHER DANIELS'
PLANKED FISH

This is one of the earliest and most delightful ways of preparing and serving fish. Clean the fish and place it skin

10. Recipes in *Natural Baking the Old-Fashioned Way*, by the same author.

down on a plank. Use a good hardwood plank, preferably oak, a little larger than the fish. Sprinkle the fish with salt and pepper. Brush lightly with melted butter or olive oil. Then bake for 25 minutes in a hot oven (425 to 450 degrees). Garnish the fish with slices of lemon and parsley. Serve it on the plank while hot.

OLD VIRGINIA-STYLE FISH SOUFFLE

Blend equal quantities of any cold, cooked fish with mashed potatoes. Stir in 1/2 cup milk and season to taste with salt and pepper. Then blend in 1 well-beaten egg. Pour this into a buttered baking dish and set in a hot oven (400 degrees). When very hot take out of the oven. Beat the white of 1 egg until it is stiff and then stir it into the yolk. Add salt and pepper to taste and pour over the fish-potato mixture. Put back in the oven and leave until browned. Serve hot.

GREAT-AUNT MARILYN'S BAKED SALMON BALLS

4 cups potatoes,
    mashed
2 cups salmon, cooked
    and shredded

2 eggs, well beaten
salt to taste
pepper to taste
garlic to taste

Blend all of the above ingredients in a large wooden mixing bowl. When well mixed, dip the hands in cold water. Then form mixture into balls of any desired size. Dip each salmon ball in melted butter and place in a shallow baking pan. Put in a moderate oven (350 degrees) and bake until browned on one side. Then turn each ball and brown the other side. Serve while hot.

PRIZED OLD-FASHIONED SALT-FISH CHOWDER

Boil a 4-pound fish until it is tender. Remove the skin and bones, and pick into fairly large pieces. Pare and dice 6 large potatoes. Peel and slice 3 large tomatoes. Put a thick layer of the fish in a saucepan. Then add a layer of potatoes, a layer of tomatoes, and a few pieces of lean ham as large as filberts. Lastly, add a sprinkling of chopped onion. Continue in this order until all ingredients are used. Then pour in 2 cups hot water. Simmer slowly for 1/2 hour and then serve while hot.

EARLY SOUTHERN CODFISH BALLS

1 cup codfish, cooked and shredded	1 tablespoon butter
2 cups potatoes, mashed	2 tablespoons cream
	1 egg

Blend the fish and potatoes while hot. Stir in the butter and cream. Set aside to cool. When cold, beat in the egg and make into small balls. Dip each ball in raw egg and then roll in seasoned bread crumbs. Deep fry in very hot fat or oil. Serve while hot.

OLD RHODE ISLAND OYSTER STEW

1 quart oysters	salt to taste
4 cups milk	pepper to taste
1/4 cup butter	

Put the oysters in an agate saucepan and let them simmer in their own liquor until the edges curl. Put the milk into a double boiler, and, when boiling, add the hot oysters. Let it stand for 10 minutes where it will keep hot, but not boil. Pour into a tureen and add the butter. Season with salt and pepper to taste. Then stir in the oyster liquor and serve.

3

Vegetable Preparation the Natural Way

Fresh vegetables in good condition do not require much elaboration in cooking to make them palatable. The majority of people never get vegetables at their best—the type not requiring full maturity and ripeness before using. These include such things as green corn, radishes, lettuce, asparagus, and peas.

According to old-timers, vegetables, so far as they are to be cooked, should find as little time as possible between the garden and the kitchen stove. All vegetables need some sort of seasoning. Some require only salt. And others need sugar, vinegar, oil, or butter. The variations and combinations of even the commoner vegetables are almost endless.

BACON AND CABBAGE IN THE OLD SOUTH

This, I need hardly say, was a favorite country dish in the South of long ago. The old-fashioned way of preparing it was to first quarter the cabbage. Then the meat and cabbage were boiled together. It was served reeking with fat. In this shape it justly earned a reputation for grossness and indigestibility that banished it, in time, from many tables. Yet it can be a savory and not unwholesome meal. The cabbage must be boiled in two waters, the second being the "pot-liquor" from the boiling meat. When the cabbage has been boiled the second time, drain it in a colander. Press out every drop of liquid without breaking any of the tender leaves. When the meat is dished, lay the cabbage neatly around it. Put a slice of hard-boiled egg on each quarter. When it is eaten, season with salt, pepper, and vinegar.[1]

GREAT-GRANDMOTHER SHAW'S POTATO RECIPES

Boiled Potatoes: After having tried both ways, my Great-grandmother Shaw decided that potatoes are less apt to be soggy if put into boiling water to cook, rather than cold water. Peel the potatoes, and let them stand a few minutes in cold, salted water. When the water in which they are to be cooked is boiling, add 1 teaspoon salt and put in the potatoes. Cover them and allow to boil, but not too hard, for 1/2 hour, or until soft. Drain off the water. Cover the potatoes with a cloth, and keep them in a warm place until ready to be served. The cloth absorbs the steam and allows the potatoes to be kept hot, while they do not absorb any moisture.

Real Old-Fashioned Mashed Potatoes: After the water is drained from boiled potatoes, add a small quantity of cream. Then add 1 tablespoon butter and a pinch of salt. Mash with a wooden potato masher. Then beat until light and creamy. Serve in a covered bowl.

Great-Granddad's Favorite Cakes: Form cakes of mashed potato between the hands. Fry in butter until they turn a golden brown. Turn them, so that both sides will be alike. This is a very nice way to use up the leftover mashed po-

---

1. Recipes in Chapter 19

tatoes. And it is an excellent accompaniment for any meat at breakfast.

Early American Baked Potatoes: Select as perfectly and evenly shaped potatoes as possible. Thoroughly wash and dry them. Bake for 45 minutes in a hot oven (400 to 425 degrees). Turn them often so they will bake evenly. Serve at once, covered with a napkin. Never cover a baked potato with a dish or dish cover as steam is created. This will make the potato wet and undesirable.

ALBERTA CATHERINE'S OLD-TIME POTATO RECIPES

Early New England Potatoes in the Shell:

8 potatoes, medium sized	salt to taste
	2 tablespoons milk
butter to suit	2 egg whites, stiffly
pepper to taste	beaten

Bake the potatoes. When done take from oven and cut in half lengthwise. Remove the insides carefully without breaking the skins. Mash and add the rest of the ingredients. Stir together lightly. Fill the skins or shells with the mixture and bake for 20 minutes in a hot oven (400 to 425 degrees). Serve while very hot.

Olden-Day Lyonnaise Potatoes:

2 cups boiled potatoes, cold and diced	1 tablespoon onion, minced
salt to taste	1 tablespoon butter
pepper to taste	1 tablespoon parsley, chopped fine

Take the cold boiled potatoes and season to taste with salt and pepper. Fry the onion in the butter and then add the potatoes. Stir until all the butter is absorbed. Add the parsley and serve while hot. *Note:* Many old-timers liked to sprinkle in a little vinegar[2] to improve the flavor.

Hollandaise Potatoes in Early New York: Peel 8 small potatoes and boil them until done. Drain well and dust with salt. Then drop 2 tablespoons butter over them. Partly cover and set aside over a low fire. Shake and baste them every few minutes. When the potatoes have absorbed most of the butter, sprinkle them with 1 teaspoon lemon juice. Then make the following old-fashioned sauce:

4 raw egg yolks	1 tablespoon vinegar
4 tablespoons water	3 tablespoons butter
pinch of salt	1 teaspoon lemon juice
pinch of red pepper	

Beat the egg yolks and stir in the water, seasoning, vinegar and half the butter. Set over a pan of hot water and stir until it begins to thicken. Then add the remainder of the butter cut into tiny bits. Stir continuously until thick as custard. Take from the fire and lightly stir in the lemon juice. Pour into a heated dish and blend in the potatoes. Serve while hot.

GREAT-AUNT DORIS MARIE'S
EARLY AMERICAN POTATO RECIPES

Old Boston Potato Casserole:

8 large potatoes, boiled and mashed	1 tablespoon butter
	3 tablespoons cream
salt to taste	2 egg yolks, well beaten
pepper to taste	1 egg well beaten

Put all of the above ingredients, except the 1 beaten egg,

---

2. Recipes in Chapter 19

into a large pan and blend. Stir over the fire until the mixture no longer adheres to the sides of the pan. Then turn it out on a flat dish. When cool enough to handle, mold the mass into any desired shape. Press it up higher around the sides to simulate a pie crust. Brush with the beaten egg and place in a hot oven (425 degrees) until lightly browned. Then remove it from the oven and fill the center with a ragout (highly spiced stew).[3] Serve immediately.

Or, the potato mixture may be pressed into a baking pan or dish that has been thoroughly greased. Allow to stand for 10 minutes. Then turn out of the pan or dish, brush with the beaten egg, and bake as above.

Original Old Vermont Delmonico Potatoes:

2 cups potatoes, boiled and cut fine
1 teaspoon salt
pinch of pepper
1 cup cream
2 tablespoons butter, melted

Season the potatoes with the salt and pepper. Put them in a shallow, buttered baking dish. Pour the cream over them and then stir in the melted butter. Put into a quick oven (425 degrees) and brown. Serve immediately.

SOUTHERN PLANTATION POTATO RECIPES

Early Alabama Fried Sweet Potatoes: Cut raw sweet potatoes in 1/4-inch lengthwise slices. Place in a pan with enough water to prevent sticking. Boil, well covered, until the water is gone. Then add 1 tablespoon butter and lard mixed. Dust with salt and pepper. Turn the pieces so that each side will be fried to a golden brown. *Note:* These potatoes were popular on the plantations as an excellent accompaniment for fried or broiled chicken.[4]

3. Recipes in Chapters 4, 5, 6, 7, and 8.
4. Recipes in Chapter 8

Old New Orleans Plantation Chips: Slice some potatoes very thin and evenly. Put them in a bowl of ice water. When cold, drain well and dry them on a coarse cloth. Fry in boiling lard, taking care to keep the slices apart. When they begin to turn a golden brown skim them out. Drain as thoroughly as possible. Sprinkle with salt and serve immediately.

Mississippi Plantation-Style Soft Fries: Slice some cold boiled potatoes and put them into a frying pan with 1 tablespoon of half butter and half lard. Dust lightly with salt and pepper. Cover and fry gently. Turn with a knife to prevent sticking. Keep covered as much as possible. When done they should be slightly browned. The covering creates steam that in turn softens the potatoes. This makes the dish a most agreeable change from the regular crisp-fried potatoes.

COOKING GREENS IN EARLY AMERICA

The most common greens (after spinach) used in the old days were dandelions and beet tops. Country people also sometimes used cowslips and mustard greens. Beet tops were apt to be infested with a grub, which deterred many people from cooking them up. Dandelion is rather bitter, but it is quite agreeable to the taste. According to my great-great-grandmother, "the first duty to a mess of greens is to see that they are washed clean." Then put the greens into salted, boiling water and cook until tender. They can be served with butter. But even this is unnecessary if they are boiled with a piece of bacon or salt pork, as so many old-timers used to do. They may be dashed with vinegar[5] when eaten, or with a little salad oil. The seasoning is a matter of individual taste.

---

5. Recipes in Chapter 19

GREAT-GRANDMOTHER MITCHELL'S
SPINACH RECIPES

Old-Time Minced Spinach: Wash the spinach carefully. Boil it until very tender. Drain and then rub through a colander, or chop it fine. Put a good lump of butter into a frying pan and melt it. Add the spinach. Season with salt and pepper to taste. When hot, beat in 3 tablespoons cream. Garnish with sliced hard-boiled eggs and serve immediately.

Common Boiled Spinach: Carefully wash—and you cannot be too careful—a half peck (4 quarts) of fresh spinach. Cut the leaves from the hard root or main stem. Put into a kettle of boiling, salted water. Boil uncovered—as this retains the color—until tender (about 1 hour). Drain off all the water and season the spinach with salt. Add 1 tablespoon butter and stir it in until it all melts. Serve with hard-boiled eggs—whole or in slices.

ESCALLOPED TOMATOES—
A FAVORITE DURING THE CIVIL WAR

Over the bottom of a deep, well-buttered baking dish scatter a layer of bread crumbs. Put in a layer of fresh, sliced tomatoes. Add a layer of finely chopped hard-boiled egg. Season with salt and pepper, and sprinkle a few drops of lemon juice over this. Then scatter small pieces of butter around. Fill the dish up in this sequence. Finish with a layer of bread crumbs over the top. Bake for 15 minutes in a slow oven (300 degrees). Then garnish, when served, with water cress, if available. *Note:* To make a small dish, use 1 pound tomatoes, 2 hard-boiled eggs, 1/2 cup butter, and the juice of 1 lemon.

ORIGINAL PLANTATION-STYLE PAN TOMATOES

To make a delightful dish of the real old-fashioned panned tomatoes, first cut a number of tomatoes into halves. Place them in a buttered baking dish or pan, skin side down. Sprinkle lightly with salt and pepper. Put a tiny bit of butter in the center of each. Bake slowly (about 300 degrees) until soft. Take the tomatoes out of the pan and place on a dish. Then add 2 cups milk to the juices in the pan. Moisten 2 tablespoons flour with a little cold milk and add it. Stir constantly until it comes to a boil. Add 1 teaspoon salt and a pinch of pepper. Pour this hot mixture over the tomatoes. Garnish with squares of toasted bread and serve while hot.

GRANDDAD'S FAVORITE BOILED ONIONS

Peel the onions and remove the hard root part. Put them in a pot of boiling water with 1 teaspoon salt. Allow the onions to boil for 1/2 hour. Drain off the water and pour in fresh boiling water. Let it boil for another 1/2 hour. When done, drain off all the water. Add 1/2 cup milk or cream and shake the pan over the fire until the milk is hot. Remove from the fire and season with salt and pepper to taste. Melt in 1 tablespoon butter. Serve at once. *Note:* According to my great-great-grandmother, this is the only way to cook onions for a family who likes onions without the rank onion flavor.

GRANDMOTHER COLLISTER'S
BEAN AND PEA RECIPES

Old-Fashioned String Bean Cookery: When preparing fresh string beans be careful to remove all the strings from them.

This is especially important if the string beans are a little old. A piece of hard, ropy string is not a pleasant thing to chew on with a mouthful of beans, no matter how well cooked or how deliciously seasoned. Boil the beans, uncovered, in salted, boiling water for 2 hours or longer. This time will vary in accordance with the age of the beans. Then simply serve well seasoned and with butter melted on them.

Old-Time Peas: Shell the fresh peas. Carefully wash and drain them. Boil in salted water for from 1/2 to 3/4 of an hour. Season with salt and pepper. Melt plenty of butter in with the peas. Serve while hot.

Early American Shell Beans: Put the beans into a pot of boiling water with a pinch of baking soda. Boil for 2 1/2 hours. Season with salt, and add plenty of butter. Serve, after the butter has all melted, in a covered dish.

OLDEN-DAY ASPARAGUS COOKERY

According to my Great-great-grandmother Horton, the fresher any vegetable is before cooking, the better it is when served on the table. This is especially true of asparagus. Cut off the hard, white part of the stalks. Wash the dirt from the tips. Put the tips into a kettle of boiling water. Add 1 teaspoon salt, and, if there is any question of the age since cutting, a pinch of baking soda "as large as a pea." Boil until tender. This should take from 20 to 45 minutes. Serve on slices of well-buttered toast. *Note:* My Great-great-grandmother often cut her asparagus in 1-inch lengths and served it with a good homemade cream sauce.[6]

----

6. Recipes in Chapter 13

COUSIN VERA'S OLD-TIME PARSNIPS

Parsnips are always said to be much sweeter in the spring of the year. Wash them and scrape off the skin. Put into a kettle of boiling water and cook them for 3/4 of an hour. Then immediately plunge into a bowl of cold water. This will enable you to rub off the remaining skin easily. Serve with a seasoning of salt, pepper, and melted butter. *Note:* Another delightful old-time method of preparing boiled parsnips is to first slice them when cold. Fry both sides in hot butter until browned. Parsnips are absolutely delicious fixed in this way.

TURNIP COOKING IN EARLY AMERICA

Peel the fresh turnips, cutting deeply enough to remove all of the hard outer skin. Put them into a kettle of boiling water and cook for 3/4 hour. Drain off all the water. Mash the turnips and season with salt. Add butter and stir it in until all melted. Pepper the top just before serving.

GRANDMOTHER PELTON'S CREAMED CARROTS

Wash and scrape the carrots. Cut them into strips. Boil in a saucepan with enough salted water to cover the carrots. Cook slowly until tender. Then drain off the water. Put in 2 tablespoons butter and a dredging (sprinkling) of flour. Season with salt and pepper to taste. When the butter has all melted, add cream enough to moisten well. Let it come to a boil and then serve while very hot. In the old days, carrots were believed to be exceedingly healthful. Physicians often prescribed them for certain ailments.

OLD-FASHIONED
ESCALLOPED CORN AND TOMATOES

Cut the kernels from 12 large ears of corn. Peel 6 large ripe tomatoes, and cut them in pieces. Put a layer of tomatoes in the bottom of a lightly buttered baking dish. Add a layer of corn. Sprinkle with salt and pepper. Then add a layer of bread crumbs and scattered bits of butter. Continue this sequence until the baking dish is full. Cover with a layer of crumbs on top. Bake for 1/2 hour in a moderate oven (350 degrees).

GREAT-GREAT-GRANDMOTHER HORTON'S
GREEN CORN RECIPES

Early Corn Cooking: Remove the husk and silk and put the ears of corn into a kettle of boiling water. Cook for from 10 to 20 minutes, or until the milk in the kernel has hardened and the corn has lost its raw taste. Season with salt, pepper, and melted butter. Serve while very hot.

Stewed Green Corn the Old-Fashioned Way: Cut the kernels from 12 ears of not-too-ripe corn. Then break the cobs in half and partly cover them with water in a stew pan. Simmer slowly for 45 minutes. Take out the cobs and add the kernels to the water. Let simmer for 15 minutes. Then add 1/2 cup cream, 1 tablespoon butter, and salt and pepper to taste. Stir well and serve at once while still hot.

Old-Time Baked Green Corn: Clean the corn cobs of the husk and silk. Break off the extreme imperfect ends. Put the ears into a shallow baking pan and baste with melted butter. Season with salt and pepper to taste. Bake for 20 minutes in a moderate oven (350 degrees). Serve while hot.

GREAT-GREAT-GRANDMOTHER NORTHRUP'S BAKED BEANS

4 cups pea beans	1/4 cup molasses
1/2 pound salt pork	1 teaspoon mustard[7]

My Great-great grandmother always said that pea beans were best for making good homemade baked beans, although larger varieties are sometimes used. Soak the pea beans overnight. The next morning put them into a kettle of fresh cold water. Parboil (boil until partly cooked) until a pin will easily pierce them. But do not cook enough to break the skins. Put them in a bean pot with the salt pork. The salt pork should be part fat and part lean. Score the rind in half-inch strips after having poured boiling water over it. For most tastes the salt pork will season the beans sufficiently. But more salt may be added, if necessary. Blend the mustard with the molasses and stir this into the beans. Then pour in boiling water enough to cover the beans. Have the piece of salt pork so arranged that only the rind is exposed. During the last hour lift the salt pork a little, to allow the rind to crisp. Bake not less than 8 hours in a moderate oven (350 degrees). Great-great-grandmother Northrup said: "The knack of baking beans is to have them come out thoroughly cooked, of a rich brown color, not too greasy, and not moist enough to destroy the individuality of the beans." *Note:* Some people made these old-fashioned baked beans without the mustard added. Try it both ways.

EARLY AMERICAN SUCCOTASH

Cut the kernels from the corn cobs. Simmer 4 cups of these kernels until they are tender. Cook 2 cups of shell

7. Recipe in Chapter 19

beans in the same manner. Then put both together in a pot and boil for 15 minutes. Drain well and add a little cream. Stir constantly until the cream is scalded. Season with salt and pepper to suit taste and serve while steaming hot.

COLONIAL RECIPES FOR COOKING SQUASH

Colonial-Style Summer Squash: Choose a squash that is tender enough to be cooked (skin, seeds and all). Wash the squash and carefully scrape off the discolored places, if there are any. Cut into 1-inch slices and boil them for 1/2 hour. Then drain off all the water. Press the squash to extract as much water as possible. Then mash it. Season with salt and pepper to taste. Stir in butter until it melts and then serve.

Colonial-Style Winter Squash: Cut the squash in pieces. Remove the seeds and pulp. Put the pieces of squash into a kettle, cover with water, and boil until tender—from 1/2 to 3/4 hour. Drain off the water. Scrape all the squash from the hard skin. Mash with "a piece of butter the size of an egg" (2 well-rounded tablespoons). Season with salt and pepper to taste. Serve while hot.

Colonial-Style Baked Squash: Cut a large squash in half. Remove the seeds and pulp. Place the halves in a buttered baking pan with the rind facing upward. Bake for 1/2 to 3/4 hour in a moderate oven (350 degrees). When soft, scrape the meat of the squash from the outer shell. Beat smoothly and season with salt and pepper. Beat in butter enough to flavor well. Serve while hot. *Note:* Old-fashioned squash prepared in this way is rather dry and sweet.

SIMPLE OLD-FASHIONED BUTTERED BEETS

Scrape the skin off some young, tender beets. Put on to boil in slightly salted water. When done (tender), take off the stove. Pour melted butter over the beets and serve while hot. Salt and pepper are not necessary.

OLD-TIME CABBAGE COOKERY

Early New England Cabbage Dishes: The best cabbage to use is a very solid head. The outer leaves are to be removed before cooking. Cut the head into quarters. Soak for 1/2 hour in salted water. Then put the quarters into salted boiling water. Change the water 2 or 3 times during cooking. This will get rid of the strong taste. Boil until tender. Serve while hot and accompany with vinegar and pepper. *Note:* Cold-boiled cabbage was commonly fried or baked as a secondary dish in the colonies. It was generally served with vinegar and pepper as above, but many people preferred it buttered.

Cream Cabbage in the Old Days: Take 1/2 head of fresh, solid cabbage. Chop it up fine with a sharp knife. Put it in a kettle with 1 cup water and cook quickly. If the water is not all cooked out when the cabbage is tender, drain it off. Season with salt to taste and add a little butter. Then stir in 1 cup of cream if you have it. If not, mix 1 tablespoon flour with 1/2 cup milk until it is smooth. Stir this into the cabbage. Serve in individual dishes.

GREAT-GREAT-GRANDMOTHER DANIELS' MUSHROOMS

In the early period of our history, fresh mushrooms were

a rather common dish. My Great-great-grandmother found them to be delicious and easily acquired, if as she said, "you know how and where to get them."

For broiling and stewing, fresh mushrooms are incomparable. When stewing, break the mushrooms into small pieces. Put them in a saucepan, sprinkle with salt, and let them stand for 1/2 hour. Then stew them in meat drippings (juices) with a little butter. When tender, add cream enough to cover. Bring to almost a boil and immediately serve on toast.

It is quite easy to properly broil mushrooms. Pare them and cut off the stems. Dip each mushroom in melted butter and sprinkle with salt and pepper. Broil on both sides until lightly browned and serve on toast. *Note:* Mrs. Daniels said that in order to test mushrooms you simply "Sprinkle salt on the gills. If they turn yellow, they are poisonous. If black, they are good."

CAULIFLOWER COOKING IN EARLY OHIO

In early times this vegetable was believed to be a sort of modified cabbage. It was used by many families where cabbage was considered taboo because of dainty olfactories or queasy stomachs. It is an attractive vegetable dish, and if cooked correctly, it is delicious. The head should be a creamy white, without spots or blemishes. Pick off the outer leaves. Soak the cauliflower head in salted water for 1/2 hour. Then put it into a kettle of boiling salted water. Skim off any impurities. Cook for 20 minutes, or until tender. It may be served with a cream sauce or a Hollandaise sauce.[8] And it is also excellent when served plain with vinegar[9] and pepper. This dish is extremely versatile and can be eaten cold with a dressing of mayonnaise.[10]

8. Recipes in Chapter 13
9. Recipes in Chapter 19
10. Recipes in Chapter 13

REAL OLD-TIME EGGPLANT

Slice an eggplant into 3 pieces to the inch. Sprinkle salt over each slice. Let the juice drain out. Then dip the slices in a mixture of bread crumbs and beaten eggs. Fry in hot lard or other grease until nicely browned. Serve hot.

RICE COOKERY THE OLD-FASHIONED WAY

Put 1 cup rice into a kettle of boiling, salted water. Do this gradually so the water will not stop boiling. Stir it with a fork, to prevent sticking. Boil for 1/2 hour, or until the rice is tender. The water should all be boiled into the rice. Then let it stand where it will stay hot until ready to serve. *Note:* Rice may be boiled in a double boiler with milk. This is excellent when cooking rice for dessert.

4

Old-Fashioned Beef Cookery

The most staple and common meat used in the United States is beef. It is perhaps the kind of flesh least likely to pall on the taste. Beef is nutritious, healthful, palatable and easily obtainable. It offers an almost infinite variety in ways of preparation for the table. And nearly everyone likes it. It is the one meat sure to be found in every market. Even back in the mid-1800s my great-grandmother said: "a housewife is ignorant, indeed, who cannot go to market for a piece of beef with some degree of intelligence."

The fattening and marketing of beef has been revolutionized in this country in the last hundred years. By 1900, domestic, home-grown beef in the Eastern States was a very small factor, even in the local rural markets. The steers and oxen that used to furnish most of the draft animals on our New England farms were seldom seen. As a consequence, New England beef was rare in the markets of that period. Indeed, most of our beef for the entire Atlantic coast then came from the west, and "Chicago dressed beef" was common. And very good beef most of it was!

Many old-timers felt that many recipes for cooking beef contained a great many ingredients that were not essential.

But if these materials are available, and agreeable to the individual taste, they may actually add to the quality of the dish in question. Included in this category are many herbs, parsley being the most common, perhaps, and a variety of vegetables, especially onions, which may be left out if not desired. When any one ingredient of this sort is considered absolutely mandatory, it will be noted as such.

The same is true of "larding," which was often prescribed in old-fashioned methods of cooking meat. Larding really meant inserting small strips of salt pork in incisions made for the purpose. And a "larding needle" was used to do it with. But most larding simply meant putting slices or strips of salt pork on the surface of the meat to be cooked.

When one particular piece of meat is prescribed in a recipe, it generally means that type of meat is preferable. But some other kind of meat will often taste as good.

OLD-TIME NOTES ON CARING FOR BEEF

The quality of a piece of beef for eating, providing it is fairly fat and not too old, depends on how it is handled between killing and cooking. The great secret of tender beef is ripeness. In 1868, my great-grandmother Sarah was a new bride at 22. A successful innkeeper in Delaware County, New York, whose steaks and chops were noted as invariably good, was asked how he managed it. He told her that he was always careful "to buy good meat," and that he kept it "long enough to insure its being tender." The time specified by him was "a week or more." According to this man, lamb needed to "hang" for some time but not as long as beef. He stored his meats where it was cold, but "never directly on the ice." An ordinary ice-closet was utilized. The innkeeper quoted above told my great-grandmother that he never used a forequarter of beef for steaks or roasts. He generally bought whole sirloins, or the tips of the sirloin, for both.

The early American homemaker, however, used much of the forequarter for both steaks and roasts. This was especially true if she lived in a rural district, and depended on "home-killed" meat or on occasional visits of the butcher's cart. The chuck ribs were considered good for either purpose. And there is a piece of the forequarter, under the shoulder, that is quite tender and juicy.

OLD-TIME BEEF COOKING POINTERS

An old-time "plate piece" of beef was simply a piece of meat from which the bones were taken after it was boiled. The whole piece was then tightly pressed and served when cold.

Young beef has a fine, firm texture and creamy-white fat. The suet (hard fat) will be dry and with little membrane. Old beef is darker in color than young beef, and coarser in fiber.

In my great-grandmother's judgement, the only sensible way to cook a sirloin or porterhouse steak is first to remove the bone. She felt it was only in the way while cooking and carving, and it added nothing to the flavor. Besides, the bone itself was much better for soup if taken out raw.

In the old days a hot platter was used to serve hot beef, and it was eaten on hot plates. These were considered necessities to the highest gastronomic satisfaction. Cold and cooling greases were felt to be very objectionable.

Beef was made tender by cooking it in a mixture of vinegar and water. Six quarts of water to 2 1/2 cups vinegar was the proportion recommended.

In turning a steak, if done with a fork, take care not to prick the lean meat as this will let out the juice.

In making gravy, my great-grandmother was always careful to first remove (skim off) the fat. Nothing was worse to her than to have a half inch of grease on the surface in the gravy boat (dish). She felt her gravy was much nicer when strained.

BEEF RISSOLES—FAVORITE OF JEFFERSON DAVIS

Finely chop up some cold roast beef.[1] Season highly with salt and pepper. To each cup meat add 1 tablespoon chopped parsley and 1/2 cup fine bread crumbs. Mix into a smooth paste with 2 unbeaten eggs. Form into balls. Dip them first in egg, and then in bread crumbs. Fry in very hot grease. Serve as plain croquettes, or with a brown sauce poured over them. *Note:* Jefferson Davis enjoyed this delicacy while he was President of the Confederacy between 1861 and 1865. He liked them best with an olive brown sauce accompaniment.[2]

GREAT-GRANDMOTHER MITCHELL'S BROILED STEAKS

Almost every part of lean beef was used for steaks in the old days. The very best steaks in a beef's carcass were believed to be the thick end of the sirloin or large "porterhouse." Then there were the small porterhouse steaks, which furnished some tenderloin. Lastly, were the sirloin steaks, rumps, chuck ribs, and round. These all furnished better or poorer steaks of varying cost. Some round steak was considered to be much better than some sirloin. It depended on the general quality and condition of the carcass, the care of the beef after killing, and the skill in cooking.

My Great-grandmother Mitchell detested people who had

1. Recipe included herein
2. Recipe in Chapter 13

to have their steak "all dried up." She believed that those who could eat rare steak knew what tasted best. "Thick and rare" was her method of steak preparation. And, as she often said, this did not mean "raw." But only a good-quality piece of meat was considered fit for a rare-broiled steak. In her estimation, the poorer cuts needed more cooking to make them palatable. Broiling takes a few minutes longer, and more care, but a steak 1 1/2 inches to 2 inches thick is far better to most people when served than one a half-inch thick. The latter is apt to be too well done and rather dry.

Great-grandmother Mitchell prepared her broiled steaks in this manner: Place the thick slice of meat in a broiler over very bright coals. Turn often to insure the quick cooking of the outside. This keeps the juices in the meat and allows each side to be broiled without burning. Test the steak by cutting through the thickest part of the meat. When done, it should be a deep pink inside. Put onto a hot platter. Season with salt and pieces of butter scattered over the top. Place in the oven a few moments before serving. *Note:* If everyone to be served likes pepper, it should be added along with the salt and butter. Otherwise, let each person pepper their own portion.

OLD SOUTHERN BEEFSTEAK
WITH OLIVES OR MUSHROOMS

1 tablespoon butter
1 tablespoon flour
1 1/2 cups soup stock
    or
1 1/2 cups beef extract[3]
salt to taste
pepper to taste

1 tablespoon Worcester-
    shire sauce[4]
1/2 cup olives, chopped
    or
1/2 cup mushrooms,
    chopped

3. Recipes in Chapter 1
4. Recipe in Chapter 13

Make a sauce with the butter and flour stirred in a sauce-pan until browned. Then gradually add the soup stock or beef extract and season with salt and pepper. Flavor with Worcestershire sauce and stir in the olives or mushrooms. Pour this sauce over the steaks after they have finished broiling. Set in a warm oven (about 300 degrees) for 20 minutes. *Note:* The olive flavor was most popular in the Old South, but the mushroom flavor is much less pronounced. Try both.

GREAT-GRANDMOTHER SHAW'S BEST ROAST BEEF

Have the oven very hot (450 degrees) for roasting beef. This cooks the outside of the meat and keeps the juices in. Put the meat on the rack of a roasting pan or "dripping pan," as it was commonly called in great-grandmother's day. Dredge (sprinkle) with flour, salt and pepper. Put 1 cup water in the bottom of the pan and place it in the oven. Turn the meat when the upper side is brown. Then start basting with the liquid in the pan, or use hot water if needed. Allow 15 to 20 minutes for every pound of beef being roasted. If the roast is to be rare, the heat must be greater at first than if the meat is to be well done. When the meat is done, take it out of the pan and lay it on a large platter. Place the roasting pan on top of the stove. Pour 1 cup boiling water into it. Allow to simmer with the brown juices already in the pan. Smoothly blend 1 tablespoon flour with 1 cup milk. Stir this into the pan. Cook, stirring all the time, until the gravy is smooth and thick. Then strain it into a tureen. *Note:* Old-fashioned Yorkshire pudding[5] is made exclusively to accompany roast beef on the dinner table. It is well worth making.

---

5. Recipe in Chapter 22

BOILED CORNED BEEF IN THE OLDEN DAYS

If the corned beef is very salty, soak it for 1/2 hour in cold water. Put it on to boil in enough fresh cold water to cover the meat. Skim occasionally when it begins to boil. Simmer until tender. Then let the meat stand in the water until it is cold. You can now pick the meat to pieces and press it in a loaf pan. But it is better to have a solid piece of meat to press. Put the solid meat under a board. Place a heavy weight on the board and set aside. This will solidify the corned beef. *Note:* My great-great-grandmother always put 4 or 5 cloves and 3 tablespoons molasses in the water in which her corned beef was to be boiled. This was especially done when the corned beef was being made to be eaten cold. After 1 hour the water was changed and more molasses and cloves were added.

GREAT-AUNT CAROL ANN'S BRISKET DELIGHT

A piece of brisket that contains the gristle is considered the best piece of meat for this old-fashioned dish. Use 7 pounds of beef. It should be trimmed and then put in a stew pan with the following ingredients:

5 slices bacon	4 allspice corns
1 onion	2 blades mace
2 carrots	2 cups beef stock[6]
bunch of herbs	or
4 cloves	2 cups water

Simmer slowly, until the meat is tender. It is then ready to serve. Garnish the meat, when served, with mushrooms, boiled turnips, and carrots.[7] Pour the flavored liquor, thickened with rice flour, around the meat.

6. Recipe in Chapter 1
7. Recipes in Chapter 3

OLD-FASHIONED FILLET OF BEEF

Prepare the beef by wiping and removing all fat and veins. Lard it (see beginning of chapter) with salt pork or nice pieces of beef fat. Dredge the meat with flour, salt and pepper. Bake in a hot oven (400 to 425 degrees) for 20 or 30 minutes. Serve with mushrooms if desired. *Note:* the fillet of beef is the tenderloin.

GREAT-GRANDMOTHER SHAW'S FABULOUS STUFFED FILLET

Cut deeply into the center of a 3-pound piece of fillet. Stuff with cooked ox tongue cut in small pieces. Lard (see beginning of chapter) the outside of the meat. Season well with salt and pepper. Cover with buttered paper. Place in a well-buttered dish. Bake in a qiuck oven (400 to 425 degrees) for 15 minutes. Then take 1/2 cup rich stock[8] and 1/4 cup port wine and pour over the meat. Cook until the meat is only slightly underdone. Then lay the meat on a bed of boiled rice.[9] Garnish with artichokes that have been cooked, cored, and filled with boiled green peas. Also garnish with whole small boiled potatoes that have been fried to a nice brown. *Note:* Boil the liquor remaining in the pan with 1/2 cup homemade tomato sauce.[10] Then strain and serve separately.

CIVIL WAR PERIOD PRESSED BEEF

During the years of the Civil War, pressed or spiced beef became very popular. It was made from the cheaper parts of the meat. And this meat dish was nourishing as well as

---

8. Recipes in Chapter 1
9. Recipe in Chapter 3
10. Recipe in Chapter 13

economical. My great-great-grandmother always used the middle cut of the shin. She removed all particles of skin and bone, and then cut the meat into several pieces. It was then covered with boiling water. She let it simmer until the meat was well cooked. It was then taken out of the pan and the liquor was seasoned with salt, pepper, and sage. This was blended with the meat and stirred well. The mixture was immediately poured or packed in a deep tin. When cold, she cut in thin slices and served. It was an ideal meat for soldiers who were on the move.

GRANDMOTHER PELTON'S FRIED PICKLED TRIPE

This is a very old recipe that was given my grandmother by the mother of a dear friend. Soak the tripe for 1 hour in lukewarm water. Then roll it in a towel and squeeze until as free from moisture as possible. Cut into small pieces, dip in beaten egg and then lightly roll in flour. Fry to a golden brown in half butter and half lard. Made properly, this can be a most appetizing dish. Many old-timers liked to fry fresh tripe better than the pickled. It had the advantage of one's being able to add vinegar (or better, lemon juice) to suit their taste. *Note:* My grandmother felt that no process would reduce the excessive acidity of pickled tripe without more or less destroying its palatablity. She preferred her tripe cooked without crumbs, batter, or even eggs. And she found tripe to also be very nice if properly broiled.

EARLY AMERICAN BEEF MOLD

Break 2 thick slices of brown bread[11] in a large wooden mixing bowl. Blend in sufficient gravy to moisten it well. Add enough minced cold beef to fill a quart mold. Season

---

11. Recipe in *Natural Baking the Old-Fashioned Way,* by the same author.

with salt, pepper and 1 teaspoon Worcestershire sauce.[12] Mix these ingredients with enough raw egg to hold it all together. Pack it firmly into the buttered and floured mold. My great-great-grandmother used a lard pail. Cover tightly and boil for 1 full hour. Empty the meat out of the mold and serve hot with homemade tomato sauce. *Note:* Molds were popular many long years ago. They were simply containers made of tin and were fitted with a tight lid or cover. They are regaining popularity today and replicas can be found in many stores, or original old-time molds can often be picked up at farm auctions, and in antique stores.

GREAT-GRANDMOTHER MITCHELL'S STUFFED ROUND STEAK

Trim the rough, fatty edges from a thick slice of round steak. Let it stand for 4 hours in cider vinegar[13] that has been spiced with salt, pepper, mustard, clove, and allspice. Make incisions half way through the slice and lard it (see beginning of chapter) with thin slices of salt pork. Make a highly seasoned stuffing.[14] Put the stuffing on the meat slice and roll it up. Tie firmly with strips of thin cloth or string. Lay the roll in a frying pan and brown it in hot grease. Half cover with boiling water. Cover and let simmer for 4 hours. Now take the roll of meat from the pan and skim the grease from the liquor. Mix 1 tablespoon flour with a little cold water. Stir this into the liquor and let it boil for 10 minutes. Strain over the meat and serve.

EARLY NORTH CAROLINA SIRLOIN TIPS

Cut 2 pounds of sirloin steak into small pieces. Dip them

12. Recipes in Chapter 13
13. Recipe in Chapter 19
14. Recipe in Chapter 22

in a mixture of cider vinegar, salt, pepper, and herbs. Dredge (sprinkle) each piece with flour. Fry in melted suet (hard fat) with 4 small sliced onions. When browned, put the meat and juices into a stew pan. Add 1 cup boiling water and 2 sliced carrots. Season with salt, pepper, and spices to taste. Cover the pan tightly and simmer for 3 hours. When ready to serve, the liquor in the pan should be thicked with 1 teaspoon rice flour.

GRANDMOTHER COLLISTER'S
BEEF STEW WITH DUMPLINGS

This is an economical old-fashioned dish that is at the same time exceedingly palatable and nutritious. There are various ways of preparing it. But the following is Grandmother Collister's own special method and it is known to be delightful. Cut 1 1/2 pounds of round steak in pieces 2 inches square. Put into a stew pan, to simmer, with 2 quarts water. Season with salt and pepper. When the water is reduced in half, add 1 slice of onion, 1 sliced carrot, and 6 whole small potatoes. Make a thickening of 1 tablespoon flour thoroughly mixed with 1/2 cup cold milk. Stir this into the pan liquor. Put in the dumplings[15] 15 minutes before serving.

GREAT-AUNT MARY'S
IRISH STEW OF THE OLD DAYS

This was often called an Irish beef stew in the days long past. My Great-aunt Mary and her mother before her did not use onions, turnips, carrots and, other common vegetables in their Irish stew. It was much plainer than the usual, and it was economical. This recipe was used to make an ad-

15. Recipe in Chapter 22

mirable stormy day dinner. Take a 3-pound piece of lean beef and cut it into 2-inch squares. Put the pieces into a pot with enough boiling water to cover them. Simmer until the meat is tender. Then skim off the grease. Put in as many sliced raw potatoes as there is meat. Do this in alternate layers of meat and potatoes. Season to taste. Cover closely and stew for 1/2 hour. Blend 1 tablespoon flour with 1/2 cup cold milk. Stir this into the pot liquor in order to thicken it.

GRANDDAD'S FAVORITE STUFFED HEART

Beef heart made a nice roast in the old days. It furnished more meat for the money than any other part of the animal. The heart is first boiled for 1 hour. It is then packed with a good stuffing[16] and roasted for 2 more hours. Stuffed beef heart was a highly prized delicacy in the days of Early America.

ABIGAIL ADAMS'S HASHED STEAK ON TOAST

This is an excellent old-time way of using up cold beef-steak or roast, of which there is often some left overs. Mrs. Adams often made this for her husband as a breakfast dish. Remove the fat, bone, and gristle from the meat. Chop the meat up until it is fine and put it in a stew pan. Add 1 tablespoon butter, a seasoning of salt and pepper, and enough boiling water to moisten it. Blend well and place the pan where it will stay warm. Toast and butter thin slices of homemade bread. Pour the warm hashed meat mixture over the toast and serve immediately.

OLD WESTERN FRIED BEEF CAKES

Mince some leftover cold beef. Mix with 1/3 the quantity

16. Recipes in Chapter 22

of mashed potatoes. Season to taste with salt and pepper. Add a little parsley, if you like it. Blend this with the beaten yolk of 1 egg. Form into cakes 1/2 inch thick. Dust them with flour. Fry in beef drippings, lard, or butter. Let the cakes brown nicely and then serve while hot. *Note:* This recipe was a favorite of many gold miners during the 1849 California rush.

GREAT-AUNT GOLDIE'S FAVORITE BEEF LIVER

Soak the liver in boiling water while the fat is being fried out of thin slices of bacon or salt pork. Then drain the liver and remove all fat and veins. Cut into small pieces and sprinkle liberally with salt and pepper. Fry in the hot bacon grease. Turn the pieces so they will be thoroughly done. Garnish with the pieces of fried bacon, cut into strips.

UNRIVALLED OLD-FASHIONED BEEFSTEAK PIE

Use about 3 pounds of the cheapest beef cut. Remove all the fat and chop the meat into pieces about 2 inches square. Put the meat into a saucepan with 2 cups boiling water and a seasoning of salt. Simmer until the meat is tender. Strain the meat from the liquor. Use 2 forks and separate the meat fibers as much as possible. Line the sides of a deep pudding dish with mashed potato or biscuit dough.[17] Put the meat in. Pour in the liquor from the saucepan, thickened with flour. Cover with 1/2-inch layer of mashed potato or biscuit dough. Place in a slow oven (300 degrees). If mashed potatoes are used, sprinkle small pieces of butter over the top and bake until browned. If biscuit dough is used, bake for 45 minutes.

---

17. Recipes in *Natural Baking the Old-Fashioned Way,* by the same author.

GREAT-AUNT MARILYN'S BRAISED BEEF

Trim a 4-pound round steak, or the face of the rump. Dredge (sprinkle) with salt, pepper and flour. Dice 2 small onions and fry in salt pork or beef drippings until a golden brown. When the onions are done, remove them from the pan. Put the beef in and brown all sides of it. Add more grease if necessary. When browned, put the steak into a braising pan (a large-mouthed bean pot answers the purpose) on skewers, so it will not stick to the bottom. Add 4 cups of boiling water and 1 tablespoon herbs tied in a muslin bag (try thyme, bay leaves, and parsley). Pour the fried onions around the beef and cover the pan closely. Cook in a moderate oven (350 degrees) for 4 hours. Baste the steak every 20 minutes. Turn the steak once during cooking. When tender, the steak should be taken out and put on a platter. Strain the liquor and add 2 tablespoons flour mixed in a little cold water. Boil until it thickens and then pour this gravy over the steak. Lemon juice, tomatoes, or mushrooms may be added to the gravy if desired. Garnish with small boiled onions or potato cakes.[18]

REAL EARLY AMERICAN KIDNEY RECIPES

Stewed Beef Kidney: Cut the kidney into slices. Season highly with salt and pepper. Fry to a light brown. Gently stew for 1/2 hour in a light milky mixture of water and a little flour. Serve with the gravy in the pan.

Fried Beef Kidney: Cut the kidney into thin slices. Soak 2 or 3 hours in warm water. Change the water twice in order to remove the strong taste. Drain the kidney slices and season with salt and pepper. Dredge (sprinkle) with

---

18. Recipes in Chapter 3

flour. Fry in butter until the slices are nicely browned. Serve with any highly seasoned gravy, or by themselves.

GREAT-GRANDMOTHER SHAW'S OX TONGUE TREATS

Boiled Ox Tongue: Soak the ox tongue for 12 hours. Boil it for 4 or 5 hours. After the tongue has thoroughly cooked, take off the outer skin by plunging it in cold water. This will enable you to remove it easily. Return the tongue to the water in which it was boiled. Allow it to slowly cool. This is the key to keeping the tongue juicy and tender. Serve it with currant jelly sauce.[19]

Roasted Ox Tongue: Soak the ox tongue for 12 hours. Boil it for 2 or 3 more hours. Skin the tongue by plunging it in cold water. This will enable you to easily remove the outer skin. Brush the tongue with a beaten egg yolk. Roll it in bread crumbs. Put on the rack of a roasting pan and roast the tongue until nicely browned. Baste it frequently with melted butter. Serve with currant jelly sauce.[20]

GREAT-GRANDMOTHER MITCHELL'S MEAT PIE

This may be made of cold roast beef or boiled beef. Or it can be made with almost any kind of cold meat. The meat is not chopped, but is cut into small 1/2-inch cubes. Season according to taste with salt, pepper, nutmeg, and other spices. Put 1 tablespoon of flour in a saucepan. Add a little butter and brown. Add 1/2 cup hot brown stock,[21] or water, if stock is not available. If water is used, put in a little more

---

19. Recipe in Chapter 13
20. Recipe in Chapter 13
21. Recipe in Chapter 1

butter to enrich the meat pie. Then put in the diced meat and cook thoroughly. Blend in 2 eggs just before taking it off the stove.

Line a buttered baking dish with a thin pie crust.[22] Fill in a layer of the meat mixture. Put on some thin slices of bacon. Alternate these layers until the dish is full. Cover with a crust. Cut a slit in the top. Bake in a moderate oven (350 degrees) until the crust has browned lightly. Serve while hot. *Note:* Carrots, turnips, onions, and other fresh vegetables may be added if desired.

GRANDMA'S BEST HAMBURG STEAK

My grandmother made her hamburger from any piece of beef. She first removed all gristle and fat. The meat was then chopped very fine. It was highly seasoned with salt, pepper, and onion juice. After thorough mixing, the meat was shaped in little square cakes. Melted butter was brushed over the meat patties and they were broiled over a good fire. Instead of always broiling, the cakes were sometimes fried in butter or pork grease. Hamburg steak was her way of utilizing lean beef not quite good enough to cook as steaks. *Note:* Some old-timers fried raw onions mixed with the meat. But in this way the onions were often burned or unevenly cooked.

---

22. Recipes in *Natural Baking the Old Fashioned Way,* by the same author.

5

Veal Cookery the Natural Way

Veal is one of the most delicious of all meat dishes. But it can be more easily ruined in cooking than beef. Great-grandmother Shaw's first canon of good veal cookery was to have the meat well done. In her own estimation, under-done veal was as bad as underdone fish. She had one other rule for good veal: "four weeks old is as young as it should ever be eaten, and six weeks is quite young enough."

There is much difference in veal as to toughness and stringiness. If tough and stringly, it is of poor quality and not very delectable. But white, tender veal, well seasoned and well cooked, is a most toothsome meat.

My great-grandmother used every part of the animal including sweetbreads, brains, head, tongue, and liver. These and her calf's-foot jelly were delights for the gourmet. And in her day, they were within easy reach of the farmer who had but a single cow or the villager who had access only to the country butcher's cart. In her own words: "What can excel a well-cooked sweetbread, or calf's liver and bacon, or calf's head with brain sauce? And a cold roast of veal, thinly sliced, with a sweet fat-and-savory stuffing?"

DELIGHTFUL OLD-FASHIONED VEAL CUTLETS

A veal cutlet is a most savory morsel whether broiled or fried, but it must be tender and well done. Start by frying 3 thin slices of salt pork. When the fat has been extracted, put a slice of veal (cut from the leg) into the pan. It should not be over 1/2 inch thick. Turn often to allow both sides to be thoroughly cooked, and browned. Season with salt. When the cutlet is taken from the pan, pour in 1/2 cup of hot water. Bring this to a boil and pour it over the meat. Serve while hot. *Note:* Flour may be added to make a thick gravy if desired. The cutlets may also be fried in crumbs or a batter. But my great-grandmother considered them better plain. She could not see any sense in "breading" a veal chop or cutlet. She felt that any meat needing thorough cooking should not be breaded or covered with a batter.

GREAT-GRANDMOTHER MITCHELL'S ROAST VEAL

A roast of veal may be treated the same as a roast of lamb, but it requires more thorough cooking. Not less than 1/2 hour to the pound is necessary. Rare lamb is all right, but rare or underdone veal is not very good. Besides the leg and loin, the breast of veal makes a delicious roasting piece. Veal is also improved by laying thin slices of salt pork on the surface before putting it in the oven.

Roasting a Loin: Put the loin on the rack of a roasting pan. Cover, heat gradually, and baste frequently—at first with salt and water, afterward with the meat juices. When the meat is nearly done, dredge (sprinkle) lightly with flour. And baste once with melted butter. When the roast is done, take from the roasting pan and lay it on a hot platter. Skim the grease from the pan liquor. Thicken the meat juices with 1 teaspoon flour. Bring to a quick boil and immeditely pour this gravy into the gravy boat (table dish). *Note:* Should the meat brown too fast, cover it with white paper.

Roast Breast: Make incisions between the ribs and the meat. Fill with a "forcemeat" (stuffing) made of fine bread crumbs,[1] bits of pork or ham chopped exceedingly small, salt, pepper, thyme, sweet marjoram, and beaten eggs. Save a little of the stuffing to thicken the gravy. Roast exactly as done for the above loin.

Roast Fillet: Make a stuffing of bread crumbs, thyme, parsley, a little nutmeg, pepper and salt. Blend in some melted butter or beef suet, and moisten with milk or hot water. Add a beaten egg to hold it more firmly together. Take out the bone from the roast. Pin the meat securely into a round with skewers. Pass a stout twine several times around the fillet, or wrap it with a band of muslin. Fill the cavity from which the bone was taken with stuffing. Make incisions in the meat with a thin, sharp knife. Pack these with stuffing also. Once in a while slip in a strip of pork or ham. Roast exactly as for the above loin.

ORIGINAL
OLD NEW ENGLAND VEAL WITH OYSTERS

Cut large, smooth slices from a fillet of veal. Trim them into a uniform shape and size. Spread each slice neatly with a dressing made of bread crumbs and a little chopped pork, seasoned with salt and pepper. Spread chopped oysters over this and carefully roll up slices. Pin each with 2 small skewers. Lay them on the rack of a roasting pan. Dash 3/4

---

1. Many excellent recipes for old-time homemade bread can be found in *Natural Baking the Old-Fashioned Way*, by the same author.

cup boiling water over them. Roast at 450 degrees, basting at least twice with melted butter. When the meat has browned, put it in a chafing dish and cover. Then add a little oyster liquor (the juice from the oysters) to the juices left in the bottom of the roasting pan. Let this simmer for 3 or 4 minutes. Thicken with 1 teaspoon browned flour, and bring to a boil. Carefully withdraw the skewers from the veal rolls. Pour the hot gravy over and around them, and serve. *Note:* If you have no skewers, bind the veal rolls with thread. Cut it, of course, before serving. This dish is delightful when eaten with gooseberry jelly or spiced gooseberries.[2]

CALF'S HEAD AND PLUCK—
A FAVORITE OF PRESIDENT JAMES MONROE
(1817–1825)

Unless you happen to live close to a farm or meat-packing plant, you will hardly find a calf's head properly dressed for cooking. Never skin a calf's head. Scald it as you would that of a pig. A little lye in the water will remove all of the hair. If the dressed head with the skin on it is not procurable, take a head from which the skin has been taken off. Assuming that you have, or can procure, a fresh calf's head, you first must clean it. Take out the brains and tongue. Put them both in a large bowl of ice cold water. Remove all of the gristle and membrane. Soak in warmish water for 2 hours. Boil the head, tongue, and heart together. Begin with cold water and slowly bring it to a boil. Pour some boiling water over the liver and let it stand for 10 minutes. Add it to the kettle when the head is nearly done. The meat and skin of the head should be removed from the bone. Serve in as well-shaped pieces as possible, with the sliced tongue, heart, and liver placed around them. They may be

2. Recipes in Chapter 18

served with a white sauce or brown sauce,[3] or, as President Monroe preferred, with brain sauce. The brain sauce he loved was made as follows:

Clean the brains. Remove the red membrane and let the brains soak in cold water for 1 hour. Then put them into lukewarm water and soak for 2 more hours. After this, put the brains into a saucepan with 2 cups cold water. Stir in 1 tablespoon lemon juice and 1/2 teaspoon salt. Boil for 10 minutes. Then take them out of the pan and plunge into ice water. Chop them into fine pieces and blend into drawn butter sauce.[4] Flavor some more with lemon juice and serve over the meat.

GREAT-GREAT-GRANDMOTHER DANIELS' VEAL STEW

Cut 2 pounds of veal into 2-inch squares. Put into a stew pan and just cover with cold water. Slowly heat and allow it to simmer until the meat is tender and the water has reduced in half. Season to taste with salt and pepper. Add 1 tablespoon flour mixed smoothly with a little cold milk. Stir in 1 tablespoon butter. Serve with crackers[5] that are to be dipped in the gravy and eaten with pieces of the meat. *Note:* Homemade dumplings[6] are often added to this stew, as well as a variety of fresh vegetables if desired.

EARLY AMERICAN VEAL STEAK

The veal for this recipe should be cut thinner than a regular beef steak. It should be thoroughly cooked through-

3. Recipes in Chapter 13
4. Recipe in Chapter 13
5. Many excellent recipes for old-time homemade crackers can be found in *Natural Baking the Old-Fashioned Way,* by the same author.
6. Recipe in Chapter 22

out. Few persons are fond of rare veal. Veal steaks should
be broiled, and they are to be turned frequently while
cooking. As the steaks are broiling, take a saucepan and put
in the following ingredients:

4 onions, minced fine
1/4 cup butter
3/4 cup boiling water

1 tablespoon tomato
catsup[7]
pinch of thyme
or parsley

Let these ingredients stew while the steaks are broiling.
Just before ready to take out of the pan, thicken the liquor
with 1 tablespoon browned flour. Add 2 tablespoons white
wine. Boil it up once hard. When the steaks are dished out,
put a small bit of butter on each. Then pour the gravy mixture over and around the steaks. *Note:* Spinach is a natural
accompaniment to veal steaks.[8]

GREAT-GRANDMOTHER SHAW'S VEAL PIE

Take 2 pounds of lean veal and cut it up into small 1-
inch cubes. Put the meat in a stewing pan and barely cover
it with water. Let it simmer until the water has been reduced in half. Then stir in 1 tablespoon flour that has been
smoothly blended in a little cold milk. Add 1 tablespoon
butter, salt and pepper to taste, and a pinch of parsley.
While the meat above is cooking, make a dough with the
following ingredients:

1 cup milk
1/2 cup lard
pinch of salt

1 1/2 teaspoon baking powder
flour to suit

7. Recipe in Chapter 3
8. Recipe in Chapter 19

Sift the baking powder with a little flour and blend this with all the other ingredients in a large wooden mixing bowl. Add flour enough to make a good dough. Roll the dough out in a 1/2-inch thick sheet. Heavily butter a deep baking dish. Line the sides of the dish with a strip of the dough.

When the baking dish is ready, strain the meat from the gravy. Shred each piece and put into the dish. Then pour the gravy over this. Make a top crust with the rest of the dough. Bake slowly (300 degrees) for 1 hour and then serve.

VEAL SCALLOP IN VICKSBURG DURING THE CIVIL WAR

Chop up some cold stewed veal until it is in fine pieces. Put a thick layer in the bottom of a well-buttered baking dish. Season with salt and pepper to taste. Next have a layer of finely powdered crackers. Strew with bits of butter and wet with a little milk. Then add more veal and season as before. And add another round of cracker crumbs, butter, and milk. When the baking dish is full, wet well with gravy or broth, diluted with warm water. Spread the top with a thick layer of cracker seasoned with salt, wet into a paste with milk and held together with a beaten egg or two. Place bits of butter thickly over this. Invert a baking pan and cover the dish with it. Bake in a moderate oven (350 degrees) for 1/2 hour if the scallop is small or 3/4 hour for a large dish. Remove the cover 10 minutes before taking the dish from the oven. Let it brown on top. *Note:* This is a simple and economical meal. It is a treat for anyone who enjoys veal. Children generally like it exceedingly well. It even tastes better on the second day.

GREAT-GREAT-GRANDMOTHER HORTON'S
OLD-TIME SWEETBREADS

Remove the membranes and the veins. Put into a saucepan of boiling water. Add salt to taste and 1 tablespoon
lemon juice. Boil for 20 minutes. Take the sweetbreads and
drop them into a bowl of ice water. This hardens them and
prepares the sweetbreads for the various styles of cooking.

Fried Sweetbreads: Dry the sweetbreads with a linen
cloth. Make incisions all around and stuff with small pieces
of salt pork or bacon. Lay them in a frying pan that has
been well buttered or greased. Cook to a fine brown, turning
frequently until the bacon is crisp. Or simply roll the sweetbreads in fine crumbs, eggs, and crumbs again. Fry in deep
fat, or in a little grease, as may be preferred. Or the sweetbreads may be cut in slices, and fried after breading, as
above.

Stewed Sweetbreads: Stew the sweetbreads in very little
water a second time. Let them simmer until tender. Then
for each sweetbread, add 1 heaping teaspoon butter, a little
parsley, salt, pepper, and 1 tablespoon cream. Let them simmer in this gravy for 5 minutes. Then take them up. Send
to the table in a covered dish, with the gravy poured over
them.

Broiled Sweetbreads: Dry the sweetbreads with a linen
cloth. Rub them with a mixture of butter, salt and pepper.
Turn frequently while broiling. Roll them over, now and
then, in a plate containing some hot melted butter. This
will prevent the sweetbreads from getting too dry and hard.
They should only be broiled about 10 minutes.

Roasted Sweetbreads: Wipe the sweetbreads until perfectly

dry. Lay them on the rack of a roasting pan and put into the oven. Baste with butter and water until they begin to brown. Withdraw them for an instant, roll in beaten egg, then in cracker crumbs. Return to the oven for 10 minutes longer. Baste twice with melted butter. Then lay them in a chafing dish while you make the gravy. The following are added to the juices in the roasting pan: 1/2 cup hot water, some chopped parsley, 1 teaspoon browned flour, and the juice of 1/2 lemon. Pour this gravy over the sweetbreads before sending to the table.

COLONIAL PERIOD
CROQUETTES OF CALF'S BRAINS

Wash the brains very thoroughly until they are free from membranous matter and perfectly white. Beat them until they become a smooth paste. Now blend in the following:

pinch of sage	2 tablespoons bread crumbs
pinch of salt	(moistened with milk)
pinch of pepper	1 egg, well beaten

Roll into balls with floured hands. Dip in beaten egg and then cracker crumbs. Fry in butter or veal drippings. *Note:* These brain croquettes make a pleasant accompaniment to boiled spinach.[9] Heap the spinach in the center of the platter. Arrange the croquettes around it.

GRANDMOTHER PELTON'S VEAL FRICASSEE

This is like any other fricassee. The meat is cut up in small pieces, and browned in butter. Put into a kettle and blend in the following ingredients:

9. Recipe in Chapter 3

VEAL COOKERY THE NATURAL WAY

2 tablespoons flour   pinch of pepper
2 cups water   salt to taste
1/4 onion, grated

Simmer gently for 1 hour. Then take out the meat and put it in the center of a platter. Surround it with boiled rice.[10] Beat the yolk of an egg and blend it in with the sauce. Pour this over the meat and serve.

ORIGINAL OLDEN-DAY VEAL CROQUETTES

1 tablespoon butter   1/2 teaspoon parsley
2 tablespoons flour   dash of onion juice
1 cup milk, scalded   1/2 teaspoon celery salt
2 cups cooked veal,   pinch of salt
    finely chopped   pinch of pepper

Rub the butter and flour smoothly together in a saucepan. Add the scalded milk and stir until it thickens. Stir in the veal. Season with parsley, onion juice, celery salt, salt and pepper. Mix well and set aside to cool. Form into balls, squares, or cones, roll in crumbs and fry in hot deep fat. Remove from the grease when browned.

GRANDMOTHER COLLISTER'S VEAL POTPIE

This can be made with the cheaper cuts of veal or the leftovers from a roast. The meat is cut into small chunks. The bones are cracked. Both are put into a saucepan and covered with cold water. Season to suit with whole cloves, peppercorns, bay leaves, and sliced onions. When the meat is tender, take it out of the saucepan and cut it up into smaller pieces. Strain the liquor and return the meat to it.

---

10. Recipe in Chapter 3

Add any combination of vegetables desired. My grand-mother liked to use potatoes, turnips, parsnips, carrots, corn, and green beans.

Make some bread dough[11] and let it rise until it is very light. Then cut the dough into small cakes. Cook them in a steamer over the broth. Or these cakes can be made like biscuits and steamed over the broth.

GRANDPA PELTON'S FAVORITE
OLD-FASHIONED VEAL LOAF

4 pounds raw veal, chopped fine	3 eggs
1/2 pound crackers, rolled into large crumbs	2 teaspoons salt
	1/2 teaspoon pepper
	pinch of allspice
	1 tablespoon butter

Blend all of the above ingredients in a large wooden mixing bowl. Pack it all into a loaf pan and bake in a moderate oven (350 degrees) for 2 hours. Let it cool in the baking pan and then serve. *Note:* This recipe was a favorite of my Grandfather Frank Curtis Pelton, who was personal secretary to Ballington Booth at the time Booth split with his father, General William Booth of the Salvation Army, and before he organized the Volunteers of America. My grandfather also did some rather important historical writing in his day. Included are *Eel Rack,* a volume of free verse on the early history of the Delaware River Valley in New York State, *Tomahawks Along the Delaware,* a novel about the battle of Minisink, and *Roughnecks of the Empire,* a verse portrayal of the Tom Quick–Sir William Johnston Revolutionary period.

---

11. Many excellent recipes for old-time homemade bread, biscuits, and crackers can be found in *Natural Baking the Old-Fashioned Way,* by the same author.

EARLY AMERICAN VEAL TERRAPIN

2 cups cooked veal, chopped fine	3 eggs, hard-boiled[12]
	salt to taste
3 tablespoons butter	pepper to taste
1 cup cream	parsley to taste, chopped

Put the chopped veal into a saucepan. Add the butter and cream. Rub the egg yolks to a paste and press the whites through a sieve. Stir both into the veal and let it come to a boil. Add the seasonings and serve while hot. *Note:* This makes a fine old-time luncheon or supper dish and is a pleasing variety to the ways of serving veal.

GREAT-GREAT-GRANDMOTHER NORTHRUP'S JELLIED VEAL

Wash a knuckle of veal, and cut it into 3 pieces. Put into a kettle with enough water to cover the meat. Boil slowly until the meat will slip easily from the bones. Then take the pieces out of the pan. Remove all of the bones and chop the meat into fine pieces. Season to taste with salt, pepper, mace, and thyme. Add 2 minced scallions. Put all of this back into the pan liquor. Let it boil until almost dry, and it is rather difficult to stir. Stir in the juice of 1 lemon just before it is taken from the stove. Turn into a mold and set aside in a cool place until the next day. Slice the jellied veal when cold, and serve garnished with parsley.

---

12. Recipe in Chapter 9

6
Old-Fashioned Lamb Cookery

In actual practice the old-time dividing line between mutton and lamb was very shadowy. "Spring" lamb was a baby sheep not exceeding 3 months in age. It was generally divided into a fore and hindquarter. The hindquarter brought the highest price, although certain parts of the forequarter were considered just as good. The earliest spring lamb was a costly luxury. It was hardly within the means of the average early American housewife. What was commonly known as mutton is nothing more than an older lamb or a full-grown sheep. This was within the reach of the average family, and it formed one of its choicest meat dishes. *Note:* In modern America we no longer have such a selection. We simply purchase what we call lamb. And this is actually similar to the cheaper cuts of mutton of earlier times.

OLD-TIME NOTES ON LAMB

What are called "lamb chops," are simply rib chops cut from the forequarter. In the old days these were trimmed.

The fat and flesh were cut away from the bone. They were then called "French chops." The leg and loin that form the hindquarter were then, and still are today, used for cutlets. The hindquarter was usually roasted whole, or if the lamb was large, the leg often was used to make a roast by itself. The "saddle" of lamb or "mutton" consists of the double loin cut from the legs, without splitting it down the back. In the old days this was used to make the finest roast, but it is not commonly used for this today. Of the forequarter, only the shoulder was used for roasting. The rest was used for stews or baked lamb dishes.

GREAT-GRANDMOTHER SHAW'S ROAST LAMB

Trim the piece selected for the roast and wash it in cold water. Wipe it dry and put on the rack in a roasting pan or "dripping pan," as it was referred to in the old days. Season it with salt and pepper. Dust with dry flour. Put 1/2 cup hot water in the pan. Cover with another pan or the roaster lid and place in the oven. The oven should be hot (425 degrees). After a few minutes, when the water has boiled away, add a little more water. Continue this up to 1/2 hour before the meat is done. At this point, remove the pan cover and occasionally baste the meat with the drippings. This will brown the roast nicely. Lamb should be roasted for about 20 minutes to the pound.

The water used in this recipe keeps the meat from drying out. And it mixes with the fat and juices making a foundation for a rich and savory gravy. If the juices in the pan are not sufficiently brown by the time the roast is done, mix 1 1/2 tablespoons browned flour with 1 cup milk. Place the roasting pan on top of the stove. Add 1 cup hot water and then stir in the flour and milk. Boil this until the gravy is thick. It should then be strained into a gravy tureen. *Note:*

Roast lamb should be eaten with mint sauce[1] or currant jelly,[2] and asparagus or green beans.[3] Lettuce salad is likewise a desirable accompaniment.

OLD NEW ENGLAND BOILED LAMB

To boil a leg of lamb the old-fashioned way, first wipe it carefully with a damp cloth. Then dust a piece of cheesecloth thickly with flour. Roll the leg in it, tie, and place in a large kettle of boiling water. Let this boil rapidly for 5 minutes. Then lower the heat and let it simmer. Cook this way for 20 minutes to each pound of lamb. When done, remove the floured cloth. Dish up the lamb and serve it with caper sauce.[1] *Note:* Boiled lamb should never be overdone.

GREAT-GRANDMOTHER MITCHELL'S LAMB FRICASSEE

The breast is the best part of the lamb for a fricassee. It should be cut up in small pieces and dredged (sprinkled) with flour. Put in a frying pan and brown with butter or meat drippings. When nicely browned, put the meat into a stew pan with a sliced onion. Cover with boiling water and simmer until any bones will easily slip out of the meat. Then take out the bones. Strain the liquor and skim off the grease. Put the liquor back in the stew pan with the meat and bring it to a boil. Add salt and pepper to taste. Stew until nearly tender. Then put in 4 cups peas (if raw they must first be boiled). Also add 2 cups boiled macaroni or 2 cups asparagus tips. Simmer for 15 minutes. *Note:* The macaroni or asparagus can be omitted if not desired.

1. Recipe in Chapter 13
2. Recipe in Chapter 18
3. Recipe in Chapter 3

EARLY AMERICAN LAMB STEW

Cut up 3 to 4 pounds of lamb into small pieces not more than 1 1/2 inches long. Crack the bones and remove all the fat. Put the meat in a kettle and cover it with cold water. Put a cover on the kettle and heat gradually. Add nothing else until the meat has stewed for 1 hour. Then put in 1/2 pound of salt pork cut into strips, a chopped onion, and some pepper. Cover and stew for 1 hour longer, or until the meat is very tender. Now make some dumplings[4] and add them to the stew. Let it all boil for 10 minutes. Season further with a little parsley and thyme. Thicken the stew by adding 2 tablespoons flour stirred into 1 cup cold milk. Bring to a boil. Then serve at once in a tureen or deep covered dish. *Note:* If green corn is in season, this stew can be greatly improved. Cut the kernels from the ears and add them to the stew about 1 hour before it is to be taken from the stove. Try this recipe as an inexpensive family dinner.

GREAT-GREAT-GRANDMOTHER HORTON'S LAMB PIE

Spread the bottom of a baking dish with bread crumbs.[5] Fill with alternate layers of thinly sliced cold roast lamb and peeled, sliced tomatoes. Season each layer with salt, pepper, and bits of butter. The last layer should be tomatoes covered with bread crumbs. Bake for 3/4 hour at 325 degrees. Serve immediately.

---

4. Recipe in Chapter 22
5. Many excellent recipes for old-time homemade bread and crackers can be found in *Natural Baking the Old Fashioned Way,* by the same author.

EARLY SOUTH CAROLINA LAMB CHOPS

The lamb chops should be neatly trimmed. Leave a fair amount of fat, but no skin or pieces of bone. Wipe with a wet cloth. If fried, put the chops into a very hot frying pan and sear one side for 1 minute. Then turn them and sear the other side. They should then be cooked more slowly. Many old-timers preferred their lamb chops rare and salted to taste. Lamb chops were also often broiled like a steak, or breaded and fried. Breading lamb chops was done quite simply in the Old South. Dip each chop in beaten egg. Roll in pounded crackers. Then fry in hot lard, butter, or meat drippings. Serve the chops while hot. If the chops are broiled instead, butter them just before serving.

GREAT-AUNT MARILYN'S BAKED LEG OF LAMB

We say "baked," although it is just as much "roasted" as any meat claiming that distinction. The only peculiarity of this recipe lies in boning the leg of lamb before putting it in the oven. This is a great comfort to the carver, and nothing is lost in the procedure. The lamb can be stuffed[6] or not, according to individual taste. Follow the directions given for *Great-Grandmother Shaw's Roast Lamb*. Bake in a hot oven (425 degrees), but watch it closely—lamb is always better when somewhat rare.

REAL OLD-FASHIONED LAMB CUTLETS

Neatly trim the cutlets of all fat and bone. Lay aside the trimmings you cut off for making a delicious gravy. Pour a little melted butter over the cutlets. Let them lie

6. Recipe in Chapter 22

in the butter for 15 minutes. Keep them just warm enough
to prevent the butter from hardening. Then dip each cutlet
in beaten egg. Roll in cracker crumbs. Lay them on the
rack in your roasting pan with a *very* little water (no more
than 1/4 cup) in the bottom. Bake quickly (425 degrees)
without covering the pan. Baste often with butter and water.

While the cutlets are baking, begin to prepare the gravy.
Put the fat, bone, and bits of meat trimmings in a saucepan with enough cold water to cover them. Stew and
season with sweet herbs, pepper, salt, and 1 tablespoon
tomato catsup.[7] Strain when all the substance has been extracted from the meat and bones. Thicken with browned
flour. Pour over the cutlets when they are served.

GRANDMOTHER PELTON'S FRIZZLED LAMB

The lamb should be cut in thin shavings from a very
"ripe" leg (one that has hung for some time after being
killed). Blend 2 tablespoons butter and 2 tablespoons currant jelly[8] in a saucepan. Heat and let melt together. Put
in the lamb shavings and highly season with salt, pepper,
and mustard.[9] Cook sharply for 5 minutes. Serve on toast
or over potatoes while very hot. *Note:* This is an excellent
recipe for chafing dish cooking.

OLD VIRGINIA ROAST CHRISTMAS LAMB

A Christmas saddle of lamb is very fine when properly
prepared. Wash it well, inside and out, with cider vinegar.
Do not wipe; hang it up to dry in a cool place. When the
vinegar has dried off, throw a clean cloth over it to keep

---

7. Recipe in Chapter 19
8. Recipe in Chapter 18
9. Recipe in Chapter 19

out the dust. On the next day, take down the meat and sponge it over again with cider vinegar. Put it back in a cool place. Repeat this process 3 times a week for 2 weeks. Keep the meat hung in a cool place, and covered, except while you are washing it.

When you are ready to cook the lamb, wipe it off with a dry cloth, but *do not* wash it. Put the meat on the rack of a large roasting pan. Pour 1 cup water in the bottom. Cover and roast—basting for the first hour with butter and water. Continue basting for 1 more hour with the meat drippings. Take off the pan cover and continue basting for 2 more hours. A large saddle of lamb will require 4 hours to roast.

When the roast is done, take it out of the pan and place on a large platter. Cover to keep hot. Skim all the grease from the juices in the pan. Add 3/4 cup walnut, mushroom, or tomato catsup,[10] 1/4 cup white wine, and 1 tablespoon browned flour. Boil it up once and immediately send to the table in a sauce boat. Always serve currant or some other tart jelly with this Christmas roast.[11] If properly cooked, a roast saddle of lamb, prepared in accordance with these directions, will strongly resemble venison in taste.

Note: An old Virginia gentleman whom my great-great-grandmother used to know always hung up the finest saddle of lamb his plantation could furnish, *weeks* before Christmas. He had it sponged off with cider vinegar every other day, until the morning of the important 25th. The excellence of his Christmas lamb was the talk of the surrounding area.

10. Recipe in Chapter 19
11. Recipe in Chapter 18

7

Pork Cookery the Natural Way

Pork has always been among our most useful meats, and for many purposes it is among the most palatable. A nice piece of pig pork, fatted on proper food, is a delight on any table, in whatever form presented. The variety of old-time dishes made from fresh and salt pork is extensive. In earlier days of our history, no part of the pig was wasted. It was utilized, according to my great-grandmother, "from the tip of the snout to the end of the tail."

To begin with, pork will "cook itself." It requires no butter or other foreign fat. It was at one time the almost universal aid in cooking other meats. And it was used as an inexpensive and popular shortening when the lady of the house did her daily baking.

Many long years ago, if one had good salt pork in the house, one was never without the makings of a delicious meal. A most appetizing meal could be prepared by using the salt pork with eggs, potatoes, milk, and cornmeal or flour. Salt pork was the foundation of all camp supplies. And it was indispenable to the more civilized community as well.

Ham, bacon, sausage, head cheese, souse (pickled pork),

104 NATURAL COOKING THE OLD-FASHIONED WAY

and other cured pork products are delicious when properly made. When improperly made they are horrid. A fresh sparerib, shoulder, cutlet or chop from well-fed pork and well cooked are unexcelled.

GREAT-GREAT-GRANDMOTHER HORTON'S ROASTED PIG

Roast pig is not a common family dish, but it was once extremely popular, especially where the family was large enough, or at least on important holidays. A well-cooked roast pig is quite as delicious as Charles Lamb described it to be. A month old pig, if it is properly raised and plump, is best for this purpose.

It is important to know how to properly dress and prepare a baby pig for roasting. Such a pig is no longer than a Thanksgiving turkey. Make ready a large kettle of scalding water. Lay the pig in ice cold water for 15 minutes. Then, holding it by a hind leg, plunge the pig into the boiling water. Shake it violently to help loosen the hairs. Take it out, wipe dry, and rub the hair off with a rough cloth or a whisk broom. Brush from the tail to the head until the skin is clean and free of all hair. Then wrap the pig in a wet cloth. Keep this cloth saturated with cold water until you are ready to stuff the pig. If these directions are implicitly followed, the pig will be fair and white.

Make your special roast pig stuffing[1] and stuff the pig into its natural size and shape. Sew it up. Bend the forefeet backwards and his hind feet forward, under and close to the body. Skewer them into the proper position. Dry the pig well and dredge it with flour. Put it on the rack of a large roasting pan. Add a little hot salted water in the bottom of the roasting pan. Baste with butter and water 3 times as the pig gradually warms up. Continue to baste

1. Recipe in Chapter 22

with the meat drippings. When the pig begins to steam, rub it every 5 minutes with a cloth dipped in melted butter. Do not omit this precaution if you want to keep the pig's skin soft and tender after it begins to brown. The oven should be slow (300 degrees) at first, but hot enough to brown (450 degrees) at the close. Baste often and bake for from 1 1/2 to 3 hours.

When the pig has finished roasting, remove it from the pan. Skim the drippings well. Add a little hot water to the juices. Thicken with browned flour. Let it come to a quick boil. Strain and add 1/2 glass of wine and the juice of 1/2 lemon. Serve in a tureen.

The pig may be served on a large platter. Have it kneeling in a bed of deep green parsley with alternate branches of whitish-green celery tops (the inner and tender leaves). A garland of this can be put around the pig's neck. And a tuft of white cauliflower goes in its mouth. Surround this with a setting of curled parsley.

In carving the pig, cut off the head first. Then split it down the back. Take off the hams and shoulders. Separate the ribs. Serve some of the dressing to each person. *Note:* The preparation of this wonderful holiday dish is erroneously considered a difficult task. Anyone can undertake it with a reasonable expectation of success.

OLD-FASHIONED SOUTHERN STEWED PORK

Take some lean slices from the leg. Dice in 1-inch squares. Put into a pot with enough cold water to cover. Put a lid on the pot and stew gently for 3/4 hour. Meanwhile, parboil 6 sliced potatoes in another pot. When the pork has stewed for the allotted time, add the potatoes. Season with salt, pepper, 1 minced scallion, 1 tablespoon catsup,[2] and a bunch of aromatic herbs. Cover again and stew for 20

---

2. Recipe in Chapter 19

minutes. The meat should be tender throughout. *Note:* This stew was extremely popular in the early 1800s, especially on cold days.

GREAT-GREAT-GRANDMOTHER NORTHRUP'S ROAST PIG'S HEAD

Take the head of a half-grown pig. Clean and split it. Take out the brains. Put them in a wooden bowl and set aside in a cool place. Parboil the pig's head in salted water. Drain the water in another bowl and set this aside. Wipe the head dry. Wash it thoroughly with beaten eggs. Dredge thickly with bread crumbs seasoned with pepper, sage, and onion. Put this on the rack of a roasting pan. Put in the oven and bake at 425 degrees. Baste twice with butter and water. Then baste with the liquor in which the head was boiled. Finally, baste with the juices that run from the meat.

Wash the brains until they are white. The washing water will have to be changed several times. Beat them to a smooth paste in a wooden mixing bowl. Add 1/4 the quantity of fine bread crumbs that have been seasoned with salt and pepper. Blend in a beaten egg and make the brains into balls. Roll them in flour and fry in hot deep fat until they are browned lightly. Arrange these brain balls around the roasted head on a large platter.

Skim the juices left in the bottom of the roasting pan. Thicken with browned flour. Add the juice of a lemon. Bring to a boil and pour over the head on the platter.

EARLY AMERICAN PORK POTPIE

You can make this with lean pork cut from any part of the pig. Crack the bones well and cut up the meat into pieces two inches long. Heavily butter a large round-bottomed pot. Line the pot with a good light puff paste.[3] Put in the meat, then a layer of parboiled potatoes, split in half. Season with salt and pepper as you continue. When the pot is nearly full, pour in 1 quart (4 cups) cold water. Put on an upper crust and cut a small hole out of the middle. This will allow you to add more hot water should the gravy boil away too fast. Then put on the pot lid. Boil for 1 1/2 to 2 hours. When done, carefully remove the upper crust. Turn out the meat and gravy into a large bowl. Spoon out the crust and lay it on a hot platter. Put the meat and potatoes on this. Pour the gravy over it. Cover with the top crust and serve. *Note:* Slips of puff paste may also be strewn among the meat and potatoes and cooked as dumplings.

GREAT-GREAT-GRANDMOTHER DANIELS' PORK-AND-PEAS PUDDING

Soak a lean piece of pork overnight in cold water. In another pot soak 4 cups of dried split peas. In the morning, put the peas on to slowly boil. When the peas are tender, drain and rub through a colander. Season to taste with salt and pepper. Add 2 tablespoons butter and 2 beaten eggs. Beat together well. Have a floured pudding cloth[4] ready. Put the pea pudding into it. Tie it up loosely—the pudding must have sufficient room for swelling. Put this into a kettle of warm water. Add the pork and bring to a boil. Let it boil for 1 hour. Lay the pork in the center of a platter. Take the pudding from the pudding cloth sack. Slice it and arrange neatly around the meat.

3. Recipe in *Natural Baking the Old-Fashioned Way,* by the same author.
4. A heavy muslin bag wrung out in hot water and floured well on the inside.

REAL OLD-FASHIONED HAM-AND CHICKEN PIE

Cut up and parboil a tender young chicken—a one-year-old is best. Line a well-buttered deep baking dish with a good pie crust.[5] Cut some thin slices of cold boiled ham.[6] Put a layer next to the crust. Arrange pieces of the chicken upon the ham. Cover this, in turn, with buttered and peppered hard-boiled eggs. Proceed in this order until your ingredients are all used up. Then pour in enough veal,[7] or chicken[8] gravy to prevent dryness. Many old-timers felt the liquor in which the chicken was boiled was best for this purpose. Bake in a moderate over (350 degrees) for 1 1/4 hours.

GREAT-GRANDMOTHER SHAW'S
ROAST LEG OF PORK

A leg weighing about 7 pounds is large enough, even for a large family. If the pig is young, the leg will be even smaller. Score the skin in squares or parallel lines running from side to side. This is done for the later convenience of the carver. Put the leg on the rack of a roasting pan with *very* little water below. Heat gradually until the fat begins to ooze from the meat. Then roast it at 450 degrees. Baste only with its own juices. Do this often to prevent the skin from becoming hard and tough. When the leg is done, take it from the roasting pan. Skim the juices thoroughly. Put in 1/2 cup boiling water and thicken with browned flour. Add salt and pepper to suit taste. Stir in the juice of 1 lemon. Serve in a gravy boat or dish.

---

5. Recipes in *Natural Baking the Old-Fashioned Way*, by the same author.
6. Recipe included herein
7. Recipe in Chapter 5
8. Recipe in Chapter 8

EARLY NEW ENGLAND CHESHIRE PORK PIE

Cut 2 or 3 pounds of fresh lean pork into strips as long and as wide as your middle finger. Line a heavily buttered, deep baking dish with puff paste.[9] Put in a layer of pork seasoned with salt, pepper, and nutmeg or mace. Next add a layer of juicy sliced apples. Cover with 2 tablespoons sugar. Add more pork, and so on until you are ready for the puff paste cover. Lastly, pour in 1 cup sweet cider or wine. Stick bits of butter all over the top. Cover with a thick lid of puff paste.* Cut a slit in the top. Brush over the dough with a beaten egg. Bake for 1 1/2 hours in a moderate oven (350 degrees). *Note:* This is a very old English dish that was extremely popular in early America. It originated in the region from where it takes its name. Many old-timers considered it to be comparable in quality to a good home-made mince pie.[10]

GREAT-AUNT CAROL ANN'S PORK STEAKS

Pork steaks cut from the loins are best, but they can also be cut from the neck. Trim the steaks neatly and season with salt and pepper to taste. Broil them over a clear fire. Many old-timer's preferred broiling these without seasoning in any manner. When finished broiling, the steaks were taken from the fire and put in a covered dish. They were then salted and peppered to taste. A little sage, minced onion, and butter were added. A cover was then put on the dish and the dish was set in the oven for 5 minutes. This allowed the seasoning to really flavor the meat. Try this method. *Note:* Spareribs can also be prepared in this same way.

---

9. Recipe in *Natural Baking the Old-Fashioned Way*, by the same author.

10. Recipe can be found in *Natural Baking the Old-Fashioned Way*, by the same author.

POPULAR OLDEN-DAY PORK CHOPS

Pork chops may be broiled, but care should be taken to cook them thoroughly. It is better to fry them in a little butter, or salt pork fat, unless, as is generally the case, they have fat enough to fry themselves. Cook slowly. Be sure they are thoroughly done, but not burned. A delicious brown gravy can be made from the pork grease if desired. This was commonly done in the old days. The gravy was poured over the chops and served in that way. A good pork chop, properly cooked, is good enough. Do not bread them.

OLD NEW ORLEANS PORK CHOPS WITH APPLE

Place the pork chops and slices of tart apples in a frying pan with a little hot grease. Salt and pepper to suit taste. Fry both the chops and the apple slices until they are nicely browned. Eat together while hot.

GREAT-GRANDMOTHER MITCHELL'S SALT-CURED BOILED HAM

Thoroughly brush and clean a large ham in lukewarm water. Soak in cold water overnight. In the morning shave off every particle of the hardened surface. Put the ham in a large kettle and cover with cold water. Let it heat slowly and bring to a boil. Remove the scum as it begins to boil. Then add:

1 bay leaf
1 onion
2 large sprigs of parsley

4 cups sweet pickle vinegar[11]
or
2 cups cider vinegar[12]

11. Recipe in Chapter 20
12. Recipe in Chapter 19

Keep the kettle barely bubbling and let it cook until the ham is tender. Allow 20 minutes to the pound from the time it starts simmering. If a fork will pierce through the thickest part and the skin will peel off easily, it is done. Let it remain in the liquor until cold. Carefully peel off the skin. Trim off any ragged edges. Sop the melted fat from the top with a soft cloth. Then blend:

1 cup cracker crumbs, fine	1/4 cup butter, melted
1/2 cup brown sugar	pinch of salt
	pinch of tarragon

Spread this mixture thickly over the surface of the ham. Put it in the oven and bake at 425 degrees until brown and crisp.

GREAT-GRANDMOTHER SHAW'S
SALT-CURED HAM BAKED IN CIDER

Use a small lean ham. Wash thoroughly in lukewarm water. Soak in cold water overnight. Wipe dry the next morning. Sprinkle over the flesh side a mixture of:

1 tablespoon onion, chopped fine	1 tablespoon cinnamon
1/4 teaspoon mace	1 tablespoon allspice
	1/4 teaspoon cloves

Make a paste dough of flour and water. Roll it out in a thin sheet and cover the flesh side of the ham. Pack it down close to the skin. Put the ham, skin side down, in a roasting pan. Pour 2 quarts cider into the pan. Add 1/2 teaspoon white pepper and 1/2 teaspoon paprika. Cover with another large pan. Bake in a moderate oven (350 degrees) for 2 hours. Baste every 20 minutes.

At the end of 2 hours remove the upper pan and allow the ham to cook for 2 more hours uncovered. When done, take the ham from the pan and carefully remove the paste dough. Take off all of the skin. Trim the ham neatly. Brush the skin side with beaten egg. Dust it thickly with bread crumbs and chopped parsley.

Skim off the grease from the cider. Put it in a saucepan and bring to a boil. Put the ham back in a quick oven (450 degrees) to brown. Boil the liquor down until you have 2 cups. Put this into a sauce bowl. When the ham is nicely browned, take it from the oven. Serve on a platter in a bed of watercress. Slices of red-skinned apples may be placed here and there in the cress as a decoration.

EARLY VIRGINIA SMOTHERED HAM

Soak the slices of ham in tepid water until sufficiently freshened. Dredge (sprinkle) with flour. Put into a roasting pan or a shallow frying pan. Bake until the fat is brown and crisp. The steam and liquid from the ham will moisten the flour and make a puffy crust. This keeps the meat soft and tender. This old method of cooking sliced ham is relatively simple to follow, yet the end result is pure delight to the taste buds.

GREAT-GREAT-GRANDMOTHER HORTON'S SCRAPPLE

In the early days of America, scrapple was made only from the head of a "porker." The head was first thoroughly scraped and cleaned. It was then cut in two. The eyes and brains were removed. The halved head was put into a kettle of cold water. It was simmered slowly until the meat fell from the bones. The grease was then carefully skimmed off. The meat was taken out of the kettle and chopped up and returned to the liquor. Seasoning was accomplished using powdered sage, salt, and pepper to suit taste. Corn meal was slowly stirred in last until the mixture was the consistency of mush. This was then slowly cooked for 1 hour. Great-great-grandmother Horton then poured it into a large shallow pan and let it cool and "set." When ready, she sliced the scrapple and fried it until nicely browned. *Note:* The real old-fashioned scrapple is nothing like that purchased commercially in the stores. Try this homemade method for a taste treat you won't soon forget.

EARLY SOUTH CAROLINA
FRIED SALT PORK AND MILK GRAVY

Cut slices of salt pork 1/4 inch thick. Fry both sides until they are crisp. Take care that it does not burn. Put the fried slices in a covered dish and set aside where it will keep warm until served. Pour all but 2 tablespoons of the pork grease out of the frying pan. Blend 1 1/2 table-spoons flour with 2 cups cold milk. Stir this into the frying pan. Beat rapidly until the gravy is thick and smooth. Heat until it boils and immediately pour into a gravy tureen. *Note:* When other meat was unavailable in the olden days, this made the basis of a very comfortable meal. It was a common Southern dish, especially during the trying years of the Civil War when good meats were seldom available to civilians.

GREAT-GREAT-GRANDMOTHER NORTHRUP'S
HOMEMADE SAUSAGE

Old-fashioned homemade sausages were either put up in "skins," or made into cakes. The "skins" were generally preferred. They were made from the small intestines of an animal. If the sausages were to be very small, the intestines of sheep were used. These were first emptied and cut into lengths of 4 to 6 feet. They were then soaked for 3 or 4 days in salt and water, or weak limewater. They were then turned inside out, scraped, and carefully rinsed. This process was repeated 2 or 3 times before the "skins" were felt ready to use. These "skins" were considered an absolute necessity for holding the sausage meat in great-great-grandmother's day. And they were made into "links" by twisting at the proper point after they were filled.

The "bags" for holding sausage meat were made of cotton cloth, about 12 inches long and 3 inches in diameter. They were always dipped in salt water and dried before using. The meat was pressed tightly into the bag. The bag was then tied and stored in a cool place until needed. When sausage was desired, the old-timers simply turned back the bag, and cut off 1/2-inch-thick slices for frying.

According to Mrs. Northrup, the meat used for making sausage should be "sweet fresh pork, nearly one-third fat." Some people added a little beef to their sausage meat but this was not considered to be the "real sausage." The pork was chopped up finely. Lean parts and fat were well blended and highly seasoned with salt, pepper, and "pounded sage." This is Great-great-grandmother North-rup's recipe for each pound of meat used in sausage: "A teaspoon of salt, a teaspoon of sage, and a scant half-teaspoon of white or black pepper."

OLD NEW HAMPSHIRE BAKED SALT PORK

This was certainly not the most popular of old-fashioned meat dishes. But when roasts of fresh meat were scarce in great-great grandmother's day, it often sufficed for the meat served at mealtime. Take a piece of salt pork large enough to feed the entire family. Soak it overnight in a bowl of milk. In the morning, score the rind with 1-inch deep cuts.

Fill these incisions with a highly seasoned bread dressing.[13] Dust with pepper. Lay the meat in a baking pan with 1 cup milk. Bake in a moderate oven (350 degrees). About 1 hour before dinner pour out most of the gravy. Surround the pork with sweet and white potatoes. Bake and brown them. Skim the grease from the gravy. Thicken the gravy with flour and season to taste. Serve it over the potatoes with thin slices of the baked salt pork.

GRANDMOTHER PELTON'S BREAKFAST SAUSAGE

Take 2 pounds of pork chops and remove all of the bones and fat. Put the meat through a grinder. Season with salt, pepper and a very little sage. Make into small cakes. While preparing the meat, put the bones and fat into a skillet and fry them. After the meat is ready, remove the bones and fat from the skillet. Fry the sausage meat in the hot grease until it is a crisp brown. Lift the sausage cakes from the grease and set them aside to drain. Then put 1 heaping teaspoon flour into the grease to form a thick gravy. Add 2 cups boiling water. When ready to serve, place the sausages on a warm platter and pour the gravy over them.

---

13. Recipe in Chapter 22

8

Old-Fashioned Poultry Cookery

The term poultry includes all domestic birds that are considered edible. In the 1800s and before, the term "fowl" generally meant a rooster or hen one year old or over. A "chicken" was the same bird under one year of age. When not above 3 or 4 months old, they were called "broilers." This term was also applied to young ducks that were frequently broiled. The old-timers were even beginning to broil young turkeys and geese as well. In the early days, poultry was generally considered a luxury, although many people preferred other meats.

I remember looking over my great-grandfather's old 1845 school reader. It contained an illustration of the extravagance of a young man who had just married. His parents had scraped and saved with great frugality. They finally amassed enough to be able to use their poultry more freely. The young couple, as the title of the story put it, "Began with a Chicken."

Poultry was cheap and plentiful in great-grandmother's day. It was an important addition to the food supply of most families of that period and before. And the farmer who owned a little land could readily raise his own fowls and eggs to advantage.

It requires some knowledge and skill to properly cook birds of any kind. And it is well worthwhile to learn and to practice the best old-fashioned methods. The Thanksgiving turkey and the popular old time Christmas goose received the best of treatment for they were then considered infrequent luxuries. Even today they are rather expensive. But fowls were often included as a weekly variation to the usual family fare. My great-grandmother especially liked to prepare it because she felt it was enjoyed more when frequently served. She often said that every morsel of meat, as well as any nutrition in the bones, could be utilized.

As for game birds, the average family had little use (nor do they today) for a multiplication of fancy recipes. In the rural districts of early America, the boys or men shot various birds for food. The basic rules for cooking domestic birds were also applied to game birds. And this is still done in today's jet-age.

OLD-TIME NOTES ON POULTRY

There was one general rule about birds that my great-great grandmother always applied to her cooking. Birds having dark meat were to be cooked rare. Birds having white meat were to be thoroughly cooked.

Domestic poultry does not improve materially by "hanging." Yet it does not harm the bird to keep it a reasonable length of time before it is cooked. Early American gourmets, however, insisted on having most game birds exceedingly "ripe" before cooking them.

There is a very old method of determining the age of a turkey. Simply press the thumb on the end of the breast bone. If it is flexible, the bird is a young one. If stiff, it is old enough to demand different treatment in cooking. Of course a very old bird is always tough. But any "fowl" can be made very nice and tender if it is parboiled or steamed for 1/2 hour before it is cooked.

The skin of a fowl or a turkey to be roasted or boiled should be carefully dressed. Every pin feather should carefully be removed. And the hairs should be singed off with a piece of burning paper or over a clear flame of some sort. The browned skin is a delicacy in a roast bird and it was, and still is today, much in demand at the dinner table.

GREAT-GRANDMOTHER SHAW'S ROAST TURKEY

Wash, clean, and dress the turkey as described above. Then fill the body and breast with a delightful old fashioned stuffing.[1] Place the bird on its back in a dripping pan into which 1 cup water has been poured. Dredge (sprinkle) the turkey with salt, pepper, and flour. Lay thin slices of salt pork, or small pieces of butter, over the breast. Bake 3 to 5 hours (about 15 minutes per pound) at 325 degrees. The roasting time will vary according to the size, age and toughness of the bird. Baste often with the drippings from the turkey. Add butter and hot water as the drippings boil away. The amount of butter needed will be determined by the fatness of the turkey. After a time the bird should be turned. Do this at least once every 1/2 hour so that it will brown evenly.

GREAT-GRANDMOTHER MITCHELL'S ROAST CHICKEN

Thoroughly wash and rinse the chicken. Fasten the wings and legs close to the body with skewers or strings. Tie the

---

1. Recipes for several kinds in Chapter 22

skin over the neck. Stuff[2] and then sew the skin of the crop and between the thighs with fine twine or coarse thread. Put the chicken on the rack of a roasting pan with the breast turned upward. Dredge (sprinkle) with salt, pepper, and flour. Lay small pieces of butter or thin slices of salt pork on the breast and legs. Put 1 cup water in the bottom of the pan to prevent burning. This will also create some steam, which softens the bird and aids cooking. Baste frequently. Add hot water as necessary.

If a fowl (older chicken) is used, cover the roasting pan and let it cook slowly (300 degrees) until the last 15 minutes. The cover should then be removed. Baste the fowl with butter and quickly brown at 450 degrees. About 1 1/4 hours will be time enough for a chicken, 2 to 2 1/2 hours for a fowl. Test by thrusting a fork into the breast. If pink juice flows, the chicken is not sufficiently done. When the chicken is finally done, and when it has been taken from the pan, make a delicious gravy by blending the following ingredients:

1 cup pan drippings,   1 cup milk
    boiling   salt to taste
1 tablespoon flour   pepper to taste

GREAT-GREAT-GRANDMOTHER DANIELS'
ROAST DUCK

Dress, wash, and wipe the ducks very carefully. To the usual stuffing[3] add a little sage and a minced scallion. Stuff and sew up. Reserve the giblets for the gravy. If the ducks are tender, they will not require more than 1 hour to roast. Baste all well during roasting. Meanwhile, stew the giblets in a little water. Chop them up fine. When the ducks

2. Recipes in Chapter 22
3. Recipes in Chapter 22

are done, and taken from the roasting pan, skim the drippings in the bottom of the pan. Add the giblets, 1 chopped scallion or onion, and 1 tablespoon browned flour. This makes a delightful duck gravy. Accompany the ducks with currant or grape[4] jelly and serve them with goose pudding.[5]

OLD NEW ENGLAND BOILED POULTRY RECIPES

Boiled Turkey the Old-Fashioned Way: The turkey may be prepared and stuffed as for roasting. Or use a plain stuffing mixture of bread crumbs, suet, parsley, and a bit of lemon peel. Soak the turkey in salted water for 1 hour before cooking. This will whiten the bird. Then plunge it into boiling water. Leave it and let simmer gently for 2 to 3 hours, according to size and age. *Note:* A delicious sauce for boiled turkey can be found in Chapter 13.

Boiled Fowl the Old-Fashioned Way: If you have a good market to select from, or a poultry yard to draw upon, get a plump and well-conditioned fowl for boiling. In any event, the bird should be thoroughly cleaned and dressed. You can stuff[6] a fowl, but most old-timers liked it better plain. Fowl may be boiled in plain water. But for a delightful old-fashioned flavor, add the following ingredients:

sprig of mace	small cinnamon stick
2 whole cloves	salt to taste
1 tablespoon vinegar[7]	

Many old-timers advised putting the fowl into cold water and bringing it to a boil. But my great-grandmother always

---

4. Recipes in Chapter 18
5. Recipes in Chapter 22
6. Recipes in Chapter 22
7. Recipes in Chapter 19

first plunged her bird into boiling water. This cooked the outside quickly and it helped to retain the juices in the meat of the bird. She also wet a napkin or clean cloth and dredged it in flour. This was wrapped around the fowl before it was placed in the boiling water. It kept the bird much juicier and made it unbelievably tender.

EARLY AMERICAN TURKEY SCALLOP

Cut the meat from a cold-boiled or roasted turkey[8] left from yesterday's dinner. Remove all bits of skin and gristle. Chop up the rest very fine. Make a batter with 1 cup cracker[9] crumbs soaked in warm milk. Season with salt. Beat in 2 eggs. The mixture should be just thick enough to spread smoothly. Set aside until needed for the upper crust.

Put a layer of plain cracker crumbs in the bottom of a buttered baking dish. Moisten slightly with milk. Spread a layer of the minced turkey, with bits of the stuffing, salt, pepper, and small pieces of butter. Add another layer of cracker crumbs. Wet down with milk as before. Continue this until the baking dish is nearly full. Dilute any leftover gravy with hot water. Season it with Worcestershire sauce,[10] catsup,[11] and butter. Pour this into the nearly filled baking dish.

Lastly, spread the previously made cracker crust batter on top of the ingredients in the buttered dish. Smooth it over and stick bits of butter plentifully on it. Put a deep plate over the entire dish and bake in a moderate oven (350 degrees) until the contents begin to bubble at the

---

8. Recipes included herein
9. Recipes in *Natural Baking the Old-Fashioned Way,* by the same author.
10. Recipes in Chapter 13
11. Recipes in Chapter 19

sides. This indicates that the scallop is thoroughly cooked. Then remove the cover (dish) and let it brown on top. *Note:* A large pudding dish full of scallop will be ready to eat in 3/4 hour. Cold chicken or any other poultry can be prepared in this same way.

OLD-FASHIONED RAGOUT OF TURKEY

This is an expensive, yet very nice old-time dish. Cut the cold turkey from the bones and into bits one inch long. Tear the meat as little as possible. Put the gravy left from the roast into a skillet or saucepan. Dilute it with hot water if the quantity is small. Stir in:

1/4 cup butter	1/2 teaspoon cloves
1/4 teaspoon nutmeg	1 teaspoon of pungent
pinch of salt	meat sauce[12]

Let the mixture boil, and then put in the meat. Stew very slowly for 10 minutes—but no more. Then stir in 1 tablespoon currant jelly,[13] and 1 tablespoon browned flour that has been wet with cold water. Lastly, add 1/4 cup dry sherry. Bring it to a quick boil. Serve in a covered dish.

GREAT-GREAT-GRANDMOTHER HORTON'S EARLY 1800 CHICKEN POTPIE

Cut up a fine large fowl and 1/2 pound of ham or salt pork. Butter a large pot lavishly or your pastry will stick to it and burn. Line the bottom and sides of the pot with a good rich puff paste.[14] Reserve enough dough for a top

12. Recipes in Chapter 13
13. Recipes in Chapter 18
14. Recipes in *Natural Baking the Old-Fashioned Way,* by the same author.

crust and for square bits to be scattered throughout the potpie. Put in a layer of the ham or salt pork. Pepper it, and cover with pieces of the chicken. Cover this with puff paste dumplings or squares. If you use potatoes, parboil them before putting any in the pie. The potatoes should be sliced and laid over the pastry squares. Add another layer of pork, chicken dumplings and potatoes. Continue this until the chicken is all used up. Cover with pastry rolled out quite thick. Slit this in the middle. Heat very slowly and let simmer for 2 full hours. When done, turn the potpie into a large bowl or platter. The lower crust will be on top and the gravy all around it. *Note:* This is the real old-fashioned potpie so popular back in the early 1800s. Veal, beef, or lamb may be substituted for the chicken. The pork will salt it sufficiently.

CHICKEN PUDDING
ON THE OLD SOUTH PLANTATION

Wash, cut up, and skin two young chickens. Put them into a large kettle with 1/2 cup butter and enough water to cover. Season well with salt and pepper. Stew slowly for 1/2 hour. Then take the chickens out of the kettle and lay them on a flat dish to cool. Set aside the water in which they were stewed. This will be used for gravy. Make a batter by blending the following ingredients:

4 cups milk	4 eggs, well beaten
3 cups flour	pinch of salt
3 tablespoons butter, melted	1 teaspoon cream of tartar

Put a layer of the chicken pieces in the bottom of a large buttered baking dish. Pour 1/2 cup of the batter over it. Add another layer of chicken, and more batter. Continue until the baking dish is full. Use whatever is left of the batter for a top crust. Bake in a moderate oven (350 degrees) for 1 hour. While the chicken is baking, beat up 1 egg and stir it into the water previously set aside. Thicken it with 2 teaspoons rice or wheat flour. Add a little chopped parsley. Bring to a quick boil and then serve in a gravy boat.

EARLY VIRGINIA FRIED CHICKEN

1/2 pound salt pork, cut up	1/2 cup cream
1 young chicken (broiling size)	1 tablespoon flour
	1 tablespoon butter
1/2 cup milk	1 teaspoon parsley, chopped

Fry the salt pork until the grease is extracted, but not until it browns. Wash and cut up the chicken. Soak it in salted water for 1/2 hour. Wipe dry, season with pepper, and dredge (sprinkle) with flour. Then fry in the hot grease until each piece is a rich brown on both sides. Take out of the frying pan and drain. Then set aside in a hot covered dish.

Add the milk and cream to the pork grease in the frying pan. Thicken it with the flour. Stir in the butter and parsley. Bring to a quick boil and pour over the chicken. *Note:* This was a standard dish in the Old Dominion. It never seems to taste as good as it does when eaten in Virginia. The creamy gravy is often omitted. The chicken is then served dry with bunches of fried parsley dropped upon it.

GREAT-GRANDMOTHER MITCHELL'S
BRAISED FOWL

Thoroughly wash and rinse the fowl. Fasten the wings

and legs close to the body with skewers or strings. Tie the skin over the neck. Stuff[15] and then sew the skin of the crop and between the thighs with fine twine or coarse thread. Dredge (sprinkle) it with salt, pepper and flour. Brown lightly in a frying pan with butter or grease. Then put the fowl in a deep pan or kettle. Half cover it with water. Also put in the giblets, 1 onion, and Bouquet Garni.[16] Cover tightly and bake until tender. Baste often. Take the fowl out of the pan and place it on a large platter. Thicken the pan juices with sufficient flour. Season to taste with salt and pepper. Then strain it into a gravy boat (bowl). Chop the giblets up and put them in the gravy. Pour this all around the fowl and serve while hot.

STEWED CHICKEN IN THE COLONIES

Wash and dress a chicken or fowl. Separate it at the joints with a sharp knife. Place the pieces in a deep agate stew pan. Barely cover with hot water. Season to taste with salt and pepper. Simmer slowly until the meat is tender. Rapid boiling destroys the flavor and toughens the meat. Smoothly blend 1 tablespoon flour with 1 cup milk or cream. Stir into the chicken liquor. This makes a very tasty gravy. Serve on a deep platter. Garnish with biscuits or crackers[17] cut in half and dipped into the gravy. *Note:* The time required for cooking depends entirely on the age of the bird. About 3/4 hour is sufficient for young chickens. Allow 1 1/2 to 2 hours for fowls.

---

15. Recipes in Chapter 22
16. Thyme, bay leaves, and parsley blended and tied in a piece of cheesecloth.
17. Recipes can be found in *Natural Baking the Old-Fashioned Way*, by the same author.

GREAT-AUNT BEVERLY JO'S FANCY FRICASSEE

1 young chicken, cut at joints	1 slice of onion salt to taste
2 stalks of celery, cut up small	pepper to taste pinch of curry
1 bay leaf	

Put the pieces of chicken in a large kettle with 4 cups hot water. Add the other ingredients. Cover and simmer until the chicken is tender, which will be about 1 hour. Take the chicken from the kettle and place it on a hot platter. Blend 1 tablespoon flour with 1 tablespoon butter. Add this to the hot pot liquor. Stir until thick and pour over the chicken. Serve immediately while hot.

GREAT-GREAT-GRANDMOTHER NORTHRUP'S BROWN FRICASSEE

This is one of the best old-time methods of utilizing a tough old fowl. It must first be parboiled (partly cooked). After this there are certain rules to follow. These instructions come from my Great-Grant-Grandmother Northrup's 1863 handwritten cooking notes: "Singe, draw and disjoint; put into a good-sized saucepan two tablespoonfuls of butter; when hot, drop in the pieces of chicken; allow them to brown gradually, taking great care the butter does not burn. As soon as the pieces are browned, draw them to one side of the saucepan, and add to the fat two tablespoonfuls of flour; mix and add one pint of stock or water. Stir constantly until it begins to boil, moving the chicken around in the sauce. Add a teaspoonful of salt and a quarter of a teaspoonful of pepper. Simmer slowly for an hour. When done, dish the rough pieces in the center, crossing the legs on the front of the platter; place the wings and the dark meat at the sides, the back and breast on top. Take the sauce from the fire, add to it the yolk of one egg, beaten with two tablespoonfuls of cream; strain this over the chicken. Garnish the dish with crescents of fried bread, dust over a little finely chopped parsley, and serve."

OLD-FASHIONED SOUTHERN BROILED CHICKEN

Select a good-sized young chicken. Split it down the back. Use skewers to pin the wings and legs down as flat as possible. Put the chicken on the rack of a roasting pan. Pour in 1/2 cup water. Dredge (sprinkle) with salt, pepper, and flour. Scatter tiny bits of butter over the chicken. Cover with a pan the same size as the roasting pan. Bake it for about 1 hour. Turn the chicken over once to have each side equally done. Then take it out of the pan and put it on a broiler. Broil over a hot fire. Turn frequently until each side is a rich brown all over. Serve on a hot platter. Spread the chicken with melted butter and chopped parsley.

COLONIAL DAYS CHICKEN JELLY

Cut the meat and crack the bones of a young spring chicken. Put it all in a stew pan with 2 quarts cold water. Boil until the meat is in shreds. Strain the pan liquor through a cloth and salt to taste. Set aside to cool. When cold, skim the hard grease from the top. There will be a firm, clear jelly left. This can be served in slices between crackers[18] or as a delightful garnish. And excellent sandwiches can be made using it.[19]

---

18. Recipes in *Natural Baking the Old-Fashioned Way*, by the same author.
19. Recipe in Chapter 15

GREAT-GREAT-GRANDMOTHER HORTON'S ROAST GOOSE

Unless the goose is very green (young) it should be parboiled (partly cooked) for 1/2 hour or more to get rid of the rank flavor and some of the fat. An 8-pound goose should bake in 1 1/4 hours. It is better not to be overdone. No butter or other grease is required to roast or bake a goose. Simply stuff the body and sew it up. Dredge (sprinkle) with salt, pepper and flour. Cover the breast with white paper until the goose is half done or use a paste of flour and water. Remove this when you are ready to brown the goose. Serve with goose pudding.[20]

UNCLE ALBERT'S SPECIAL CREAMED CHICKEN DELIGHT

1 small chicken cooked	1 tablespoon butter
	1 tablespoon parsley, minced
1 tablespoon cornstarch	salt to taste
1 1/2 cups milk	white pepper to taste

Cut the chicken meat into small pieces. Blend the cornstarch with a little of the milk. Heat the rest of the milk in a double boiler. Thicken this, when hot, with the cornstarch mixture. When smooth, add the rest of the ingredients. Put the chicken pieces in this sauce and let it simmer for 5 to 8 minutes. Serve on slices of buttered toast. Garnish with parsley. *Note:* This made a fine luncheon dish in the old days.

---

20. Recipes in Chapter 9

OLD-TIME CHICKEN TERRAPIN

2 cups cooked chicken,   3 eggs, hard-boiled
   chopped fine   salt to taste
3 tablespoons butter   pepper to taste
1 cup cream   parsley to taste, chopped

Put the chicken pieces in a saucepan. Add the butter and
the cream and heat. Rub the egg yolks to a paste and press
the whites through a sieve. Stir both into the chicken and
let it all come to a boil. Season with salt, pepper, and
parsley. Serve while hot. *Note:* This always made a pleasing
luncheon dish in the days gone by and it was a popular
variation to the ordinary ways of serving chicken.

EARLY AMERICAN PRESSED TURKEY OR CHICKEN

Boil the turkey or chicken in a little water until the meat
falls from the bones. Take out all the meat. Season with
salt and pepper. Add a little celery salt and lemon juice
and bring to a boil. Let it all boil until there is 1 cup of
liquid left in the pan. Stir it thoroughly and blend in the
meat. Butter a mold. Place slices of hard-boiled eggs on
the bottom and sides (or use pieces of boiled tongue or
ham, cut into fancy shapes). Then tightly pack in the
chicken mixture. Let it completely cool. Serve cold with a
parsley garnish. Or serve it with lettuce, radishes, or beets.

OLD NEW ORLEANS BLANQUETTE OF CHICKEN

2 cups cooked chicken,   1 tablespoon parsley,
   cut small   chopped
1 cup drawn-butter sauce[21]   2 tablespoons cream
2 egg yolks, well beaten

21. Recipe in Chapter 13

Put the pieces of chicken in a double boiler with the drawn-butter sauce. When hot, add the egg yolks, parsley, and cream. Take off the stove, cover, and let stand for 3 minutes. Then serve in a border of boiled rice.[22]

CHICKEN PILAU—OLD PLANTATION STYLE

2 cups cooked chicken, cut small	onion to taste, chopped
2 cups stewed tomatoes,[23] strained	curry to taste
	1 cup rice
salt to taste	1/2 cup cream
	or
pepper to taste	1/2 cup butter

Put the chicken in a saucepan with 2 cups hot water. Stew until the meat is very tender. Then take the chicken pieces out of the pan and skim the liquor. Add the tomatoes, salt, pepper, onion and curry. Bring to a boil and put in the rice. Let it boil until the rice is soft. Put the chicken back in and add the cream or butter. Stir well and serve while hot.

22. Recipes in Chapter 3
23. Recipes in Chapter 3

9

Egg Cookery the Natural Way

In the late 1800s the hens in America were estimated to be laying in the neighborhood of 14 billion eggs annually. When we reflect on this figure, the importance of eggs in the average home of that period, and even long before, is most obvious.

In how many ways were eggs cooked and eaten in the old days? How many ways there might have been is a still more formidable question. My great-grandmother and her mother before her believed eggs to be the compactest, most convenient, most unadulterated, most easily digestible, and most readily cooked little parcel of nutrition available in their kitchens.

Let's take a close look at an egg. It concentrates within its clean shell the very essence of food. And it is shaped so that it may readily be used by itself, or in innumerable combinations. There are but few recipes in which the egg does not sometimes reinforce or supplement. Is there a weak sauce or gravy? An egg enriches it! A meager cake? An egg helps it! A barren breakfast table? An egg supplies the need! Nourishment needed for an invalid? An egg does the job well! The egg seems to be the universal resource for whatever may be lacking.

A COLONY FAVORITE—EGGS WITH MAPLE SYRUP

The French people in the Colonies liked to cook their eggs with maple syrup. The maple syrup was poured into the frying pan and heated. When hot, an egg was dropped in and cooked exactly the same as a poached egg dropped in water. A dish of eggs was often cooked in this way as a dessert. It not only tasted good but looked tempting. Try it yourself if you would like to have an authentic Colonial treat.

1824 OMELETTE AUX FINES HERBES— A LAFAYETTE FAVORITE

6 egg whites, beaten
   stiffly
6 egg yolks, beaten
   smoothly
1 cup milk
salt to taste
pepper to taste

2 tablespoons parsley,
   chopped
2 tablespoons thyme,
   chopped
2 tablespoons marjoram,
   chopped

The egg whites must be beaten until they will stand alone. When the yolks are beaten to a smooth thick batter, stir in the milk, salt and pepper. Then lightly stir in the stiff whites. When the omelet is mixed and ready to go into the hot frying pan, lightly stir in the herbs. Pour into the buttered frying pan. It should cook no more than 10 minutes. Do not stir, but slip a broad-bladed knife under the omelet to guard against burning at the bottom. As soon as the middle of the omelet has "set," place the pan in a hot oven (425 degrees) and let it finish cooking. When done, lay a hot dish bottom upward on top of the frying pan. Turn the pan over on the plate to bring the browned side of the omelet uppermost. Eat immediately as it will soon fall. *Note:* My Great-Great-Grandmother Huldah Horton fixed this dish at the request of General Lafayette when he visited her home in Newburgh, New York, in 1824, on his second and last visit to America.

GREAT-GREAT-GRANDMOTHER HORTON'S OTHER RECIPES

Old-Fashioned Cauliflower Omelet: Chop some cold, cooked cauliflower[1] very fine. Make your basic omelet as above, but leave out the herbs. Mix the cauliflower in when the omelet is ready to go into the hot frying pan.

Old-Fashioned Asparagus Omelet: Mince some cold, cooked asparagus tips.[2] Make your basic omelet as above, but leave out the herbs. Mix the asparagus tips in when the omelet is ready to go into the hot frying pan.

Old-Fashioned Tomato Omelet: Make your basic omelet as above, but leave out the herbs. Spread stewed tomatoes over the surface of the omelet as it is frying. Fold it in half before placing in the oven to finish cooking.

EARLY AMERICAN POACHED EGGS A LA CREME

1 tablespoon cider
    vinegar[3]
1/2 teaspoon salt
1/2 cup cream

1 tablespoon butter,
    well rounded
salt to taste
pepper to taste

1. Recipes in Chapter 3
2. Recipes in Chapter 3
3. Recipe in Chapter 19

Nearly fill a clean frying pan with boiling water. Add the cider vinegar and salt to the water. Take the frying pan from the stove. Slip the eggs from a saucer onto the top of the water. Boil for 3 1/2 minutes. Drain the eggs and lay them on buttered toast in a hot dish. Empty the frying pan and pour in the cream. If you use milk instead, thicken it with very little cornstarch. Let it come to a boil. Stir constantly to prevent burning. Add the butter, salt and pepper. Bring to a quick boil and immediately pour over the eggs. *Note:* A little broth was often added in the old days to give the dish an even more delightful flavor. Try it both ways.

OLD SOUTHERN SWEET FRIED OMELET SOUFFLÉ

4 tablespoons powdered sugar	6 egg whites
	1 teaspoon vanilla
6 egg yolks	2 tablespoons butter

Add the sugar to the egg yolks, a little at a time, as you thoroughly beat them. Then beat the egg whites until they will stand alone. Blend together and stir in the vanilla. Put the butter in a frying pan and heat to boiling. Pour the omelet in and cook it quickly. Slip the knife frequently under it, to loosen from the sides and bottom. It is more likely to scorch than an omelet without sugar. Turn out, when done, on a hot dish. Sift powdered sugar over the top. Serve instantly, or it will fall and become heavy. *Note:* This was a popular dish on the plantations of the Old South. It was made up as a special Sunday morning treat for the enslaved blacks. And it was also served in the owner's home with some degree of regularity.

GREAT-GREAT-GRANDMOTHER NORTHRUP'S SWEET BAKED OMELET

6 tablespoons powdered
   sugar
6 egg yolks

6 egg whites
juice of 1 lemon
1/2 lemon peel, grated

Gradually add the powdered sugar to the egg yolks and beat them until they cease to froth. The yolks should be thick and smooth. Beat the whites until they are stiff enough to cut with a knife. Stir the beaten yolks and whites together lightly with the lemon juice and peel. Pour this mixture into a warm, well-buttered, deep baking dish. Bake in a quick oven (425 degrees) for 5 or 6 minutes. Serve with a spoon. Let each person help himself before it cools and falls.

EARLY NEW ENGLAND APPLE OMELET

6 large ripe apples
1 tablespoon butter
6 tablespoons sugar
nutmeg to taste

3 egg yolks, well beaten
1 teaspoon rosewater
3 egg whites, stiffly
   beaten

Pare and core the apples and then stew them as for applesauce.[4] Beat them very smooth while still hot. Stir in the butter, sugar and nutmeg. Allow to cool. When cold add the beaten egg yolks and rosewater. Lastly, stir in the beaten egg whites. Pour the mixture into a warm, well-buttered, deep baking dish. Bake in a moderate oven (350 degrees) until delicately browned. Eat while warm with homemade bread.[5]

---

4. Recipe in Chapter 17
5. Recipes in *Natural Baking the Old-Fashioned Way*, by the same author.

ORIGINAL CIVIL WAR PERIOD
OMELET WITH JELLY

4 tablespoons cream	5 egg yolks, well beaten
1 teaspoon rice flour	1 teaspoon bitter almond
2 tablespoons powdered sugar	5 egg whites, stiffly beaten

Blend the cream and rice flour until it is smooth. Add this and the powdered sugar to the custardlike beaten egg yolks. Then stir in the bitter almond. Lastly, stir in the stiff egg whites with a few soft strokes. Grease the frying pan with butter and let it get hot. Pour in the omelet. Take the pan from the fire as soon as the omelet is done. Quickly spread the top with currant jelly or some other tart jelly.[6] Slip your knife under one side of the omelet and double it over. Put on a warm dish. Sift powdered sugar over it and eat at once.

OLD SOUTH CAROLINA FRICASSEED EGGS

6 eggs, hard-boiled	1/2 teaspoon mustard[7]
2 tablespoons ham, minced or	1 cup veal gravy[8] or
2 tablespoons chicken, minced	1 cup chicken broth[9]
1 teaspoon parsley, chopped	salt to taste
1 teaspoon butter, melted	pepper to taste
	3 tablespoons cream

Cut the boiled eggs in half crosswise. Take out the yolks. Rub them to a paste with the ham or chicken, 1/2 teaspoon parsley, butter and mustard. Blend well and use to fill the empty egg whites. Set them close together in a deep, covered

6. Recipes in Chapter 18

dish, the open ends up. Then take the veal gravy or chicken broth and heat it in a saucepan. Stir in the other 1/2 teaspoon parsley, salt and pepper to taste, and the cream. Bring to a boil. Pour smoking hot over the eggs in the dish. Put the cover on and let stand for 5 minutes. Send to the table. *Note:* This is not an expensive dish. Eggs are always a cheaper dish for a small family than meat. And this was true one hundred years ago when eggs were priced at fifty-cents a dozen. Remember, always drop hard-boiled eggs into cold water as soon as they are done. This will prevent the yolks from turning black.

GREAT-GREAT-GRANDMOTHER DANIELS' BREADED EGGS

Boil some eggs until they are hard. Remove the shells. Let the eggs cool and then cut them up in thick round slices. Salt and pepper each slice. Dip each in beaten raw egg. Roll each slice in fine bread crumbs or powdered cracker. Deep fry in clean meat drippings or butter that is hissing hot. Take the fried slices out of the grease when nicely browned and let them drain well. Put on a hot dish and serve with sauce, as made above, poured over them.

COLONIAL-STYLE POTATO OMELET

1/2 cup milk
1 teaspoon flour,
   heaping
1 cup potatoes,
   mashed

1 teaspoon salt
pinch of white pepper
3 egg yolks, well beaten
3 egg whites, stiffly
   beaten

Smoothly blend the milk and flour in a saucepan. Stir in the mashed potatoes, salt and pepper. Gently stir until free from lumps. Pour this mixture over the beaten egg yolks and stir rapidly. Whip the whites into this mixture. Heat and butter a frying pan, and quickly pour the omelet into it. Fry until the underside is browned. Set the pan on the rack in the oven to brown it on top. Serve immediately.

GREAT-GRANDMOTHER MITCHELL'S TIPS ON BOILING EGGS

The best way of "boiling" eggs (which is a misnomer, in that an egg is not boiled, but poached) is to cover with boiling water. Allow 1 cup water to each egg. Cover and let stand for 10 minutes. This makes a good, soft-boiled egg. If the eggs are desired hard, add a little more boiling water to the first water as it begins to cool. Wrap the saucepan in a thick cloth and leave the egg in the water for 20 minutes.

TASTY OMELET PUFF IN EARLY AMERICA

1 1/2 cups milk
1 tablespoon flour
1 tablespoon butter
salt to taste
pepper to taste
4 egg yolks, well beaten
4 egg whites, stiffly
     beaten

Put 1 cup milk into a saucepan. Bring to a boil and add the flour mixed smoothly with 1/2 cup cold milk. Stir in the butter, salt and pepper. Let this simmer gently. Stir all the time until it is thick and free from lumps. Take it from the stove and pour over the egg yolks while stirring rapidly. Whip the beaten egg whites lightly into the other ingredients. Grease a hot frying pan or griddle with a small piece of butter. Pour some of the egg in the center and shake well to allow it to spread. When fried to a golden brown, fold over once and serve immediately. *Note:* These omelet puffs are cooked the same as pancakes. If a fancy omelet is desired, place in the oven just before folding. This will dry the top. Then spread with chopped ham, parsley, grated cheese, or jelly and fold.

GREAT-GRANDMOTHER SHAW'S HASH WITH EGGS

1 cup boiled ham,[10] chopped fine	1/2 teaspoon butter, melted
1 cup potatoes, mashed or chopped	salt to taste
1 cup cracker crumbs	pepper to taste
1/2 teaspoon parsley, chopped	eggs to suit

This is a very tasty old-fashioned dish that is pretty as well. Blend all of the above ingredients except for the eggs with a little water to make a soft paste. Put into a deep, buttered baking dish and smooth over the top. Make dents all over the top. They must be just large enough to hold an egg. Put it in a moderate oven (350 degrees) and heat it through. Then take it from the oven and drop an egg into each of the dented places. Sprinkle each egg with powdered crumbs. Return the pan to the oven and leave it until the eggs are nicely cooked. Serve while hot.

---

10. Recipes in Chapter 7

10

Old-Fashioned Fried Cakes and Fritters

In this chapter are included various old-fashioned preparations that are cooked by frying. Some are fried in deep fat and some in shallow. The list of recipes might be much longer—but it embraces, as it is, some of the most unique yet practical concoctions of days long past.

BREAD GRIDDLE CAKES IN EARLY AMERICA

3 cups stale bread[1]
2 1/2 cups milk
1 teaspoon salt
2 tablespoon sugar
1 cup flour

pinch of nutmeg
1/2 teaspoon baking
   powder
3 eggs, well beaten

Put the stale bread in a large wooden mixing bowl and soak it with the milk for 12 hours. Keep the mixture in a warm place where it will sour slightly. Rub through a sieve.

---

1. Many excellent recipes for old-time homemade bread can be found in *Natural Baking the Old-Fashioned Way,* by the same author.

Add the salt, sugar, flour, and nutmeg. Dissolve the baking powder in a little hot water. Blend it in the mixture and then stir in the beaten eggs. Drop in cakes on a hot, buttered griddle and fry until browned. Serve while hot with jelly,[2] a good pudding sauce,[3] or syrup.

COLONIAL BUCKWHEAT CAKES

Since the commercialized self-rising buckwheat preparations came on the market so many many years ago, the buckwheat cakes our great-grandmothers used to "bake" have been relegated to the attics of our memories. They are called old-fashioned and slow. The olden-day mixtures had to be raised overnight with yeast. It did take more time, but they were so much better that it paid for the extra time and trouble. Here is how they were made in the early 1800s:

In an open earthen jar or deep dish put one pint of warm water, one teaspoonful of salt, one-half cake of yeast dissolved in a little warm water, one tablespoonful of molasses, and enough buckwheat to make a batter as thick as cream. Stir until free from lumps; let it rise overnight, and in the morning add a scant teaspoonful of soda dissolved in a little water.

Pour this batter in small cakes on a hot buttered griddle. Fry both sides a golden brown. Serve with butter and maple syrup. *Note:* If buckwheat pancakes are wanted every morning for breakfast, put aside 1 cup of the batter. This can then be used to raise the new batch, instead of always using fresh yeast. And in the past, these buckwheat cakes were baked in a hot oven (425 degrees) rather than fried. Try both ways.

2. Recipes in Chapter 18
3. Recipes in Chapter 12

GREAT-GRANDMOTHER MITCHELL'S
PRIZE RAISED FRITTERS

1 cup milk, warm
1/2 yeast cake
flour to suit
4 tablespoons butter,
   melted
6 eggs, well beaten

1/2 cup sugar
1/2 cup almonds,
   chopped
jelly, jam or fruit to
   suit[4]

Blend the warm milk, the yeast (dissolved in a little cold water), and enough sifted flour to make a batter that will drop from a spoon. Stir well and set aside to rise. When quite light add the melted butter, beaten eggs, sugar and almonds. Knead hard and again set aside to rise. Knead and let it rise a third time. When risen, roll out in a thin sheet and cut in circular shapes. Spread half the discs with jelly, jam, or fruit.[5] Cover these with the remaining discs. Press the edges firmly together. Let them stand until they rise. Fry in deep fat until browned. Take care not to cook too quickly. When done, roll in powdered sugar and serve.

OLD NEW ORLEANS FRENCH PANCAKES

3 egg yolks, well
   beaten
1 cup milk
1/2 teaspoon salt
1 teaspoon sugar

1/2 cup flour
3 egg whites, stiffly
   beaten
1/2 tablespoon olive oil

Blend the beaten egg yolks with the milk, salt, and sugar in a large wooden mixing bowl. Put one-third of this mixture into a separate bowl with the flour. Stir until it becomes a

4. Recipes in Chapter 18
5. Recipes in Chapter 18

smooth paste. Add the remainder along with the beaten egg whites. Beat harshly again and stir in the oil. Heat and butter a small frying pan. Pour in enough of the batter to cover the bottom. Cook and brown both sides of the pancakes. Remove from the skillet when they are done. Spread the cakes with butter and jelly, jam or fruit.[6] Roll up and sprinkle with powdered sugar. *Note:* These delightful old-fashioned French pancakes are often served with meat dishes.

GREAT-AUNT SHIRLEY'S OLD-TIME WAFFLES

2 cups flour, sifted
milk to suit
2 eggs, well beaten

1 tablespoon butter,
  melted
salt to taste

Gradually blend the flour with sufficient milk to make a thin batter. Mix in the beaten eggs and the melted butter. Salt according to taste. *Note:* These require a greased waffle iron. Cook each side for about 30 seconds. Serve while hot with syrup, or butter and sugar. They make a fine supper or breakfast dish.

EARLY PLANTATION-STYLE DOUGHNUTS

1 cup sugar
1 egg
4 tablespoons butter,
  melted
pinch of cinnamon
1/4 nutmeg, grated

pinch of salt
1 cup milk
1 teaspoon baking soda
flour to suit
2 teaspoons cream of
  tartar

6. Recipes in Chapter 18

Blend the sugar, egg, melted butter, cinnamon, nutmeg, and salt. Mix the baking soda and milk and stir it in. Sift 1 cup flour with the cream of tartar. Add to the blend. When this is beaten to a smooth paste, add enough flour to make a dough stiff enough to be rolled. Roll out in a half-inch thick sheet. Cut into strips and twist or form in rings. Fry in hot deep fat until browned. Sprinkle with powdered sugar before they cool.

GREAT-GREAT-GRANDMOTHER HORTON'S FRIED DROP CAKES

2 cups milk	1 teaspoon salt
3 eggs	flour to suit

Our old New England nomenclature called them "pan cakes." On the average Yankee table they often made a dessert dish served with bottled cider and sugar. Sherry and sugar were also used to make a delicious dessert.

Simply blend all of the above ingredients. Use enough flour to make a thin batter. Drop from a large spoon into hot deep fat. Let cook until browned.

GREAT-GREAT-GRANDMOTHER DANIELS' SPONGE FRITTERS

Back in the early 1860s my Great-Great-Grandmother Daniels had a number of her most practical dishes published in the local weekly paper of that day. Among them was her delicious "sponge fritter" recipe. It reads as follows:

Pour seven-eighths of a cup of scalded milk over one-third cup of sugar. Cool and add one cake yeast dissolved in two tablespoonfuls warm water. Add one and one-third cups flour, and let it rise until it doubles its bulk. Then add two beaten eggs, the grated rind of one-half lemon, one-fourth teaspoonful salt and one and one-third cups flour. Let it rise again, cut down, roll out and cut in small round fingers, and let it rise again. Put two rounds together, forming a depression in the center of each. Place a little quince marmalade and currant jelly on the under one and wet the edges with milk. Press very firmly together with floured fingers and drop into fat hot enough to brown a small cube of bread in sixty seconds. When cooked, drain on brown paper and sprinkle with powdered sugar. The fritters will require twelve or fifteen minutes to cook, turning them occasionally.

Note: A mixture of 1/3 currant jelly and 2/3 quince, Banbury or orange marmalade was commonly used by Mrs. Daniels in the above recipe.[7] They were beaten together until smooth. All kinds of home-canned fruit, drained from its juices, was also used by her for a filling variation.

COLONIAL-TIME CORN FRITTERS

5 large ears green corn	(if milk is used)
3 eggs, well beaten	1 teaspoon salt
2 tablespoons cream	flour to suit
or	1 teaspoon baking powder
2 tablespoons milk	1/4 teaspoon baking soda
1 tablespoon butter, melted	

Scrape the kernels from the ears of green corn. Put the beaten eggs in a large wooden mixing bowl. Add the corn, cream and salt. Blend a little flour with the baking powder and baking soda. Add this and enough extra flour to make a thick paste. Fry in hot deep fat until nicely browned.

---

7. Recipes in Chapter 18

COUSIN ELIZABETH'S QUICK BANANA FRITTERS

Peel 2 bananas and cut in half lengthwise. Cut each piece crosswise. Sprinkle with lemon juice and let stand for 1 hour. Take the following ingredients and blend in a large wooden mixing bowl:

1 tablespoon sugar	1 cup flour
2 tablespoons butter, melted	1/2 cup milk
	2 egg whites

Dip the pieces of banana into the batter. Fry in hot deep fat until nicely browned. For a sauce use 1 cup sugar and 1/2 cup boiling water. Boil together and flavor with vanilla.

OLD-FASHIONED RAISED DOUGHNUTS

2 cups milk bread dough[8]	2 egg whites
1 egg	1 cup milk, warm
1/2 cup sugar	flour to suit

Put the milk bread dough in a wooden mixing bowl. Blend in the egg, sugar, egg whites, and warm milk. Add flour enough to make a dough. Knead hard. Set aside, cover with a thick cloth, and let it rise until morning. In the morning the dough should be cut and deep fried without any more kneading.

---

8. Recipe for old-fashioned milk bread can be found in *Natural Baking the Old-Fashioned Way,* by the same author.

GRANDMOTHER PELTON'S BEST RICE WAFFLES

4 cups flour
1 teaspoon salt
4 egg whites
1 cup boiled rice,
    cold

1 tablespoon butter,
    melted
2 eggs, well beaten
milk to suit

Sift the flour with the salt. Blend in the egg whites, cold rice, and melted butter. Stir in the beaten eggs. Pour in enough milk to make a thin batter. Bake in a well-buttered wafflle iron. Serve with maple syrup.

11

Salad-Making the Natural Way

The place that salads occupied in the early American family's diet was not very important. In fact, it was less noticeable in our own country than almost anywhere else in the civilized world. But a more general interest in and an acceptance of salads began to quickly grow in the mid-1800s. Some historians of the day considered this change to be one of the evidences of advancing civilization.

The old-fashioned salads of our great-grandmother's day were one of the truly artistic creations in American cookery. A proper homemade mayonnaise[1] was the aesthetic manifestation of the early homemaker's culinary artistry. It afforded an endless opportunity for invention and combination before the turn of the century.

LOBSTER SALAD AS JOHN ADAMS LIKED IT BEST

Pick out every bit of the meat from the body and claws of a cold boiled lobster. Mince the meat and set it aside

---

1. Recipe in Chapter 22

while you make the dressing. For this old fashioned dressing you will need the following ingredients:

4 egg yolks, hard-boiled	2 teaspoons sugar
2 tablespoons salad oil	1/2 teaspoon red pepper
1 teaspoon mustard[2]	1 teaspoon Worcestershire sauce[3]
1 teaspoon salt	celery vinegar to suit

Rub the egg yolks to a smooth paste in a bowl with a wooden spoon (in the days of John Adams they used a mortar and a pestle). They must be free from all lumps. Add gradually, rubbing all the time, all the other ingredients. Proceed slowly and carefully in blending the ingredients. Moisten with cider vinegar as they stiffen. Increase the vinegar as the mixture grows smooth. You should end up with 3/4 cup and it should be thin enough to pour over the minced lobster. Pour it over the lobster meat and stir long and hard. The meat must be thoroughly impregnated with the dressing. *Note:* John Adams sometimes liked chopped lettuce mixed with this salad. But unless it is to be eaten within a few minutes after mixing, the vinegar will wither the tender leaves. It is best to heap a glass dish with the inner leaves of several heads of lettuce. Lay crushed ice among them, and pass with the lobster so each guest may add the lettuce according to their individual taste.

When lettuce was out of season, Mr. Adams enjoyed this salad with cabbage and onion. The recipe calls for 4 table-spoons of good white cabbage, chopped fine, with 2 small onions, minced into almost invisible bits.

All lobster salad should be eaten as soon as possible after the dressing has been added. Garnish the dish with a chain of rings made with the whites of the boiled eggs.

2. Recipe in Chapter 19
3. Recipe in Chapter 13

GREAT-GREAT-GRANDMOTHER HORTON'S
BEST CHICKEN SALAD

2 cups cold chicken,
    minced[4]
1 1/2 cups celery,
    1/4-inch bits
3 hard-boiled eggs[5]
1 teaspoon salt

1 teaspoon pepper
2 teaspoons sugar
3 teaspoons olive oil
1 teaspoon mustard[6]
1 egg, well beaten
1/2 cup cider vinegar[7]

Blend the chicken and the celery in a wooden mixing bowl and set it aside in a cool place while you prepare the dressing. Rub the egg yolks to a fine paste. Add the salt, pepper and sugar. Then stir in the olive oil, a few drops at a time, while grinding the mixture hard. The mustard goes in next. Set aside a moment while you whip the raw egg to a froth. Beat this into the dressing. Spoon in the vinegar, whipping the dressing as you do it. Then sprinkle a little salt and pepper over the meat-celery mixture. Toss it lightly with a fork. Pour the dressing over it. Toss and mix until the bottom of the mass is as well saturated as the top. Turn into a salad bowl. Garnish with the boiled egg whites, cut into rings or flowers, and sprigs of bleached celery tops.

Note: If you cannot get celery, substitute crisp white cabbage, and use celery vinegar in the dressing. You can also, in this case, chop some cucumbers and stir them in. Turkey makes an even better salad than chicken. Try both ways.

---

4. Recipes in Chapter 8
5. Recipe in Chapter 9
6. Recipes in Chapter 19
7. Recipes in Chapter 19

COLD SHRIMP SALAD
IN THE LOUISIANNA TERRITORY

1/4 pound cheddar
   cheese, grated
1 tablespoon olive oil
1 teaspoon red pepper
1 teaspoon salt
1 teaspoon sugar
1 teaspoon mustard[8]

4 tablespoons celery
   vinegar
   or
4 tablespoons onion
   vinegar[9]
1/2 pound shrimp, minced

Put the grated cheese in a large wooden mixing bowl. Blend in the other ingredients in the order given above. Let it all stand together for 10 minutes before adding the shrimp. When this is done, stir well for 1 1/2 minutes. Serve in a glass dish garnished with slices of lemon. Or serve this salad in a clean crab shell if you can obtain one.

GREAT-GRANDMOTHER MITCHELL'S
OLD-TIME SALMON SALAD

1 1/2 pounds boiled or
   baked salmon[10]
3 hard-boiled eggs
1 teaspoon salt
1 teaspoon red pepper
1 teaspoon sugar

2 tablespoons olive oil
1 teaspoon mustard[11]
1 teaspoon Worcestershire
   sauce[12]
3/4 cup cider vinegar
2 heads lettuce

Mince three-quarters of the salmon. Set aside 4 or 5 pieces of salmon 1/2 inch wide and 4 or 5 inches long.

---

8. Recipe in Chapter 19
9. Recipes in Chapter 19
10. Recipes in Chapter 2
11. Recipe in Chapter 19
12. Recipe in Chapter 13

Prepare the dressing as follows. Rub the egg yolks to a smooth paste while gradually adding the salt, pepper, and sugar. Add the olive oil, a few drops at a time, while grinding the mixture hard. Stir in the mustard[13] and the Worcestershire sauce.[14] Lastly, add the cider vinegar and whip the dressing well.

The reserved pieces of salmon should be soaked in this dressing for 5 minutes, and then dipped in cider vinegar. Set aside while completing the salad.

Pour the dressing over the minced salmon. Shred the lettuce, handling as little as possible. Heap it in a separate bowl with crushed ice. This must accompany the salmon. Guests may help themselves to their liking. Or you may blend the lettuce with the fish, if it is to be eaten immediately.

When you have transferred your salad to the dish in which it is to be served, round it into a mound. Lay the strips of salmon upon it in such a manner as to divide it into triangular sections. The bars should all meet at the top, and diverge at the base. Between these have a chain made with the whites of the boiled eggs. Each circle of egg should overlap the one next to it. *Note:* Halibut can also be prepared in this way.

OLD-FASHIONED OYSTER SALAD

Put 2 cups fresh oysters in a saucepan. Bring to a boil. Drain them from the liquor. When cold, chop up fine and mix with 2 finely cut stalks of celery. Place on a bed of lettuce leaves or water cress. Serve with mayonnaise.[15]

---

13. Recipes in Chapter 19
14. Recipe in Chapter 13
15. Recipe in Chapter 22

GERMAN POTATO SALAD
IN EARLY AMERICAN HOMES

6 large potatoes
1/2 pound lean bacon,
   diced
salt to suit

pepper to suit
1/2 onion, diced
1/2 cup corn vinegar[16]

Boil the potatoes until they are soft. Peel and slice while still hot. Fry the diced bacon until it browns. Season the potatoes with salt, pepper, and the diced onion. Mix this in with the bacon and bacon grease. Stir in the vinegar (cider vinegar may be substituted). Turn out on a warm dish and garnish with sliced hard-boiled eggs. *Note:* My great-great-grandmother often had the opportunity of eating this salad as it was prepared by her German cooks. She was loud in her praise and claimed it is far better than when made in other ways.

OLD ATLANTA SIMPLE CHICKEN SALAD

This is a very old Southern recipe that was given to one of my distant relatives by an old colored woman in Atlanta back during slavery times. According to this woman, it is by no means necessary to have celery for a chicken salad. Other vegetables give an excellent and novel flavor. Crisp fresh cucumbers, for instance, combine well with the chicken. And French peas added to this make it even more attractive. Use 2 large cucumbers, and 2 cups cooked peas to every 4 cups chopped chicken. Stir in a suitable amount of mayonnaise,[17] and serve. *Note:* It is best to chill all ingredients before making this salad.

16. Recipes in Chapter 19
17. Recipe in Chapter 22

EARLY ALABAMA SWEETBREAD SALAD

Soak a pair of sweetbreads in cold salted water for 3/4 hour. Cook until tender in boiling water containing 1/2 teaspoon salt and 1 teaspoon cider vinegar.[18] After taking from the stove, drop the sweetbreads into cold water to harden them. Chop up into little pieces and put away to thoroughly chill. When it is time to serve, mix the sweetbreads with 2 thinly sliced cucumbers. Lay this in a bed of lettuce leaves and dress with mayonnaise.[19]

PRESIDENTIAL GRAPE SALAD— A FAVORITE OF ANDREW JACKSON

2 pounds green grapes	1/2 cup cucumber pickles,[20]
1 cup celery, chopped	chopped

Seed, skin, and cut the grapes in halves. Blend with the celery and cucumber pickles. Set aside until you make the following dressing:

2 eggs, well beaten	1 tablespoon butter, well
1 cup cider vinegar*	rounded
1/2 cup sugar	1 teaspoon cornstarch, wet
salt to taste	with cream
pepper to taste	3/4 cup cream
1 teaspoon mustard[21]	

Put all of the above ingredients, except for the cream, into a saucepan. Stir until it comes to a boil. Set aside, stirring occasionally, until it cools. Beat the cream with a little

---

18. Recipes in Chapter 19
19. Recipe in Chapter 22
20. Recipe in Chapter 20
21. Recipes in Chapter 19

sugar and stir in last. Pour the dressing into a wooden serving bowl. Add the grape salad mixture and blend them together. Serve when chilled.

FRUIT SALAD IN OLD TENNESSEE

3 oranges, pared
  and sectioned
12 walnuts, shelled
  and halved

24 green grapes, seeded
1 small pineapple, shred-
  ded with a fork
2 bananas, sliced and cut up

Blend all of the above fruits well and cover with a mixture of cider vinegar[22] and sugar. Chill thoroughly and then arrange on lettuce leaves. Garnish with mayonnaise.[23] Serve immediately as it is best when cold.

---

22. Recipe in Chapter 19
23. Recipe in Chapter 22

12

Old-Fashioned Puddings and Sauces

The number of early American puddings and sauces is almost endless. My great-grandmother, and those who came before her, made all sorts of homemade puddings—baked, boiled, steamed, fried, hot, cold, and raw.

Pudding is a historical dish, and it has been the garnisher of many a romance. Dickens made the Christmas Pudding[1] immortal. Burns made the Scotch haggis, which is a pudding, a national culinary monument. The margin between the plainest and the richest puddings is a wide one, and there is every grade between. The average family dinner table in early America was thought to be incomplete without its pudding. But in New England, pie still held its supremacy.

YE OLDE PLUM PUDDING, 1820

2 cups butter	1/2 tablespoon mace
2 cups sugar	2 nutmegs, grated
12 egg yolks, well beaten	6 cups raisins, chopped, dredged in flour

1. Recipes included herein

2 cups milk
10 cups flour
12 egg whites,
    stiffly beaten
1 cup brandy
1/2 tablespoon cloves

6 cups currants, chopped,
    dredged in flour
1 cup citron, shredded,
    dredged in flour
1 pound suet, chopped
    fine

Cream the butter and sugar in a large wooden mixing bowl. Beat in the egg yolks. Next stir in the milk. Then add the flour, alternately, with the beaten egg whites. Stir in the brandy and the spices. Lastly, stir in the fruit and the suet. Blend everything thoroughly. Wring out a heavy muslin cloth (called a "pudding cloth" in the old days) in hot water. Flour well inside. Pour in the mixture. Boil it for 5 hours. *Note:* I can confidently recommend this as the best old-time plum pudding I have ever tasted. It does not readily spoil if kept in a cool place, and any leftover plum pudding can be sliced and fried in butter.

GREAT-GRANDMOTHER MITCHELL'S BAKED APPLE PUDDING

3 tablespoons butter
1/2 cup sugar
4 egg yolks, well
    beaten
juice of 1 lemon
1/2 lemon rind, grated

6 large tart apples,
    grated
4 egg whites, stiffly
    beaten
nutmeg to suit

Cream the butter and sugar in a large wooden mixing bowl. Stir in the egg yolks, lemon juice, rind and grated apples. Lastly, blend in the egg whites. Put into a buttered baking dish, sprinkle nutmeg over the top, and bake in a moderate oven (350 degrees) until nicely browned. Eat when cold with a topping of whipped cream, or with cream poured over the pudding.[2]

CORNSTARCH PUDDING
DURING THE CIVIL WAR PERIOD

4 tablespoons cornstarch	nutmeg to suit
4 cups milk	cinnamon to suit
1 tablespoon butter	4 egg whites, stiffly
4 egg yolks	beaten
3/4 cup sugar	powdered sugar to suit

Dissolve the cornstarch in a little cold milk. Heat the rest of the milk in a kettle. Bring it to a boil. Stir in the cornstarch and boil for 3 minutes. Stir continually. Remove from the stove, and while still very hot, put in the butter. Set aside until cool. Now beat the egg yolks with the sugar and seasonings. Add them and the stiffly beaten whites to the cold mixture in the kettle. Beat thoroughly until it is a smooth custard. Pour into a buttered dish. Bake for 1/2 hour in a moderate oven (350 degrees). Eat when cold with powdered sugar sifted over it.

GREAT-GREAT-GRANDMOTHER NORTHRUP'S
FRUIT BREAD PUDDING

1 3/4 cups fine bread crumbs, stale	3/4 cup raisins, chopped and dredged in flour
4 cups milk	3/4 cup currants, dredged in flour
5 egg yolks	1/4 cup citron, shredded and dredged in flour
2 tablespoons sugar, heaping	5 egg whites, stiffly beaten
2 tablespoons butter, melted	

2. Recipe in Chapter 22

Soak the bread crumbs in the milk. Beat the egg yolks with the sugar until they are custard-like. Put into a large wooden mixing bowl and stir in the soaked bread crumbs along with the melted butter. When smooth, stir in the fruit. Then add the frothy egg whites and stir well. Pour into a buttered baking dish. Bake until browned in a moderate oven (350 degrees). *Note:* Cover this pudding while baking if it threatens to harden too soon on top. Send it to the table in the baking dish. Or turn it carefully out on a hot platter. Eat while warm with a good pudding sauce.[3]

EARLY VIRGINIA RICE PUDDING WITH EGGS

1 cup rice, boiled[4]
4 cups milk
4 egg yolks, well beaten
3/4 cup sugar
1 tablespoon butter, melted

4 egg whites, stiffly beaten
1/2 cup raisins, cut in two
nutmeg to suit

Soak the boiled rice in 2 cups of the milk for 1 hour. Put into a saucepan and bring to a boil. Let it boil for 5 minutes. Take from the stove and allow to cool. Put the well-beaten egg yolks in a large wooden mixing bowl. Stir in the sugar, melted butter, rice-milk blend, the other 2 cups cold milk, beaten egg whites and finally the raisins. Blend well and put into a buttered baking dish. Grate nutmeg on top. Bake in a moderate oven (350 degrees) for 3/4 hour, or until the custard is well set and light brown. Eat when cold.

---

3. Recipes included herein
4. Recipe in Chapter 3

ORIGINAL OLD-TIME LEMON PUDDING

2 cups milk
2 tablespoons cornstarch,
    wet with cold water
1 tablespoon butter

1 cup sugar
4 egg yolks, well beaten
juice of 2 lemons
rind of 1 lemon, grated

Heat the milk to boiling. Stir in the cornstarch. Boil for 5 minutes. Stir constantly. While hot, mix in the butter and set it aside to cool. Stir the sugar into the beaten egg yolks. Stir thoroughly and add the lemon juice and rind. Beat this to a stiff cream. Gradually add it to the cooled cornstarch-milk mixture. Blend until smooth. Put into a buttered baking dish. Bake in a moderate oven (350 degrees). Eat when cold with a good lemon sauce.[5]

GREAT-GREAT-GRANDMOTHER HORTON'S ORIGINAL INDIAN PUDDING

6 cups milk
1 cup Indian meal
1/4 cup butter
1 cup molasses
1 egg

1 teaspoon salt
1/2 teaspoon ginger
1/2 teaspoon cinnamon
1 cup water, boiling

Put 4 cups of the milk into a kettle and bring it to a boil. Stir in the Indian meal, butter, molasses, egg, salt, ginger and cinnamon. When blended thoroughly, pour the mixture into a bean pot. Add the other 2 cups milk and the boiling water. *Do not stir.* Bake in a slow oven (300 degrees) for 4 full hours. *Note:* This is the kind of Indian pudding commonly made in the early 1800s and before. And as my own great-great-grandmother once said, "It is the best pudding you ever put in your mouth."

5. Recipe included herein

REAL OLD-FASHIONED MACARONI PUDDING

4 cups milk	3/4 cup sugar
1 cup macaroni	juice of 1/2 lemon
2 tablespoons butter	rind of 1/2 lemon, grated
4 egg yolks	4 egg whites, stiffly beaten

Put 2 cups of the milk into a saucepan and bring to a boil. Add the macaroni and let simmer until tender. While hot, stir in the butter. Then beat the egg yolks with the sugar, lemon juice, and rind. Stir these into the macaroni mixture. Lastly, add the whipped egg whites. Pour into a buttered baking dish. Bake in a moderate oven (350 degrees) for 1/2 hour, or until nicely browned. Serve with a nice pudding sauce.[6]

GREAT-GREAT-GRANDMOTHER DANIELS' NEAPOLITAN PUDDING

1 1/2 cups fine bread crumbs	6 egg whites, stiffly beaten
1/2 cup milk	1/2 pound almond macaroons[7]
1 tablespoon butter, melted	1 cup sherry wine
3/4 cup sugar	1/2 pound stale sponge cake,[8] thinly sliced
6 egg yolks, well beaten	1/2 cup jelly or jam[9]
juice of 1 lemon	
rind of 1 lemon, grated	

---

6. Recipes included herein
7. Recipes can be found in *Natural Baking the Old-Fashioned Way,* by the same author.
8. Recipes can be found in *Natural Baking the Old-Fashioned Way,* by the same author.
9. Recipes in Chapter 18

Soak the bread crumbs in the milk. Rub the butter and sugar together in a large wooden mixing bowl. Add the beaten egg yolks. Stir in the soaked bread crumbs, lemon juice, and rind. Beat to a smooth, light paste. Lightly stir in the stiff egg whites. Butter a baking dish *very* well. Put a light layer of bread crumbs on the bottom. Next put down a layer of macaroons, placed evenly and close together. Wet these with wine. Cover with a layer of the pudding mixture. Add thin slices of the sponge cake, spread thickly with jelly or jam. Next add another layer of macaroons, wet with wine, more pudding, sponge cake, and jelly or jam. Continue until the dish is full. Cover with a layer of pudding over the top. Put a lid on the dish and steam in the oven for 3/4 hour. Then remove the cover and brown the top. Turn out carefully on a dish. Pour a sauce[10] over it and serve. Or make a special sauce by beating warm currant jelly with 2 tablespoons melted butter and 1/4 cup pale sherry. *Note:* This old-fashioned pudding is exceptional when boiled in a buttered mold as was so often done in times long past.

OLD MASSACHUSSETT'S
BAKED PLUM PUDDING DELIGHT

5 egg yolks
1 cup sugar
1/2 pound suet, finely
    chopped
1 teaspoon nutmeg
1 teaspoon cinnamon
1 teaspoon cloves
5 cups flour

milk to suit
3 cups raisins, halved,
    dredged in flour
2 tablespoons citron,
    shredded
5 egg whites, stiffly
    beaten

Beat the egg yolks and sugar together until a smooth, custard-like consistency. Stir in the suet and spices. Add the

10. Recipes included herein

flour. Moisten the mixture gradually with milk until you can move the spoon around in it. Slowly stir in the fruit. Finally, stir in the stiff egg whites. Beat *very* hard and long before putting into a deep, buttered baking dish. Bake in a moderate oven (350 degrees) for 1 1/2 hours. Then turn it out onto a large dish and serve with a rich sweet sauce.[11]

EARLY SOUTHERN PLANTATION
PEACH BATTER PUDDING

Use sound, ripe peaches for this pudding. Peel and remove the pits from enough peaches to fill a large bowl. Place the peaches close together. Pour 1/2 cup water over them. To make the batter you will need:

2 cups flour	1 cup milk
2 tablespoons sugar	2 eggs, well beaten
pinch of salt	3 tablespoons butter,
2 teaspoons baking powder	melted

Blend the flour, sugar, salt, and baking powder in a wooden mixing bowl. Rub through a fine sieve and then add the milk and eggs. Stir until a smooth batter is formed. Stir in the melted butter. Pour this batter over the peaches in the bowl. Bake uncovered, or cover and steam the pudding. It should be eaten hot with a rich sweet sauce.[12]

GRANDMOTHER PELTON'S
DAINTY STEAMED FIG PUDDING

2 cups rolled oats	1 cup figs, finely
1/2 cup cream	chopped
1/4 cup sugar	1 cup milk

11. Recipes included herein
12. Recipes included herein

Moisten the oats with the cream. Blend in the sugar, figs, and milk. Pour into a buttered baking dish. Cover, place in moderate oven (350 degrees) and steam for 2 1/2 hours. Serve with whipped cream[13] or a hot pudding sauce.[14]

GREAT-GRANDMOTHER SHAW'S
OLD-TIME CHRISTMAS PUDDING

10 crackers, pounded fine	1 tablespoon salt, heaping
4 cups milk	1 tablespoon nutmeg
8 eggs	1/2 tablespoon mace
2 cups sugar	1 tablespoon cloves
1 cup molasses	1 lemon rind, grated
1 cup brandy	1/4 cup citron
1 pound suet, chopped fine	3 cups currants
	4 1/2 cups raisins

Blend the crackers and the milk in a porcelain kettle. Let this stand overnight. In the morning, rub it through a colander and then add the rest of the ingredients. Blend well and then boil the pudding for 5 hours. Or you may steam it for 3 hours or more. *Note:* This is an extremely good fruit pudding. It is appreciated more when served with a foamy sauce.[15]

Early American Pudding Sauces

GREAT-GREAT-GRANDMOTHER HORTON'S
CREAMY HARD SAUCE

1 cup butter	juice of 1 lemon
3 cups powdered sugar	2 teaspoons nutmeg
1/2 cup wine	

13. Recipe in Chapter 22
14. Recipes included herein
15. Recipe included herein

Put the butter and sugar in a wooden mixing bowl. Stir until it becomes smooth and creamy. Blend in the wine, lemon juice, and nutmeg. Beat long and hard until it turns several shades lighter than at first. It should be extremely creamy. Smooth into shape with a broad-bladed knife dipped in cold water. Set on ice until the pudding is served. *Note:* This sauce goes well with any of the puddings in this chapter.

WHITE WINE SAUCE IN THE CONFEDERACY

2 1/2 cups powdered
   sugar
1/2 cup butter
1/2 cup boiling water

1/2 cup pale sherry or
   white wine
1 teaspoon nutmeg

Put the sugar in a wooden mixing bowl. Work the butter into the sugar until it is a smooth cream. Moisten as you go, with the boiling water. Beat long and hard until your bowl is nearly full of the creamy mixture. Then gradually add the wine and nutmeg, still beating hard. Turn into a small saucepan and set this in a larger pan of boiling water. Stir frequently until the sauce is hot (but *not* until it boils). Take the large pan from the stove. Leave the smaller pan standing in the hot water. Stir the contents occasionally until you are ready to serve the pudding. *Note:* If properly made, this sauce will be as white as milk. It goes well with any pudding.

UNRIVALLED OLDEN-DAY LEMON SAUCE

1/2 cup butter
1 1/4 cups sugar
1 egg, well beaten
1/2 lemon rind, grated

juice of 1 lemon
1 teaspoon nutmeg
3 tablespoons water,
   boiling

Cream the butter and sugar in a small bowl. Beat in the egg, lemon rind, lemon juice and nutmeg. Beat hard for 10 minutes. Then beat in, a spoon at a time, the boiling water. Set the bowl within the uncovered top of a tea-kettle. Bring the kettle to a boil. Keep it boiling until the steam heats the sauce. Stir constantly but do not let the sauce boil.

GREAT-AUNT BEVERLY JO'S MILK PUDDING SAUCE

1 1/4 cups sugar
1 teaspoon butter
2 eggs, well beaten
1 teaspoon nutmeg or
    mace

1/2 teaspoon cornstarch,
    wet with cold milk
5 tablespoons milk,
    boiling

Put the sugar in a small saucepan. Rub the butter into the sugar until it is creamed nicely. Stir in the beaten eggs, and whip the mixture to a creamy froth. Add the nutmeg and the wet cornstarch. Finally, beat in, a spoon at a time, the boiling milk. Set the pan within a larger pan of boiling water. Leave for 5 minutes, continually stirring. Do not let the sauce come to a boil. *Note:* This is an excellent sauce for bread and other simple puddings.[16]

GREAT-GRANDMOTHER MITCHELL'S BRANDY SAUCE DELIGHT

2 eggs, well beaten
1 cup powdered sugar
2 cups milk, boiling

nutmeg to taste
1 teaspoon vanilla
2 tablespoons brandy

Put the thoroughly beaten eggs into a small pan and beat the sugar into them. Gradually whip in the boiling milk.

16. Recipes included herein

Stir in the nutmeg and vanilla. Set the small pan within a large pan of boiling water. Stir until it begins to thicken. Take it off the stove and gradually stir in the brandy. Leave it, until needed, in the pan of hot water. Pour over the pudding and serve while hot.

MARTHA WASHINGTON'S
OLD-FASHIONED JELLY SAUCE

1/4 tablespoon cornstarch	1 tablespoon butter,
3 tablespoons water,	melted
boiling	1/2 cup currant jelly[17]
1/4 cup pale sherry	

Wet the cornstarch in a little cold water. Stir this into the boiling water. Heat, stirring continuously, until it thickens. Stir in the butter, and set aside until it is almost cold. Beat in, 1 teaspoon at a time, the jelly. It should be a smooth pink paste when blended enough. Pour in the wine and beat hard. Heat in a small pan set within a larger pan of boiling water. Let the sauce get very hot, but don't let it boil. *Note:* This sauce is great when poured over and around Neapolitan and bread pudding.[18]

CIVIL WAR PERIOD CREAM SAUCE SPECIAL

2 cups cream	2 egg whites, stiffly beaten
4 tablespoons powdered	1 teaspoon vanilla
sugar	or
1 teaspoon nutmeg	1 teaspoon bitter almond

Heat the cream slowly in a small saucepan set in a larger

17. Recipe in Chapter 18
18. Recipes included herein

pan of boiling water. Stir often. When the cream is scalding, but not boiling, take it from the stove. Put in the sugar and nutmeg. Stir 3 or 4 minutes and then add the egg whites. Blend thoroughly and flavor with vanilla or bitter almond. Set the pan back in the larger pan of hot water until the pudding is served. Stir occasionally until time to use it.

EGG SAUCE IN EARLY NEW ORLEANS

2 cups sugar
1 cup butter

2 eggs, well beaten
1/2 cup wine

Cream the sugar and butter in a saucepan. Blend in the beaten eggs and the wine. Beat hard and then set the pan into a larger pan of boiling water. Stir continually until the sauce is thick and creamy. Pour it over and around the pudding.

GRANDMOTHER COLLISTER'S OLD-FASHIONED FOAMY SAUCE

3 tablespoons butter
1 1/2 cups powdered
  sugar
1 egg white

1 egg white, stiffly
  beaten
4 tablespoons sherry wine
3 tablespoons water,
  boiling

Cream the butter and sugar in a saucepan. Stir in the unbeaten egg white and the stiffly beaten egg white. Beat it all together until very light and fluffy. Add the wine and the boiling water. Set on the stove and heat slightly. Stir until the sauce becomes frothy. Serve at once.

13

Fish and Meat Sauces the Natural Way

A large portion of the modern sauces that are put into cook-books for fish and meats are impractical to make and use in the average home. There are, however, many old-fashioned sauces that add so much to the palatableness of the dishes served that they should be utilized, even at the cost of a little extra time and trouble. Such is *John Quincy Adams' Favorite Hollandaise Sauce,* which he liked Louisa Catherine to fix when she served him fresh brook trout. And the *Early American Drawn Butter Sauces,* enjoyed so much by Zachary Taylor when served with white-meated boiled fish dishes, are treats. The *Original Old-Time Tartar Sauce* for fried fish and soft-shelled crabs and *Granddad's Best Oyster Sauce* for boiled fowl or turkey are both excellent. Then too, my *Great-Grandmother Shaw's Currant Jelly Sauce* for roast lamb, *Old Plantation Mint Sauce* for all lamb dishes, and the *Old New England Caper Sauce* for boiled lamb are unique "taste-teasers."

169

UNCLE ART'S BASIC MEAT SAUCE

2 tablespoons horseradish, grated
24 peppercorns
1 tablespoon salt
1 tablespoon sugar
pinch of red pepper

3 large pickled onions,[1] minced fine
1 tablespoon allspice
1 nutmeg, grated
4 cups vinegar from walnut or butternut pickles[2]

Mix all of the above ingredients together, except for the vinegar. Put them in a stone jar and crush with a billet of wood or a heavy wooden mallet. Pour the vinegar over this, cover with a cloth, and let stand for 2 full weeks. Pour the liquor into a porcelain kettle and heat to boiling. Immediately strain and set aside until the next day so that it will settle well. Bottle and cork very tightly. *Note:* This makes an extremely good sauce for all kinds of meat and it can be used to season any gravy or stew.

EARLY AMERICAN DRAWN BUTTER SAUCES

Take 1 tablespoon flour and 2 tablespoons butter. Beat smoothly together in a saucepan. Gradually add 1 cup boiling water, and stir continually to keep it smooth. Let it come just to a boil, but do not let it boil. Add 1 tablespoon lemon juice and a small pinch of pepper to improve its flavor. *Note:* Using this simple drawn butter sauce for a foundation, the following sauces for fish and meats will be found quite easy to make.

Drawn Butter Egg Sauce: Finely chop 2 hard-boiled eggs and stir into the above drawn butter sauce. Blend well. It

1. Recipe in Chapter 20
2. Recipe in Chapter 20

FISH AND MEAT SAUCES

is excellent for baked or boiled fish. This sauce was a favorite of our twelfth President, Zachary Taylor.

Drawn Butter Asparagus Sauce: Take a small bunch of fresh asparagus tips and boil with 1 teaspoon lemon juice in the water. Drain well and press through a colander. Set aside. Then take 2 cups of the above drawn butter sauce and add 1 slice of onion, a sprig of parsley, 1/2 tablespoon of grated carrot and a small blade of mace. Place in a saucepan and let it simmer for 20 minutes. Lastly, strain this hot mixture over the previously prepared asparagus tips. Stir well and put back into the saucepan. Let it come to a boil. Immediately take from the stove. Longer cooking will destroy the color of the sauce.

Drawn Butter Celery Sauce: Take a bunch of celery and cut the stalks and leaves into small pieces. Boil until tender, drain well, and press through a colander. Stir the celery and 2 well beaten egg yolks into the above hot drawn butter sauce. Do not cook after the eggs have been added.

Drawn Butter Lobster Sauce: Shred 2 cups of lobster meat. Add this to the above drawn butter sauce with 1 tablespoon lemon juice and a pinch of red pepper. Blend well.

Drawn Butter Parsley Sauce: Add 2 tablespoons chopped parsley to 1 cup of the above drawn butter sauce. Blend well and it is ready to use.

GRANDDAD'S BEST OYSTER SAUCE

1 tablespoon butter
1 tablespoon flour
25 oysters
1/2 cup cream

salt to taste
pepper to taste
lemon juice to taste

Blend the butter and flour smoothly together in a saucepan. Boil the oysters in their own liquor until their edges curl. Strain 1 cup of the oyster liquor into the butter-flour mixture. Stir until smooth and thick. Chop the oysters and add them with the cream to the hot sauce. Bring to a good boil. Take off the stove and season with salt, pepper, and lemon juice. *Note:* This sauce is excellent with boiled turkey[1] or any boiled fowl dish.

JOHN QUINCY ADAMS'S
FAVORITE HOLLANDAISE SAUCE

3 tablespoons lemon juice
pinch of salt
pinch of pepper

6 egg yolks, well beaten
1 cup butter

Put the lemon juice, salt and pepper into a saucepan and boil until it has been reduced in half. Take off the stove and add a little cold water and the beaten egg yolks. Blend well and then put the pan back on the stove. Then add the butter, a little at a time, stirring it steadily with a wooden mixing spoon. Do not let it come to a boil. If the sauce becomes too thick, simply add a little cold water to prevent curdling. *Note:* This is an excellent sauce for use with cauliflower dishes or with salmon and brook trout.

ORIGINAL OLD-TIME TARTAR SAUCE

1 tablespoon cider
   vinegar[2]
1 tablespoon lemon juice
pinch of salt

1 tablespoon Worcester-
   shire sauce[3]
1/3 cup browned butter

---

1. Recipe in Chapter 8
2. Recipe in Chapter 19
3. Recipe included herein

Put the vinegar, lemon juice, salt, and Worcestershire sauce in a double boiler and blend together. When well mixed and hot, add the browned butter.

or

1 tablespoon capers, chopped fine	1 tablespoon cucumber pickle,[4] chopped fine
1 tablespoon olives, chopped fine	1 tablespoon parsley, chopped fine
few drops onion juice	

Blend all of the above ingredients in a wooden mixing bowl. Stir into mayonnaise. *Note:* Either of these recipes are excellent for fried fish, soft-shelled crabs, etc. The first recipe is especially good with broiled fish and it should always be served hot.

GREAT-GRANDMOTHER SHAW'S BASIC BROWN SAUCE

1 tablespoon butter	pepper to taste
1 tablespoon flour	1 cup hot stock[5]
salt to taste	1 tablespoon lemon juice

Smoothly blend the butter with the flour. Heat and stir until it becomes a golden brown color. Season with salt and pepper. Gradually stir in the stock, or, if you have no stock, 1 cup hot water into which 1 teaspoon beef extract[6] has been dissolved. Add the lemon juice last and blend well.

---

4. Recipe in Chapter 20
5. Recipe in Chapter 1
6. Recipe in Chapter 1

Note: Using this brown sauce as a basic foundation, Great-Grandmother Shaw's other delightful old-fashioned sauces will be found rather easy to make.

Great-Grandmother Shaw's Currant Jelly Sauce: Take 1 cup of the above brown sauce and add 1/2 cup melted currant jelly.[7] Stir until the jelly is well blended and serve while hot. This is very nice with roast lamb[8] and other lamb dishes.

Great-Grandmother Shaw's Mushroom Sauce: Make a brown sauce as above, but use 1/2 cup stock and 1/2 cup mushroom liquor, instead of all stock. When thick and smooth, add 1/2 cup of mushrooms cut into small pieces. Season with salt, pepper, and 1 teaspoon Worcestershire sauce.[9] Simmer for 5 minutes. Add 1 tablespoon sherry wine and serve hot.

Great-Grandmother Shaw's Olive Sauce: Take 12 green olives and soak them in warm water for 1 hour to extract the salt. The olives may then be cut around close to the stone, leaving the meat in a single piece. Or they may be cut into little pieces. Add them to the above brown sauce and let it simmer for 10 minutes. Serve while hot.

OLD PLANTATION MINT SAUCE

Mint sauce was extremely popular in the old days as a dressing for roast lamb.[10] My great-grandmother used 1 cup of chopped mint, 1/4 cup sugar, and 1/2 cup cider vinegar.[11] Others used less mint and more sugar. It can be varied to suit the individual taste. The ingredients were all put in

7. Recipe in Chapter 18
8. Recipe in Chapter 6
9. Recipe included herein
10. Recipe in Chapter 6
11. Recipe in Chapter 19

a saucepan and heated. When the sugar was dissolved, the sauce was ready to serve.

REAL OLD-FASHIONED WORCESTERSHIRE SAUCE

3 teaspoons red pepper
3 scallions, minced
3 anchovies, chopped
    fine
4 cups cider vinegar[11]

2 tablespoons walnut
    or tomato catsup[12]
    strained through
    muslin

Blend all of the above ingredients and rub them through a sieve. Put into a stone jar and set this in a pot of boiling water. Heat until the liquid in the stone jar is so hot you cannnot keep your finger in it. Immediately strain and let stand in the jar, closely covered, for 2 days. Then put into bottles and seal until needed.

OLD NEW ENGLAND CAPER SAUCE

1 tablespoon flour
1 tablespoon butter
2 cups lamb broth

1 tablespoon lemon juice
2 tablespoons capers

Blend the flour with the butter until it is a cream. Gradually add the hot lamb broth to this. Stir until smooth and thick. Then pour into a gravy tureen (table bowl) and stir in the lemon juice and capers. This sauce is wonderful with boiled lamb[13] and most other meat dishes.

---

12. Recipes in Chapter 19
13. Recipe in Chapter 6

EARLY NEW HAMPSHIRE TOM ALLEY SAUCE

A veteran New England fishing boat pilot gave this recipe to my Great-Great-Grandmother Horton many years ago. I have found this sauce to be excellent. The boat pilot's instructions were: "Take the 'Tom Alley,' or green fat, of five or six freshly boiled lobsters, and season with salt, red pepper, lemon juice or vinegar, and add a tablespoon of either good salad oil, or melted butter. Stir all well together, and dress the plain lobster. The proportions of the seasoning will vary with the taste of the mixer, and the amounts with the size of the lobsters."

SEED VINEGAR SAUCE, 1825

Gather some green nasturtium seeds when they are full grown but not yet yellow. Dry them in the sun for 1 day. Put into small jars or wide-mouthed bottles. Cover the seeds with boiling corn vinegar or cider vinegar.[14] Allow to cool and then tightly close the containers. The sauce will be fit for use in about 6 weeks. It gives an agreeable taste to drawn butter for fish, or when put on beef and lamb.

COLONIAL-STYLE CHESTNUT SAUCE

Stew 2 cups fresh chestnuts (after shelling) with some good stock[15] until they are tender. Drain and rub them through a sieve or colander. Put back into the saucepan with enough cream to make a thick sauce. Stir in 1/2 cup butter and season to taste with salt and pepper. Serve while hot. *Note:* This chestnut sauce was a great favorite in early Colonial times and it was spoken highly of by Willem Kieft, one of the Colonial governors of New York.

14. Recipe in Chapter 19
15. Recipe in Chapter 1

GRANDMOTHER COLLISTER'S
SPECIAL CUCUMBER SAUCE

100 cucumbers, medium
    size
12 onions, medium
    size
2 cups salt
corn vinegar or cider
    vinegar to suit[16]

1/4 cup black mustard
    seed
1/4 cup white mustard
    seed
2 cups ground mustard
1 tablespoon celery seed

Pare and slice the cucumbers very thin and chop the onions until they are fine. Put both into a stone jar in layers, salting each layer. Let this stand overnight in a cool place. The next morning drain well in a colander for several hours. Then sprinkle in all the above spices. Put enough good vinegar on the mixture to soak it well. Pack tightly in jars and cover with salad oil. *Note:* This can be made without the onions if you dislike their flavor. It is a tasty addition to any fish or meat dish.

GREAT-GRANDMOTHER MITCHELL'S
FANCY TOMATO SAUCE

1/4 cup butter
1/4 cup flour
1 cup brown stock[17]
1 1/3 cups tomatoes,
    stewed and strained
1 slice carrot
1 slice onion
1 sprig of thyme
1 sprig of parsley

bit of bay leaf
2 whole cloves
6 peppercorns
1/4 cup cheddar cheese,
    grated
2 tablespoons sherry wine
salt to taste
pepper to taste

---

16. Recipe in Chapter 19
17. Recipe in Chapter 1

Brown the butter in a saucepan and stir in the flour. Brown again and then pour the brown stock into this. Stir in the tomatoes. Add the carrot, onion, thyme, parsley, bay leaf, cloves, and peppercorns. Cook for 15 minutes. Strain and then blend in the cheese, wine, salt and pepper. Serve while hot.

UNCLE ALBERT'S FAVORITE BAKED FISH SAUCE

1 tablespoon butter, melted
1 1/2 teaspoons cornstarch
3/4 cup milk
1/2 pound sharp cheddar cheese, grated

salt to taste
pepper to taste
mustard[18] to taste
1 egg, well beaten

Bake a 2- or 3-pound piece of halibut or other type fish. Baste freely with milk while baking and then serve with a delightful old-fashioned cheese sauce made from the above ingredients. The procedure is as follows: Blend the melted butter and cornstarch in a saucepan. Slowly pour on the milk. Put over the fire and when hot, add the grated cheese, salt, pepper, and mustard. Add the beaten egg as soon as the cheese has all melted. Blend well and pour over the baked fish while both are still hot. This combination with other fish dishes, as well as various meat dishes, is fabulous.

18. Recipe in Chapter 19

14

Old-Fashioned Beverages

Coffee-Making during The Civil War Period

There has always been an endless variety of coffee pots around. But given a good quality bean, properly roasted and ground, anyone can make good old-fashioned coffee in a tin pail or anything else handy. And this can easily be accomplished even without a strainer, filter, or bag.

The soldiers during the Civil War became adepts at making good coffee—and these men had only a tin cup for a coffee pot. They would fill the cup nearly full of cold water and put in enough coffee to make it sufficiently strong. It was then left to soak until very moist and finally set on the camp fire. The liquid was brought to a boil. The soldier then poured a long stream of cold water from a canteen held high above the cup to "settle" it. Uncle Sam was said to furnish very good coffee, as a rule, to his military men. And they thoroughly enjoyed it, according to my Great-Grandfather Elias, himself a veteran at 26 in 1865.

Coffee-Making Pointers From The Old Days

My great-grandmother broke an egg in her coffee before it was ever brought to a boil. This, she said, made the coffee clear. She believed the cheaper grades of coffee could not possibly be made into a decent beverage. In her estimation, only the best beans made drinkable coffee. Proper roasting of the coffee beans was a cardinal rule. Burnt coffee beans ruined the flavor of a cup of coffee. The beans also had to be fresh, for this alone insured a delightful aroma. Good water for making the coffee was another of her prerequisites. As she so often said: "you can spoil the best coffee with bad water." Clearness was important, for this grand lady detested a "muddy" cup of coffee.

Neither sugar nor cream are absolutely essential to a satisfactory cup of coffee, although many people use both. But if you are going to use anything besides sugar, cream alone will suffice. Skim milk in coffee is a damaging addition. And so are brown sugar and molasses, such as many a family had to use during the Civil War period of our history.

Boiling certainly does not ruin coffee. Indeed, some of the nicest coffee to be had is made by boiling. Try the following recipe for a real old fashioned treat.

TO MAKE OLD-FASHIONED BOILED COFFEE

1 egg shell, crushed	4 cups boiling water
1 egg white, beaten	1/2 cup ice-cold water
1 cup ground coffee	

Stir up the crushed eggshell and the beaten egg white with the dry coffee. Add a very little cold water to moisten. Gradually blend this with the boiling water in the saucepan or pot (or what was called a "coffee-boiler" in the old days). Stir from the sides and top as it boils up. Boil pretty fast for 12 full minutes. Then pour in the ice-cold water and take from the fire. Gently set aside to settle the grounds. In 5 minutes it will be ready to drink. In the old days, the boiled coffee was then poured off carefully into a silver, china, or Britannia coffee pot. This serving pot was always scalded well before it was to be used. The coffee was sent to the table *hot*.

OLD-TIME TIPS ON BUYING COFFEE

Coffee quickly loses its aroma after it is ground. It is well worth your while to buy the whole bean. Get it either in small quantities freshly roasted, or raw and roast it yourself as the old timers so often did. You can roast the beans in a pan in the oven. Or the beans can be roasted in a pan on top of the stove. However it is done, stir every few minutes and roast quickly to a bright brown—not a dull black. Beat the white of an egg with 1 tablespoon melted butter. Stir this into the coffee beans while they are still hot. This is a very old trick used to preserve the flavor. Grind just enough beans at a time to make a single pot.

TEA IN THE COLONIES

2 teaspoons tea   1 cup boiling water

Scald the teapot well before using. Put in the tea leaves and cover tightly. Set the pot on the stove and warm it for 1 minute. Pour on enough boiling water to cover the leaves. Let it stand for 10 full minutes to "draw." Keep the lid of the pot shut, but do not let the tea boil. Now fill up the pot with as much boiling water as you will need. Pour into a heated china or silver pot. Send to the table steaming hot.

The ruination of good tea in many households is unboiled

water. It can never extract the flavor as it should, although it may be left to steep for hours. The kettle should not only steam, but bubble and puff in a hard boil before you add water from it to the tea leaves.

Never boil the tea after it is made. This injures the natural flavor, either by deadening it or making it rank.

REAL OLD-FASHIONED HOT CHOCOLATE

2 cups water	2 cups milk
6 tablespoons chocolate, grated	sugar to taste

Put the water in a saucepan and bring it to a boil. Rub the chocolate smooth in a little cold water. Stir into the boiling water. Boil for a full 20 minutes. Add the milk and let it all boil for another 10 minutes. Stir frequently. You can sweeten with the sugar by adding it while boiling the chocolate or later in the individual cups.

GREAT-GRANDMOTHER SHAW'S RASPBERRY SHRUB

Select about 12 quarts of the juiciest, plumpest raspberries. Put them in a large stone jar or a huge mixing bowl. Pour enough cider vinegar[1] over them to reach as far as the berries, but no more. Let the raspberries soak in the vinegar for 36 hours. Lay a coarse muslin cloth in a colander and set this over another stone jar. Dip the raspberry-vinegar mixture into it. Mash the raspberries a little to extract all their juice.

Now remove the colander and dip the juice blend out of the stone jar. Measure the juice as you put it in a porcelain-lined kettle. Place on the stove and bring to a boil. Once

---

1. Recipe in Chapter 19

it begins to boil, add 2 cups sugar for every pint (2 cups) of liquid in the kettle. Allow this mixture to boil for 10 minutes. Immediately bottle and seal. *Note:* use 2 tablespoons of this syrup in a glass of water. Add 2 tablespoons of crushed ice. Stir and serve with the most delicate white sponge cake or with simple wafers.[2] It is a most refreshing and pleasant drink.

GREAT-GRANDMOTHER MITCHELL'S CURRANT SHRUB

Extract the juice from 2 quarts of rich ripe red currants. Sweeten with 1 cup sugar to every 2 cups juice. Beat the mixture well with a large wooden spoon. Dilute the juice with twice as much crushed ice and ice water as there is currant juice. *Note:* My great-grandmother often added a little grated nutmeg to each glass of this shrub.

EARLY AMERICAN RAISIN WINE

2 cups sugar
6 cups seedless raisins, chopped fine
1 lemon, all the juice
and half the grated peel
2 gallons boiling water

Blend all of the above ingredients in a large stone jar. Stir every day for 1 week. Then strain and bottle it. The wine will be fit to drink in 10 days after bottling.

CAFÉ AU LAIT IN THE COLONIES

2 cups very strong coffee, fresh and hot
2 cups milk, boiling

2. Recipes can be found in *Natural Baking the Old-Fashioned Way,* by the same author.

This was an extremely popular "after church drink" in the early days of our glorious history. The coffee was boiled[3] and then carefully poured off the grounds. This was done through a fine strainer (thin muslin was considered to be the best material) into what was known as the "table coffee-pot," or serving pot. The milk was added and the serving pot was placed back on the stove for 5 minutes before serving. But care must be taken that it does not boil.

GRANDMOTHER PELTON'S BLACKBERRY CORDIAL

Stew some blackberries until they have become soft and strain them through a fine sieve. Do not allow any of the seeds to get into the blackberry juice. Measure the juice and put it in a porcelain kettle. Add 1 cup sugar to every 4 cups of the strained juice. Stir in 1/2 tablespoon grated nutmeg and 1 tablespoon cinnamon. Allow this mixture to simmer until it becomes thick. Then take off the stove and set aside to cool. When cold, add 1 pint of brandy to each quart of the syrup and bottle it. *Note:* Some old-timers also added a pinch of allspice and a pinch of cloves. Others used another cup of sugar for every quart of the juice. Try it both ways.

EGGNOG CHRISMAS SPECIAL, 1776

1/2 cup sugar	1 cup brandy (a half pint)
6 egg yolks, well beaten	3 egg whites, beaten until very stiff
1 quart rich milk	nutmeg to suit taste

Beat the sugar into the egg yolks until they reach a custard-like consistency. Stir this into the milk. Add the

3. Recipe included herein

brandy. Lastly, whip in the stiffly beaten egg whites and add nutmeg to suit individual taste.

GREAT-GREAT-GRANDMOTHER HORTON'S CALF'S FOOT BROTH[4]

2 calves' feet	pepper to taste
8 cups cold water	8 eggs
salt to taste	1 cup milk

Put the calves' feet into a saucepan with the cold water. Boil the feet to shreds and then strain the liquor through a double muslin bag. Season to taste with the salt and pepper. Put the eggs in a large wooden mixing bowl and add the milk. Beat the egg-milk mixture very hard. Put equal quantities of this in each cup of the broth until it is all used up. Serve while hot. *Note:* This broth was often served at luncheons and teas in the old days. It was also drank with many meals as well as considered excellent for anyone who was sick. In such cases, the broth was served with thin, crisp slices of toast. A dash of lemon juice was sometimes added to the broth before the egg-milk mixture was beaten in. Many old timers believed it improved the taste of the drink.

---

4. Also see Calf's Foot Jelly recipe, Chapter 17

15

Sandwich-Making the Natural Way

Like salads in the olden days, sandwiches were at first generally made only for luncheons or a picnic basket. They were seldom, if ever, prepared for the dinner-table and served at regular meals. They were from the first varied almost indefinitely and concocted of practically everything edible.

My Great-Great-Grandmother Horton believed it was more of an art to make a good sandwich than most people thought—even a sandwich of the plainest sort. A thick, dry, stuffy sandwich was considered objectionable (of course homemade bread[1] was always used in her day). In her estimation, the bread used in sandwich-making should be just a little stale, but not dry (it would hold together better). And the slices should be cut thin. If buttered, or if the sandwich was to be made with a paste, it had to be evenly spread. The crust was cut from the bread and the 2 pieces that form the sandwich were firmly pressed together. If a slice of meat was used, it was cut very thin.

---

1. Many excellent recipes for old-time homemade bread can be found in *Natural Baking the Old-Fashioned Way,* by the same author.

The meat was never quite as large as, and certainly no larger than, the bread.

Mrs. Horton, after removing the crust from the bread, spread the whole slices. When finished with spreading the filling, she put the 2 slices together and cut them in triangles, to make smaller, more easily handled sandwiches.

Special recipes need not be given for the plain old-fashioned meat sandwiches—such as tongue, ham, corned beef, and the like. If mustard[2] is used, it should be carefully and evenly spread on the meat, and it should always be freshly mixed. The use of pronounced flavors in sandwiches is usually not desirable, since so many people do not care for them. And it is offensive to bite into a sandwich and find onion or any other flavor that is disliked. It goes without saying that the butter used should be fresh and of the best quality. Rank butter is even worse than rank onion or mustard. All sandwiches were made with homemade bread in the old days. Many excellent recipes for old-time breads can be found in *Natural Baking the Old-Fashioned Way*, by the same author.

GREAT-GRANDMOTHER MITCHELL'S SALMON SANDWICHES

A piece of freshly baked salmon should be finely shredded. It may be seasoned as one likes, but Mrs. Mitchell used salt, pepper, and a little lemon juice. Both the upper and lower bread slices should be spread with the fish. Then add sliced cucumbers that have been soaked in French dressing.[3]

---

2. Recipe in Chapter 19
3. Recipe in Chapter 22

OLD WESTERN EGG AND CHEESE SANDWICHES

Take the yolks of 6 hard-boiled eggs and rub 1 table-spoon grated cheddar cheese into them. The sharper the cheese, the better it turns out. Add a little cream to form a thick paste. Season with salt, paprika, and a bit of red pepper. Spread on thinly sliced, buttered bread. *Note:* In the old west, this sandwich was often toasted in a buttered frying pan over an open fire. It was a favorite of the chuck wagon cooks.

GREAT AUNT RUTH'S
OLD-TIME DEVILED EGG SANDWICHES

12 eggs, hard-boiled[4]
1 tablespoon olive oil
1 tablespoon mustard[5]
1 tablespoon boiled ham,[6] minced

1 teaspoon parsley, chopped fine
dash of celery vinegar[7]
salt to taste
pepper to taste

Remove the shells from the hard-boiled eggs and cut into halves lengthwise. Take out the yolks and rub them to a smooth paste with the olive oil, mustard, minced ham, parsley, and cider vinegar. Season to taste with salt and pepper. Blend well. Spread on both halves of the sandwich. Add slices of the egg whites and some lettuce leaves. *Note:* This same mixture can be used to fill the hollowed-out egg white halves. These are then arranged on a dish in a bed of crisp lettuce and served as a luncheon snack or dinner accompaniment.

---

4. Recipe in Chapter 9
5. Recipe in Chapter 19
6. Recipe in Chapter 7
7. Recipe in Chapter 19

POPULAR OLD-TIME OLIVE SANDWICHES

Butter the bread lightly and spread on a thick layer of chopped green olives. Cover with a little mayonnaise.[8] Lay the slices together and press firmly. Trim off the crusts and cut the sandwiches into 4 squares. *Note:* These sandwiches are even better when chopped nuts are added.

GRANDMOTHER PELTON'S WALNUT SANDWICHES

A sandwich that always brought high praise in my grandmother's home was made of cream cheese and walnuts. Butter the bread lightly. Spread over each slice a layer of cream cheese about 1/8 inch thick. Put on a thick layer of chopped walnuts. Sprinkle lightly with salt before putting the slices together.

EARLY AMERICAN NASTURTIUM SANDWICHES

Butter the bread and then lay on one side of the slices a medium-sized nasturtium leaf. Spread a thin layer of mayonnaise[9] over it. Fold the slices of bread together. Cut out the sandwich in the shape of the leaf and let the stem stick out. Only the least bit of mayonnaise should be used as the nasturtium has a great deal of flavor of its own. This is one of the oddest and daintiest of old-time sandwiches. Unfortunately it can usually be made only during the summer when the leaves are readily obtainable. But these leaves can be secured from a florist in the winter season. It will pay any hostess to try and get them.

---

8. Recipe in Chapter 22
9. Recipe in Chapter 22

GREAT-GRANDMOTHER MITCHELL'S
CELERY-CHEESE SANDWICHES

A delightful celery sandwich is made from crisp celery, whipped cream[9] and sharp grated cheese. Do not attempt to make it unless you can get celery that is tender and fresh. Chop the celery fine and set it on ice. Mix it and the grated cheese with the whipped cream. Spread on buttered slices of bread and press together.

COLONIAL CHICKEN JELLY SANDWICHES

Trim all the crust from the bread to be used. Spread the thinly sliced bread with butter and chicken jelly.[10] Roll the slices up and serve. If a flat sandwich is desired, simply press the prepared slices firmly together.

GREAT-GREAT-GRANDMOTHER DANIELS'
LETTUCE SANDWICHES

Boil some eggs until they are hard. Chop them fine and season with salt and pepper. Get nice tender lettuce and pick it to shreds with the fingers. It ruins lettuce to chop it. Mix the egg and lettuce evenly. Spread daintily on thin slices of buttered bread. Put on some nice salad dressing.[11] Cover with another thin slice of buttered bread. *Note:* Sandwiches were always made very thin in the old days.

OLD SOUTHERN SALAD SANDWICHES

This delightful old-fashioned sandwich is made by combining lettuce, cucumbers, and capers. They should all be

9. Recipes in Chapter 22
10. Recipe in Chapter 8
11. Recipes in Chapter 22

finely chopped together and then blended with a little mayonnaise.[12] Spread between two unbuttered slices of bread.

UNCLE ALBERT'S
FAVORITE CREAM CHEESE-OLIVE SANDWICHES

On buttered slices of bread spread a thick layer of cream cheese. Put on a thin layer of chopped green olives. Add salt and pepper to suit taste and press the bread slices firmly together.

GREAT-AUNT BEVERLY JO'S
CHICKEN SANDWICHES

Chop only the white meat taken from a boiled chicken.[13] Add 3 finely chopped olives. Mix together into a smooth paste with mayonnaise.[14] Spread between very thin slices of bread and sprinkle lightly with finely chopped walnuts.

OLDEN-DAY CUCUMBER SANDWICHES

Remove the skin from a good-sized green cucumber. Cut the cucumber in lengthwise slices and put in a bowl of ice water for 1/2 hour. Drain the slices. Dip in French dressing[15] or mayonnaise. Place each slice between very thin slices of bread. Cut the bread into the shape of the cucumber slice. Serve immediately.

---

12. Recipe in Chapter 22
13. Recipe in Chapter 8
14. Recipe in Chapter 22
15. Recipes in Chapter 22

GREAT-GRANDMOTHER SHAW'S
OMELET SANDWICHES

An excellent sandwich can be made from a cold omelet.[16]
Press the omelet firmly between 2 thin, well-buttered slices
of bread. Trim the crusts from the bread. Cut diagonally,
making triangular sandwiches. *Note:* Lettuce leaves or any
other green leaf were often added to this sandwich. Mrs.
Shaw often made it with nasturtium leaves, raw spinach,
or collard leaves. And she sometimes spread a tart jelly[17]
on the omelet.

16. Recipe in Chapter 9
17. Recipes in Chapter 18

16

Old-Fashioned Ice Cream

GREAT-GRANDMOTHER SHAW'S
ICE CREAM POINTERS

My great-grandmother had a standard rule for her home-made ice cream. She liked to make it rich and at the same time economical. Her best recipe, which was handed down from her mother, can be used as an excellent base for all fruit ice creams. It will make 2 quarts when frozen. Here is the way to prepare ihe ice cream.

2 cups cream	1 cup sugar
2 cups milk	flavoring to suit taste

Put the cream and milk into a double boiler. When just at the boiling point, quickly remove from the stove and stir in the sugar until it is thoroughly dissolved. Allow this mixture to cool before you add any fruit or flavoring. Put into the freezer and freeze. *Note:* More sugar may be added when the fruits to be used are sour. When we use the term "freeze" today it is a simple matter to accomplish. But back in the old days it was a quite different and more complex process. The above cream was poured into a freezing "tin" or can that had a hand crank for turning a "dasher" or beater inside the can. This can was then placed in a wooden "freezing box" and tightly packed around with a mixture of ice and salt. The cream mixture was brusquely stirred by turning the crank for 10 minutes. Fruit or flavoring was then blended in with the partly frozen cream and it was cranked (stirred) some more until a heavy custard-like consistency was obtained. The "dasher" or beater was then removed from the freezing can, the ice cream smoothly packed in the can, and the "freezing box" was tightly covered. The ice cream was left to stand in the ice for around 2 hours. When ready to serve, the can or tin was removed from the "freezing box," dipped in warm water, and turned out on a dish.

Another interesting sidelight of early America is that the cold winter months were always looked upon as "ice cream making time." Ice making had not yet been commercialized, and common snow was utilized for packing the "freezing box." This was widely known as "snow-packing."

OLD-FASHIONED BANANA ICE CREAM

Take 6 bananas and peel, mash and beat to a smooth paste. Add this to the above cooled cream. Then freeze.

OLD-FASHIONED PEACH ICE CREAM

Press enough fresh, ripe peaches through a sieve to make 4 cups of pulp. Add this with the juice of 1 lemon to the above cooled cream. Then freeze. *Note:* Apricot ice cream is made in this same exact way. Simply substitute apricots for the peaches.

OLD-FASHIONED PISTACHIO ICE CREAM

Blanch, chop and pound to a paste 1 cup pistachio nuts and 1/4 cup almonds. Add this to the above cooled cream. Then freeze. *Note:* Any kind of nuts may be substituted for a delicious variation to this recipe.

GREAT-GRANDMOTHER MITCHELL'S CUSTARD ICE CREAM

2 cups cream	1 cup sugar
2 cups milk	1 tablespoon lemon juice
6 egg yolks	

Put the cream and milk in a double-boiler and heat. Beat the egg yolks with the sugar. Add this to the cream-milk mixture just as it reaches the boiling point. Stir until it thickens. Immediately remove from the stove. Then blend in the lemon juice. Allow to cool and then freeze it.

OLDEN-DAY PHILADELPHIA PEACH ICE CREAM

18 ripe peaches	1 cup milk
sugar to suit	1 tablespoon gelatin
4 cups cream	

Skin the peaches and remove the pits. Mash them as fine as possible. Sweeten to taste with sugar. Add the cream and milk. Then dissolve the gelatin in a little water and add it. Blend thoroughly and immediately freeze.

GRANDMOTHER PELTON'S RASPBERRY GRANITE

1 cup water	8 cups raspberries
1 cup sugar	juice of 1 lemon

An old-fashioned "granite" is a grained ice that is served like a sherbet in little glasses, usually just before or after a roast. Boil the water and sugar together for 5 minutes. Take from the stove and stir in the strained juice of 6 cups of the raspberries and the lemon juice. Allow to cool. Put in a freezing container and set in the freezer. At the end of 1 hour, scrape the sides of the freezing container with a long, flexible knife. Blend what has been frozen with the rest of the more-liquid portion. Do not beat it. The mixture should be coarse and grainy with ice particles throughout. Close and set in the freezer again. Open and mix again 3 times in as many hours. At the end of that time, stir in 2 cups of whole raspberries.

OLD NEW ORLEANS FROZEN MACEDOINE

1 cup cherry juice	1 pineapple, shredded
1 cup sugar	1 cup cherries, cut up
2 oranges, pulped	1 cup cider, boiled
1 grapefruit, pulped	

This is a delightful mixture of fruits for any dessert treat. Blend the cherry juice and sugar in a saucepan. Bring this to a boil and pour over all the varied fruits. Then add the boiled cider and allow to cool. When cold, put in a freezer container and set in the freezer. Allow to stand for 3 hours, stirring occasionally. Then serve.

GRANDMOTHER COLLISTER'S FROZEN LEMONS

Select large, fresh lemons. Wash and polish them well. Cut in two and remove all of the pulp. Separate the fiber and seeds. Put the scooped out skins into a pan of ice water to make them firm. Then to each quart (4 cups) of pulp and juice, put in 1 cup cold water and 2 cups sugar. Pour this into a freezer container and place in the freezer. When frozen, scoop the mixture out and pack in the individual rind halves. Use these as the serving cups. Frozen lemons look very pretty when served on small plates garnished with green leaves.

EARLY AMERICAN COFFEE ICE CREAM

1/4 pound ground coffee   2 cups milk
2 cups cream   1 cup sugar

Put the coffee, cream and milk in a double boiler. Bring to a boil and immediately remove from the stove. Let it stand until cold. Strain and then blend in the sugar. Put into a freezer container and freeze.

GREAT-AUNT SHIRLEY'S CHOCOLATE ICE CREAM

2 cups milk   2 cups cream
1 cup sugar   1/2 teaspoon vanilla
1 tablespoon chocolate,
    grated

Put the milk, sugar and grated chocolate in a double boiler and bring it to a boil. Let this boil for 10 minutes. Remove from the fire and let cool. When it is cold, blend in the cream and vanilla. Immediately freeze.

GREAT-GREAT-GRANDMOTHER HORTON'S
MILK SHERBET

2 cups sugar   juice of 1 orange
Juice of 3 lemons   4 cups milk
Peel of 1 lemon, grated

This seems to be half way between an ice and an ice cream. It is a very desirable recipe. Blend the sugar, lemon juice, grated lemon peel and the orange juice. Set aside and let it dissolve to a syrup. Then pour in the milk *without* stirring, and freeze.

COUSIN ELIZABETH'S FAVORITE COFFEE FRAPPÉ

4 tablespoons fresh coffee, finely ground	2 cups milk
	6 egg yolks
3/4 cup sugar	3/4 cup cream, whipped

Put the fresh roasted coffee into a saucepan. Add the sugar and milk. Bring to a boil. Set aside to cool. Put the egg yolks in a double-boiler. Strain the previously boiled liquid over the yolks. Stir over the stove until it thickens to a custard. Set aside to cool again. When quite cold, work in the whipped cream. Freeze the mixture and keep it on ice until the time of serving.

OLD-TIME NEW HAMPSHIRE GRAPE SHERBET

4 cups milk	1 cup sugar
or	1 cup water
4 cups cream	1 cup grape jelly[1]

Put the milk in a freezing container and chill it in the freezer. When slightly iced, add the rest of the ingredients. Stir well and immediately freeze. *Note:* A purple jelly makes a very handsomely tinted sherbet. It was a favorite years ago.

---

1. Recipe in Chapter 18

GREAT-GRANDFATHER MITCHELL'S
FAVORITE FROZEN RICE

1/2 cup rice, boiled[2]   1/4 cup powdered sugar
1 1/2 cups cream   flavor with vanilla

Boil the rice until tender. Whip the cream to a froth and add the powdered sugar. Flavor with the vanilla to suit individual taste. Blend the boiled rice with the cream mixture and put in a freezing container or mold. Place in the freezer 3 or 4 hours before serving. *Note:* Any desired wine can be added to this in place of the vanilla.

REAL OLD-FASHIONED FROZEN PUDDING CREAM

Great-Grandmother Shaw received this old recipe from her aunt many years ago. The ingredients are as follows:

2 cups milk   2 tablespoons gelatin
1/2 cup flour   4 tablespoons wine
2 cups sugar   4 cups cream
2 eggs   1 cup candied fruit

Let the milk come to a boil in a double boiler. Beat the flour, 1 cup sugar and the eggs together. Stir this into the boiling milk. Cook for 20 minutes while soaking the gelatin in water enough to cover it. Then add the gelatin and set the mixture aside to cool. When cold, add the wine, cream, and other cup of sugar. Freeze for 10 minutes. Stir in the fruit and finish freezing. Serve with whipped cream.[3]

---

2. Recipe in Chapter 3
3. Recipe in Chapter 22

17

Dessert-Making the Natural Way

Here is another widely diversified department of early American cookery. The versatile jet-age housewife can now make an infinite number of excursions down long forgotten pathways of the exciting past. The following selection of choice old-fashioned dessert recipes provides ample opportunity to try some of our great-grandmothers' most delightful dishes.

OLD-TIME RULES FOR GOOD CUSTARD-MAKING

A good rule for custard is 5 eggs to a quart of milk, and 1 tablespoon sugar to each egg. But a delicious plain custard can be made with 1 egg for each cup milk, and 4 tablespoons sugar to the quart.

Always boil milk and custard in a pan set in another pan of boiling water. If you do not have a "custard kettle," my Great-Great-Grandmother Horton suggested improvising one by "setting a tin pail inside of a pot of hot water, taking care it does not float, also that the water is not so deep as to bubble over the top." Custards are tastier and lighter if the egg yolks and egg whites are always beaten separately. The whites are to be stirred in last.

DOLLY MADISON'S BOILED CUSTARD OF 1810

4 cups milk	2 teaspoons vanilla
5 egg yolks	1 tablespoon powdered
6 tablespoons sugar	sugar, heaping
5 egg whites, stiffly beaten	2 egg whites

Heat the milk almost to boiling. Stir the sugar into the beaten egg yolks. Take the scalding milk from the fire. Instead of pouring the beaten egg yolks into it, put a spoon or two of the hot milk in them. Beat well while doing this. Add more and more milk until there is no longer any danger of sudden curdling. Now stir in the 5 stiffly beaten egg whites. Return the pan to the fire and boil gently until the mixture becomes thick (10 to 15 minutes should suffice). Stir constantly while boiling. Stir in the vanilla and pour the custard into heated glass cups. Whip the powdered sugar and 2 egg whites to a thick meringue. When the custard is cold, pile a little of this on top of each cup. *Note:* Mrs. Madison garnished her custard with a preserved (home-canned) strawberry or cherry, a bit of fresh melon, or a little bright jelly. It was placed on top of each cup of custard.

CHERRY PYRAMID—
MARTHA WASHINGTON'S SPECIALTY DESSERT

Wash and stone (take out the pits) 2 quarts of cherries. Make some good light pie crust.[1] Roll it out to about 1/4

1. Recipes in *Natural Baking the Old-Fashioned Way,* by the same author.

inch thick. Cut a round piece about the size of an 8-inch dinner plate. In the old days they often used the top of a tin pail for a cutter. Spread your cherries on the round piece of dough. Sprinkle heavily with sugar. Leave a 1/2-inch border all around. Roll out a second sheet of pie crust and cut it 1 inch less in diameter than the first. Lay it carefully on top of the fruit and sugar. Turn the border of the lower piece of dough up over this one. Spread this, in turn, with cherries and sugar. Cover with a third and smaller piece of round pie crust. Proceed in this sequence until the sixth and topmost cover is not more than 3 inches across. Take a conical-shaped, stout muslin bag adapted to the proportions and dimensions of your pyramid pile. Dip it in boiling water. Flour the inside. Draw it gently down over the pyramid. It should be large enough to meet and tie under the base without cramping the pyramid. Place this gently in a large kettle of boiling water. Boil for 2 hours. Serve while hot. It should be eaten with a sweet sauce. *Note:* Husband George liked this same dessert made with currants as well as he did with cherries. And he preferred it best accompanied with a good hard sauce, or his wife's own delightful cream sauce.[2]

GREAT-GRANDMOTHER SHAW'S
GOOSEBERRY FOOL

1 quart ripe gooseberries
1 tablespoon butter
1 cup sugar
4 egg yolks, well beaten

3 tablespoons powdered
    sugar
3 egg whites

Put the gooseberries into a porcelain saucepan. Stew in just enough water to cover the berries. When the gooseberries become soft and broken, rub them through a sieve to remove the skins. While still hot, beat in the butter,

2. Recipes in Chapter 12

sugar, and custard-like whipped egg yolks. Pile in a glass
dish, or in small dessert glasses. Now beat the powdered
sugar with the 3 egg whites until it forms a stiff meringue.
Heap this on top of the gooseberries and serve.

EARLY AMERICAN TRANSPARENT LEMON PIE

1 cup butter
2 cups sugar
6 egg yolks, well
    beaten
juice of 1 lemon

rind of 2 lemons,grated
1 nutmeg, grated
1/4 cup brandy
6 egg whites, stiffly
    beaten

Cream the butter and sugar in a large wooden mixing
bowl. Whip in the custard-like beaten egg yolks, lemon
juice, rinds, nutmeg, and brandy. When well blended, stir
in the stiffly beaten egg whites. Fill an unbaked pie shell[3]
(crust) and bake in a hot oven (450 degrees) for 10
minutes. Finish baking in a moderate oven (350 degrees)
for 25 more minutes. You do not need a top crust. *Note:*
Such a pie is even more delightful if you fix a good
meringue to go on it. Simply beat 4 egg whites, 4 tablespoons sugar, and a little lemon juice together. When the
whites will stand alone, spread it thickly over the top of
the pie. Place the pie back in the oven to "set" the meringue.
Eat when cold.

GRANDMOTHER PELTON'S
STRAWBERRY DUMPLINGS

3 cups flour
1 teaspoon baking
    powder, heaping
milk to suit

2 tablespoons butter
1/4 teaspoon salt
strawberries to suit, fresh

3. Recipes in *Natural Baking the Old-Fashioned Way*, by the same
author.

Blend the flour, baking powder, and enough milk to make a nice soft dough. Rub in the butter and salt. Roll the dough out to a 1/2-inch thick sheet. Cut into 4-inch squares. Place 3 or 4 large fresh strawberries in the center of each square of dough. Gather up the dough around them and pinch together at the top. Set these on a greased tin and steam for 25 minutes. They should be eaten with a special strawberry sauce made with:

2 tablespoons butter	3 drops lemon juice
1 cup powdered sugar	1 cup fresh strawberries

Beat the butter and the powdered sugar together until it makes a smooth cream. Flavor with the lemon juice and then stir in the fresh strawberries. Pour this sauce over and all around each dumpling and serve.

OLD-FASHIONED BLACKBERRY FLUMMERY

2 cups ripe blackberries	4 tablespoons cornstarch
2 cups water	1/2 cup sugar

This is a delicious dessert dish for hot weather eating. It is easily made and always a success. And it is a welcome change when one tires of berries with cream and sugar. Put the blackberries and water into a saucepan. Let simmer, but do not stir. The berries should be ready in 10 minutes. Blend the cornstarch with a little cold water. Carefully stir into berry mixture. When thick, take the pan off the stove and let cool for 2 minutes. Stir carefully so as not to break the berries. Then add the sugar and blend it well. When cool enough, pour into a glass dish and chill. Eat icy cold with sugar and cream over it.

GREAT-GREAT-GRANDMOTHER HORTON'S
BAKED CUSTARD

5 tablespoons sugar
4 egg yolks, well beaten
4 cups milk

4 egg whites, stiffly beaten
2 teaspoons vanilla
nutmeg to suit

Blend the sugar with the custard-like beaten egg yolks. Scald but do not boil the milk. Add the hot milk, by degrees, to the yolks. When well mixed, stir in the fluffy egg whites. Blend in the vanilla. Pour the mixture into a deep, buttered baking dish, or white stone china custard cups. Set these in a pan of hot water. Sprinkle nutmeg over the custard. Bake in a moderate oven (350 degrees) until firm. Eat from cups when custard is cold.

GREAT-GRANDMOTHER MITCHELL'S
OLD-TIME PEACH TRIFLE

4 egg yolks
2 tablespoons sugar
2 cups milk
1/2 teaspoon vanilla
1/2 teaspoon almond

Sponge cake[4] to suit,
    stale, sliced thin
6 large, ripe peaches,
    peeled and sliced
powdered sugar to suit

Beat the egg yolks with the sugar until they are custard-like and light. Put the milk in a saucepan and heat it to almost boiling. Gradually add the hot milk to the egg yolks and thoroughly beat. Set aside to cool. When cold, flavor with vanilla and almond. Put on ice.

Lay the slices of sponge cake in the bottom of a glass dish. Cover the cake with 1/4 of the cold custard blend. Spread the peach slices over this. Dust thickly with pow-

4. Recipe in *Natural Baking the Old-Fashioned Way,* by the same author.

dered sugar. Pour on the rest of the iced custard. Smooth over the top and set aside until you make a meringue. This is quickly and easily accomplished by whipping 4 egg whites with 4 tablespoons powdered sugar. When it is very stiff, cover the top of the custard. *Note:* A few drops of almond flavoring can be added to the meringue if desired.

CALF'S-FOOT JELLY, 1800—
A FAVORITE OF THOMAS JEFFERSON

4 calves' feet, cleaned carefully	3 egg whites, stiffly beaten
4 quarts water	2 teaspoons nutmeg
2 cups wine	juice of 1 lemon
3 cups sugar	rind of 1/2 lemon, grated

Boil the calves' feet in the water until it is reduced in half. Strain the liquor and let it stand for 10 to 12 hours. Then skim off every particle of grease and remove the dregs. Pour into a porcelain kettle and simmer slowly. Stir in the wine, sugar, whipped egg whites, nutmeg, lemon juice, and rind. Boil fast for 12 minutes. Skim well and strain into a large bowl through a double flannel bag. In the days of Jefferson, the flannel bag was suspended between the legs of an upturned high stool or backless chair. The bowl was set directly under the bag. Do not squeeze or shake the bag until the jelly ceases to run freely. Take the first bowl up and put another one in its place. Gently press what remains in the bag. The first bowl will have clearer jelly. But the second dripping will taste quite as well. Wet your molds and pour in the jelly. Set in a cool place.

There are still some country folk and old-timers who insist that jellies made from modern gelatin are not nearly comparable in beauty and flavor to the old-fashioned kind prepared from calves' feet. In my Great-Great-Grandmother

Horton's time, the commercial gelatin was darkly asserted to be "made of horn-shavings and hoofs and the like, and no more fit to be used for cooking purposes than so much glue."

GREAT-AUNT MARY'S STRAWBERRY FLOAT

4 egg whites
1/2 cup sugar
3 egg yolks, well beaten
4 cups milk
pinch of salt

1/2 teaspoon vanilla
strawberries to suit
1 tablespoon powdered
    sugar

Beat 2 of the egg whites with the 1/2 cup sugar. Blend with the custard-like egg yolks. Scald the milk and gradually pour it into the eggs, stirring continually. Pour this mixture into a double boiler. Stir over the fire until it thickens. Add the salt. When partly cooled, flavor with vanilla. Put a thick layer of fresh strawberries in a serving bowl. Pour 1/2 of the custard over them. Add another thick layer of strawberries. Pour on the remainder of the custard. Whip the other 2 egg whites with the powdered sugar until stiff and glossy. Heap over the custard. Dot the top with a few strawberries and serve. *Note:* Raspberry floats are made this same way. Simply substitute raspberries for the strawberries called for in the recipe.

EARLY NEW ENGLAND
GREEN GOOSEBERRY TARTS

Top and tail the gooseberries. Put them into a porcelain kettle with just enough water to prevent burning. Stew slowly until they break. Take them off the stove, sweeten to taste, and set aside to cool. When cold, pour into small unbaked pastry tart shells.[5] Cover with a top crust of puff paste, pinch down the edges, and bake in a hot oven (400 degrees) for about 40 minutes, or until browned lightly. When almost done, take from the oven and brush tops with a beaten egg. Place back in the oven to glaze for 3 minutes. Eat when cold. *Note:* A large green gooseberry pie can be made this same way.

GRANDMOTHER COLLISTER'S
CREAMY OLDEN-DAY PRUNE WHIP

1 pound prunes	2 cups cream
1 cup sugar	3 egg whites

This is very rich, nice to look at, and extremely tasty. Cook the prunes with 1/2 cup sugar. When they are done, let cool, and then cut up fine and remove the pits. Whip 1 cup cream and blend with the prunes. Beat the egg whites with 1/2 cup sugar until they are stiff and fluffy. Stir this into the prune mixture. Put into small serving glasses. Whip the other cup cream. Pile this on top of the dessert and serve.

---

5. Recipes in *Natural Baking the Old-Fashioned Way,* by the same author.

18

Old-Fashioned Preservatives and Jellies

The embellishments of the early American table are included in this unique chapter. There are innumerable old-time recipes covering this much varied ground. From the beginning, America's housewife displayed great ingenuity for inventing new and often better concoctions. The change in this line of cookery during the 1800s came rather quickly. It was primarily due to great advances in the art of preserving edibles by canning. Or, as our English cousins called it, "tinning." In our country, however, glass was more a factor than tin, in safely preserving fruits and vegetables.

GREAT-GRANDMOTHER MITCHELL'S
CANNED FRUIT TIPS

According to Great-Grandmother Mitchell, the most appetizing and attractive canned fruit or berry is that which retains, as nearly as possible, its fresh natural flavor. And that which looks solid and best keeps its shape. In order to procure this flavor and firmness, the following old fashioned process will be found very successful: Carefully prepare the fruit or berries, having them as dry as possible. Fill the jars and shake lightly. Make a very sweet syrup with 1 cup sugar and 1 cup hot water for every quart of fruit or berries. Heat this syrup and bring it to a boil. When boiling, pour it slowly over the fruit or berries in the jars. Seal the jars as soon as they are filled with the syrup. Place the jars on the rack in a large boiler. They must not rest on the bottom of the pan or they will break. Pour in enough boiling water to cover them. Put heavy cloth or blankets over the top of the boiler. Set aside and allow to stand for 24 hours. Then remove the jars from the boiler pan and carefully wipe dry. Put away until needed.

Another important rule applies if the fruit is hard (such as pineapple, hard peaches, or pears). The water in which the jars are set in the boiler should be boiled for 45 minutes. Then cover the pot as above and leave alone for a day and a night before removing and wiping the jars.

BLACKBERRIES WITHOUT SUGAR
THE OLD-FASHIONED WAY

Select and wash your blackberries carefully. Put them into a porcelain kettle. Set on the stove and simmer until the juice flows freely. Bring to a boil. Cook only long enough to heat the fruit thoroughly. Immediately put the berries and juice into sterilized jars and seal. *Note:* These blackberries will be delicious for they will be found to have retained their full natural flavor. Sugar, if desired, can be added at the table, or 1/2 hour before serving, if preferred.

GREAT-GRANDMOTHER SHAW'S
PRESERVED PEARS

Pare the pears and cut in half. Immediately place the

fruit in cold water or it will discolor. Weigh the pears. Use 2 cups sugar for every 3 pounds of pears. And use 4 cups water for every 6 cups sugar. Put the required amount of sugar and water in a porcelain kettle. Heat and bring to a boil. When boiling, take the pears from the cold water and drop them into the hot syrup. Cook until they can be easily pierced with a fork. Fill sterilized jars with the fruit. Pour in syrup to the brim of each jar. Cover and seal the jars. *Note:* You may use a small strainer when pouring the syrup into the jars. This will make it much clearer.

REAL OLD-TIME SPICED CURRANTS

8 cups currants	3 tablespoons cinnamon
5 cups sugar	1 1/2 cups cider vinegar[1]
3 tablespoons cloves	

Blend all of the above ingredients in a porcelain kettle. Bring to a boil. Let simmer for 2 1/2 hours. You may let it simmer longer and make the mixture thicker. Immediately put it in sterilized glass jars and seal.

SPICED GOOSEBERRIES IN EARLY NEW ENGLAND

6 quarts green gooseberries	2 tablespoons cloves
8 cups sugar	2 tablespoons cinnamon
	2 cups cider vinegar[2]

Remove the stems and blossoms from the fresh gooseberries. Put them into a porcelain kettle with the sugar, cloves, cinnamon and cider vinegar. Bring to a boil and then simmer slowly for two full hours. Be careful that it does

1. Recipe in Chapter 19
2. Recipe in Chapter 19

not burn. Immediately put into sterilized jars and seal. *Note:* This is excellent with all meat dishes.

Jellies, Jams and Marmalades

OLD-FASHIONED POINTERS
ON JELLIES, JAMS AND MARMALADES

After making jellies, jams, and marmalades, the following directions should be carefully heeded: Pour the mixture into sterilized glasses (sometimes called tumblers). The tumblers should be sitting on a hot cloth that has been soaked in boiling water to prevent them from breaking. Or they may simply be dipped in hot water before filling. Allow to cool for 24 hours after filling. Cover with a thin layer of melted paraffin. Store in a cool place.

GREAT-GREAT-GRANDMOTHER HORTON'S
CURRANT JELLY

The following recipe is one that never seems to fail. Pick the currants as soon as possible after they turn red. Put the currants in an agate or porcelain kettle. Place on the stove. When thoroughly heated, mash them with a large spoon or masher. Turn them into a flannel jelly bag. Extract the juice, being careful not to squeeze too hard or the jelly will turn out to be cloudy. Measure the juice as soon as it is put back in the kettle. Let it come to a boil. Simmer for 20 minutes. Allow 1 cup sugar for every cup of juice. Have the sugar measured (and heated in the oven) and add it to the boiling juice. Stir rapidly until dissolved. Boil for 5 more minutes. Pour, while hot, into sterilized glasses, as directed at the beginning of this section of the chapter.

Note: 11 quarts of currants will make 17 nice jars of jelly.

EARLY AMERICAN WHITE GRAPE JELLY

In 1841, my great-great-grandmother attended a country dinner party. She was served some delicious white grape jelly. In her own words: "I begged the recipe. The grapes were a native white variety, highly flavored, but had no real name. Probable the recipe, which is a simple one, might answer for any grape. The color of the jelly, which was a clear, light amber, and the delicious flavor, were what attracted my attention."

Here is how the wonderful jelly is made: The grapes should be picked clean and washed. Place on the stove in a porcelain kettle. Add water enough to keep the grapes from burning. Simmer until the grapes are quite soft. Remove from the stove and strain them through a cloth strainer. Measure the juice. Then measure and set aside an equal quantity of sugar. Simmer the strained juice for 1/2 hour. Then stir in the sugar and let it all simmer for 10 minutes, or until you can see it coming to a jelly consistency. Remove from the stove. Pour, while hot, into sterilized glasses, as directed at the beginning of this section of the chapter.

ORIGINAL OLD-TIME GREEN GRAPE JELLY

This is recommended as an excellent recipe for disposing of any grapes that are sure not to ripen. Take 8 quarts green grapes and put into a porcelain kettle. Add 4 cups water and stew until soft. Strain the grapes through a flannel bag and simmer for 20 minutes. Then measure the juice and add 1 1/2 cups sugar (heated in the oven) to every 1 cup juice. Boil the mixture for 1 minute after stirring in the sugar. Pour, while hot, into sterilized glasses, as directed at the beginning of this section of the chapter.

GREAT-GREAT-GRANDMOTHER NORTHRUP'S BLACKBERRY JELLY

Select firm, fresh wild blackberries. Put into a porcelain kettle and heat gently. Squeeze the berries through a linen strainer cloth until all the juice has been extracted. Measure the juice and put it back in the kettle. Add 1 cup sugar for every 1 cup of juice. Bring to a boil and let it simmer together for 20 minutes, or until it begins to jell. It shouldn't take longer than 1/2 hour at the most. Pour, while hot, into sterilized glasses, as directed at the beginning of this section of the chapter.

GOOSEBERRY JELLY IN OLD VIRGINIA

Use green gooseberries to make this delightful jelly. Remove the stems and flowers. Place them in a porcelain kettle and allow to simmer until soft. Mash the gooseberries to extract the juice. Strain the juice through a coarse flannel bag. Measure the juice. Allow 1 1/2 cups sugar for every 2 cups of juice. Boil the strained juice for 20 minutes. Stir in the sugar (warmed in the oven) and simmer it for 10 minutes longer. Pour, while hot, into sterilized glasses, as directed at the beginning of this section of the chapter.

ORIGINAL OLDEN-DAY APPLE JELLY

Take large, ripe cooking apples and remove the stems, cores and imperfections. Do not pare the apples. Cut them into slices and put into a porcelain kettle. Allow a very small amount of water and simmer slowly until soft. Turn into a flannel or muslin jelly bag to drain. Measure and allow 3/4 cup sugar for every cup of juice. Simmer the juice for 20 minutes and stir in the sugar. Continue stirring until the sugar has all dissolved. Boil up once. *Note:* To give an indescribably delicious flavor to this jelly, my Great-Great-Grandmother Horton dropped a small, tender rose geranium leaf into each empty glass. She then poured the hot jelly over it. When it floated to the top, she removed it from the hot jelly. The jelly was allowed to cool for 24 hours after filling the glasses. She then covered each glass with a thin layer of melted paraffin and stored it in the cellar until needed.

UNCLE ARTHUR'S FAVORITE
ORANGE AND RHUBARB JAM

22 rhubarb stalks	2 cups sugar
2 oranges	

Wipe the rhubarb stalks until they are clean and dry. Cut them into fine pieces without peeling. Peel the oranges. Cut away all the white under the skin. Take out the seeds. Divide the oranges into quarters. Open each section that holds the pulp and take that out, being careful to save all the juice. Grate the peelings. Put the rhubarb into a porcelain kettle. Add the orange pulp, juice, and grated peel with 2 cups sugar. Heat and stir the mixture until the sugar has all dissolved. Then simmer slowly until it begins to thicken. Pour, while hot, into sterilized glasses, as directed at the beginning of this section of the chapter.

OLD SOUTHERN PLANTATION BLACKBERRY JAM

The blackberries should be very ripe (mellow), but in perfectly sound condition. Put them into a porcelain kettle and heat gently. Mash the berries and then weigh them. To each pound of pulp allow 1 1/2 cups sugar. Blend the pulp and sugar together in the kettle. Bring to the boiling point. Let simmer for 20 minutes. Stir frequently to prevent any scorching. Pour, while hot, into sterilized glasses, as directed at the beginning of this section of the chapter. *Note:* This same recipe can also be used for plum and raspberry jam.

REAL OLD-FASHIONED BANBURY MARMALADE

7 pounds currants
2 oranges, chopped fine
12 cups sugar

6 cups raisins,
  chopped fine

Put the currants into a large porcelain kettle. Crush and squeeze the juice from them. Add the sugar, raisins and oranges. Bring to a boil and let it all simmer for 1 1/2 hours. Pour, while hot, into sterilized glasses as directed at the beginning of this section of the chapter. *Note:* According to my great-great-grandmother, "the only trouble with this marmalade is that it is too good to last very long."

GREAT-GREAT-GRANDMOTHER DANIELS'
ORANGE MARMALADE

12 sour oranges
16 cups sugar
16 cups water

juice of 2 lemons
rind of 2 lemons, grated

Put the oranges in a porcelain kettle and cover with water. Let simmer until tender. Take oranges out of kettle. Cut open. Remove seeds and part of white inside skin. Separate the pulp from the rind. Chop the rind up very fine. Now proceed to make a syrup with the sugar, water, lemon juice, and lemon rind. Put all of these ingredients into a porcelain kettle and let simmer until quite thick. Bring to a boil and add the orange rind and pulp. Boil for 1/2 hour or until it jells. Over boiling this marmalade will spoil the color. Pour, while hot, into sterilized glasses as directed at the beginning of this section of the chapter.

19

Catsup, Mustard, and Vinegar the Natural Way

CORN VINEGAR AS MADE IN THE COLONIES

2 cups fresh corn   1 cup sugar

Put the corn in 1/2 gallon (8 cups) pure rain water and bring to a boil. Allow to continue boiling until the kernels break. Empty this mixture into a large stone jar. Add another 8 cups of warm rain water. Dissolve the sugar in 1 cup boiling rain water and pour this into the stone jar. Cover the jar with a heavy blanket or 3 layers of cheesecloth. Set aside in a warm place (about 80 degrees). Leave it for 30 days. Strain through cheesecloth and put into bottles or jugs. Cork or cover the mouth of the bottle in some other way. Store until needed in a warm, dry place. *Note:* This simple old-time vinegar was used as the basis for making other types of vinegar. It must be tightly sealed when stored or the air will make the vinegar lose its sour taste.

GREAT-GRANDMOTHER MITCHELL'S BRANDY CATSUP

8 quarts tomatoes,
 stewed and strained
6 tablespoons pepper
6 tablespoons salt
4 tablespoons mustard

1 tablespoon cloves
1 tablespoon ginger
4 cups cider vinegar[1]
1 cup sugar
1 cup brandy

This is a very old recipe we have used in our family for a good many years. It is quite simple to make. Blend all of the above ingredients in a large kettle. Boil very slowly until it has been reduced in half. Cool, put into bottles, and seal.

OLD-TIME HOMEMADE MUSTARD

4 tablespoons dry mustard
2 teaspoons salad oil
celery vinegar to suit[2]
2 teaspoons salt

1 teaspoon white pepper
2 teaspoons sugar
1 small garlic, minced

Put the mustard in a wooden mixing bowl. Wet with the oil, and rub it in with a wooden spoon until it is absorbed. Wet with sufficient celery vinegar until it becomes a stiff paste. Add the salt, pepper, sugar and garlic. Work all together thoroughly, wetting little by little with the vinegar until you can beat it as you do cake batter. Then beat very hard for 5 minutes. Pour into wide-mouthed bottles (empty mustard jars if you have them). Pour a little oil on top. Cork tightly. Set away in a cool place. It will be mellow enough to use in a couple of days. *Note:* My Great-Grand-mother Shaw used this tasty mustard for years in her own

---

1. Recipe included herein
2. Recipe included herein

family. She made it in a Wedgewood mortar with a pestle. It was her favorite and most highly prized mustard recipe. This homemade mustard will keep for many weeks.

GREAT-GRANDMOTHER SHAW'S TOMATO CATSUP

This recipe is my great-grandmother's very own. The proportions are for 4 quarts of ripe tomatoes, which are relieved of their skin and blemishes, and put into scalding water. Stir up the pulp and slowly boil until it has been reduced in half. Strain through a sieve and a strainer cloth and set aside. Now you need:

2 cups corn vinegar[3]
2 nutmegs, grated
1 tablespoon black pepper
3/4 tablespoon red pepper
1 tablespoon ground
  mustard
1 tablespoon cinnamon

Take the vinegar and put it in a saucepan. Then put all the spices in a cloth bag and tie the top tightly closed. Place this spice bag into the vinegar. Bring this to a boil. Skim off any impurities and then let it simmer (not boil) for an hour or two. Add the strained tomatoes. Let it all cook slowly for a few minutes. Take off the stove. When cold, add salt to taste. Cover and set aside for 24 hours. The next day put into bottles and seal. It will keep a long time.

CELERY VINEGAR OF THE GOOD OLD DAYS

1 bunch fresh celery
    or
1/4 pound celery seed
4 cups corn vinegar[4]
1 teaspoon salt
1 tablespoon sugar

---
3. Recipe included herein
4. Recipe included herein

Cut up the celery into small bits or pour the seeds into a stone jar. Scald the vinegar and blend in the salt and sugar. Pour this over the cut up celery stalks or seeds. Let cool and tightly cork or cover the stone jar. Set aside for 2 weeks. Strain through cheesecloth and pour into small bottles or jars. Cork tightly and store in a warm, dry place.

GRANDMOTHER PELTON'S
SECRET WALNUT CATSUP

Select young, unshelled walnuts tender enough to be pierced with a pin or needle. Prick them in several places. Lay the walnuts in a stone jar with a handful of salt to every 25 and water enough to cover them. Break the nuts with a billet of wood or a wooden masher. Let them lie in the liquid for 2 weeks. Stir twice each day. Then drain off the liquor into a saucepan.

Cover the shells with boiling corn vinegar[5] to extract the remaining juice. Crush to a pulp and strain through a colander into the saucepan. Add the following ingredients for every quart (4 cups) of liquid:

1 tablespoon black pepper	pinch of red pepper
1 tablespoon ginger	1/2 scallion, minced fine
1/2 tablespoon cloves	1/2 teaspoon celery seed,
1/2 tablespoon nutmeg	tied in a bag

Boil all of these ingredients together for 1 hour. Set aside to cool and bottle when cold. *Note:* Butternuts also make delightful catsup. Simply substitute them for the walnuts and follow the above directions.

---

5. Recipe included herein

OLD NEW ENGLAND APPLE CIDER VINEGAR

Get some ripe apples and cut off all spots. Wash and then crush in a cider mill. Squeeze out all of the juice in a press. Strain into a stone jar or clean keg. You will need 1 yeast cake for every five gallons of apple juice. Soak the yeast cake in 1 cup of the juice. When soft, stir it into the juice in the stone jar or keg. Cover with a towel or piece of cheesecloth. Set aside in a warm place (about 80 degrees). It should finish fermenting or "working" in less than 1 week. When the juice stops bubbling, set the jar in a warm dark place. Cover with a clean cloth but do so in such a way that air can readily enter. Do not disturb the film that forms on the top of the liquid. Taste the vinegar at least once each week. This is the only way to tell if it has become sour enough. Strain it through cheesecloth and put into bottles or jugs. Cork or tightly cover the mouth of each container. It must be airtight or the vinegar will soon lose its flavor. *Note:* Many old-timers add 1 gallon of good, strong corn vinegar[6] to every 5 gallons of the fermented juice. This was done when the juice stopped bubbling within the first week. It is said to make the cider vinegar more satisfactory. But it isn't really necessary.

GREAT-GRANDMOTHER MITCHELL'S OYSTER CATSUP

4 cup oysters	1 teaspoon red pepper
3/4 cup cider vinegar[7]	1 tablespoon salt
3/4 cup sherry wine	6 teaspoons mace

Chop the oysters and boil in their own liquor with the

---

6. Recipe included herein
7. Recipe included herein

cider vinegar. Skim off the scum as it rises. Let this boil
for 3 full minutes. Strain through a cheesecloth. Return
the liquor to the fire and quickly add the wine, pepper,
salt, and mace. Boil another 15 minutes. Set aside and allow
to cool. When cold, pour into bottles and cork. Seal the
corks by dipping them in melted wax.

EARLY AMERICAN LEMON CATSUP

rind of 12 large lemons,
    grated
4 tablespoons white
    mustard seed
1 tablespoon tumeric
1 tablespoon white
    pepper
1 teaspoon cloves

1 teaspoon mace
pinch of red pepper
2 tablespoons sugar
2 tablespoons horseradish,
    grated fine
1 scallion, minced fine
2 tablespoons salt
juice of 12 lemons

Blend all of the above ingredients together, except for
the salt and lemon juice. When well mixed, strew the salt
over the top and add the lemon juice. Do not stir. Set aside
and let stand in a cool place for 3 hours. Boil in a porcelain
kettle for 1/2 hour. Immediately pour into a covered vessel
—china or stone. Let stand for 2 full weeks. Stir well at least
once each day. Then strain, bottle, and seal. *Note:* This
lemon catsup is a fine addition for fish sauces, fish soups,
and ragouts.

OLD-FASHIONED ONION VINEGAR

6 large onions, minced
1 tablespoon salt

1 tablespoon sugar
4 cups corn vinegar[8]

8. Recipe included herein

Put the onions in a stone jar. Strew on the salt. Let them stand for 5 or 6 hours. Dissolve the sugar in the vinegar and heat until it scalds. Immediately pour this mixture over the onions and salt in the stone jar. Cover tightly and set aside to steep for 2 full weeks. *Do not stir.* Strain into bottles and seal.

GREAT-GREAT-GRANDMOTHER HORTON'S AGELESS CATSUP

12 anchovies, washed, soaked, and pulled to pieces	4 cups mushrooms, minced or
12 small onions, peeled and minced	4 cups ripe tomatoes, sliced
1 tablespoon mace	3 tablespoons black pepper, whole
3 tablespoons salt	1 tablespoon cloves
2 tablespoons ginger	3 tablespoons sugar
1 tablespoon red pepper	8 cups cider vinegar[9]

This early American recipe was Mrs. Horton's pride and joy. She put all of the above ingredients into a kettle and boiled them slowly for 4 hours, or until the mixture was reduced to one-half the original quantity. It was then carefully strained through a flannel bag. She never bottled it until the next day. The "flasks" or bottles were filled to the very top. And she dipped the corks in beeswax and rosin to make them airtight. *Note:* This wonderful homemade catsup is said to keep for years. It simply doesn't spoil. Mix it with drawn butter[10] and use it as a sauce for boiled fish. It is also a fine flavoring essence for gravies of almost every kind. And it is delightful with most meat dishes.

---

9. Recipe included herein
10. Recipe in Chapter 13

PEPPER VINEGAR IN EARLY AMERICA

4 cups corn vinegar[11]
2 tablespoons sugar
36 black peppercorns

6 red pepper pods,
broken up

Scald the vinegar in which the sugar has been completely dissolved. Pour this over the pepper. Put into a stone jar, cover tightly, and let steep for 2 full weeks. Immediately strain and bottle. *Note:* This vinegar is generally eaten with boiled fish and raw oysters. And it is useful in the preparation of all vegetables or other salads calling for vinegar.

UNCLE ART'S BEST RAW TOMATO KETCHUP

4 quarts ripe tomatoes, finely chopped (skins, seeds, and all)
1 cup horseradish, grated
2 teaspoons black pepper
1 teaspoon cloves
2 teaspoons cinnamon
2 celery roots, chopped fine
1 teaspoon mace

3/4 cup salt
1 cup mustard seeds
1 cup sugar
4 cups cider vinegar[12]
1 cup green nasturtium seeds and onions, chopped together
2 ladyfinger red peppers, chopped fine
1 tablespoon celery seed

The peculiarity of this early American recipe lies in the word "raw." It is not cooked at all. Blend all of the above ingredients in a large wooden mixing bowl. Make certain they are thoroughly mixed. Quickly put into bottles and tightly seal. Use as needed.

11. Recipe included herein
12. Recipe included herein

JEFFERSON'S FAVORITE HORSERADISH VINEGAR

4 cups corn vinegar[13] 6 tablespoons horseradish,
1 tablespoon sugar scraped or grated

Scald the vinegar in which the sugar has been dissolved. Pour while boiling hot over the horseradish. Put into a good stone jar, cover tightly, and let it steep for 1 full week. Immediately strain and bottle. *Note:* Thomas Jefferson is said to have preferred the taste of this vinegar over all others. And he was known to make his own batch when the supply ran low.

GREAT-GRANDMOTHER SHAW'S ELDERBERRY CATSUP

4 cups corn vinegar[14] pinch of ginger
4 cups elderberries 2 tablespoons sugar
6 anchovies, washed, 1 teaspoon salt
  soaked, and pulled 1 tablespoon black
  to pieces peppercorns
1/2 teaspoon mace

The elderberries must be washed and picked free of all stalks. Put them into a large stone jar. Scald the vinegar and pour it over the elderberries. Cover the jar with a pane of glass and set it in the hot sun for 2 full days. Then strain off the liquor from the stone jar. Pour it into a large saucepan and blend in all the other ingredients. Bring to a boil while continually stirring the mixture. Let it boil for 1 hour. Keep the pan covered except while stirring. Take it off the stove and set aside to cool. When cold, it is ready for bottling. Strain into bottles and cork tightly. *Note:* This catsup is best when used for flavoring brown gravies, soups and stews. Stirred into browned butter, it makes a stimulating sauce for broiled or baked fish.

13. Recipe included herein
14. Recipe included herein

20

Old-Fashioned Pickling

Good cider vinegar[1] or corn vinegar[2] is highly recommended for making any of the following pickling recipes. In my great-grandmother's day, people were told to avoid the commercially bottled varieties for it was widely believed to be nothing more than "a sharp colorless liquid sold under that name."

In fact, so strong was the prevailing feeling against any "store bought" cider vinegar, that a popular cookbook of 1862 claimed it was:

> warranted to riddle the coat of any stomach, even that of an ostrich, if that bird were so bereft of the instinct of self-preservation as to make a lunch of bright-green cucumber-pickle seven times a week.

My great-grandmother had several general rules that apply to pickle-making. She said to always keep pickles in glass or hard stoneware. Check them over at least once a month and remove any soft ones. And if there are several

---

1. Recipe in Chapter 19
2. Recipe in Chapter 19

of these, drain off the vinegar and scald it. These rules apply to pickles of both the sweet and sour varieties.

There were a few other important rules to apply only to sour or "dill" pickles. When you drain off and scald the vinegar, add 1 cup sugar for each gallon of the liquor. Pour the hot vinegar-sugar mixture back over the pickles. If, however, the pickles are keeping well, simply throw a liberal handful of sugar in for every gallon of liquid and cover them over again with the lid. This tends to help preserve the pickles and it mellows the sharpness of the vinegar. Always be sure to keep your pickles well covered with vinegar. And if you use ground spices in making pickles, tie them up in thin muslin bags before putting into the pickling solution.

Great-Grandmother Shaw said that a well-made pickle is better when a year old than at the end of 6 months. She claimed to have eaten pickled walnuts and pickled butter-nuts[3] that were 10 years old—and they were said to be fine.

GREAT-GRANDMOTHER SHAW'S
PICKLED BUTTERNUTS AND WALNUTS

2 quarts butternuts	36 whole cloves
2 quarts walnuts	36 peppercorns
or 4 quarts of either	18 allspice berries
1 gallon cider vinegar[4]	12 blades of mace
1 cup sugar	

Gather the nuts when they are soft enough to be pierced with a pin. Put them in a stone jar and cover with a strong brine (1 cup salt to every quart water). Leave for 36 hours. Empty out the brine and replace it with a fresh batch. Again leave for 36 hours and again replace the brine. On

---

3. Recipe included herein
4. Recipe in Chapter 19

the fifth day drain the nuts and wipe each with a coarse cloth. Pierce each nut by running a large needle through it. Lay them in cold water for 6 hours.

After 6 hours of soaking, pack the nuts in sterilized glass fruit jars. Now take the cider vinegar[5] and put it into an enameled kettle. Add the sugar and spices. Boil for 5 full minutes. Pour this, while scalding hot, over the nuts in the jars. Repeat this twice more within the week. Then seal the jars and store. *Note:* These nuts will be ready to eat in 1 month. This unique recipe was given Mrs. Shaw by her grandmother. It is very, very old.

VINTAGE PICKLED WATERMELON RIND, 1820

Take the thickest watermellon rind you can get. Pare off the hard green rind and the soft inner pulp. Lay the pieces—narrow strips or fancy cuttings—in brine strong enough to float an egg. Let them remain in this for 10 days. Then soak in fresh water for 10 more days (change the water daily). On the eleventh day, put the rinds in a large enameled kettle and cover with fresh water. Heat slowly and let boil gently for 5 minutes. Take out and plunge instantly into ice water. Leave the rinds in this until the next day.

The next morning, put the rinds in a kettle of fresh water and again bring it to a gentle boil. Simmer carefully for 5 minutes, as a hard boil will injure the rinds. Take them directly from the boiling water and again plunge into ice water. Do not disturb them for 4 more hours. Change the water and boil them a third time for 5 minutes. Leave the rinds in the kettle overnight.

In the morning, take the rinds out of the kettle. Add enough sugar to the water to make it sweet but not quite

---

5. Recipe in Chapter 19

a syrup. Put the rinds back in and simmer for 10 minutes. Drain and put on dishes to cool.

Meanwhile, start preparing your second and final syrup. First weigh the rind. For every pound of rind you will need the following ingredients:

2 cups sugar   2 cups cider vinegar[6]
1/2 cup water

Blend the required amounts of sugar and water in the large enameled kettle. Carefully measure and add 1 table-spoon ginger for every gallon of the syrup. Put on the stove and heat. When the sugar has melted and the syrup is quite hot (not boiling), put in the rinds. Let it simmer until they look clear. Take the pieces of rind out and spread on dishes again. Now add the cider vinegar. And add 1 tablespoon tumeric for every gallon of the syrup previously measured. Spice to taste with mace, cloves, and cinnamon. Bring to a boil and put the rinds back in. Let simmer for 15 minutes. Take out the rinds and immediately put them into sterilized glass jars. Fill the jars with hot syrup and seal. It will be ready to eat in 2 weeks.

GREAT-AUNT RUTH'S
OLD-TIME PICKLED ONIONS

Peel some small white onions. Let them stand in strong brine (1 cup salt to every quart of water) for 4 days. Change the brine twice during the 4 days. On the fifth day, heat more brine to a boil. Put in the onions and let them boil for 3 minutes. Immediately take the onions out and put them in ice water. Leave them there for 4 hours. Then take them out and pack in sterilized jars. Intersperse with whole mace, peppercorns, and cloves.

6. Recipe in Chapter 19

Prepare sufficient cider vinegar[7] to fill the jars. Blend with 1 cup sugar for every gallon used. Bring to a boil. Pour while scalding hot over the onions and fill each jar. Seal the jars while hot. *Note:* The pickled onions will be ready to eat in a month, but are much better at the end of 3 months.

GREAT-GREAT-GRANDMOTHER HORTON'S WAY TO CORN BEEF

In early times, everyone knew how to properly corn beef. The method is quite a simple process and it was often done right in the home. To corn a piece of beef, the meat should be allowed to hang 3 or 4 days after the animal has been killed. Then put it in a brine made of:

4 cups water	2 cups molasses
6 cups salt	or
1/2 tablespoon saltpeter	2 1/2 cups coarse brown sugar

The above ingredients should be thoroughly mixed while cold. The meat should be entirely submerged, and then turned once in a while. A week in the brine will corn it enough for most tastes. But for many people, a longer time is better. In cold weather the brine may be used several times. In warm weather it is safe to use it but once. On the early New England farms a considerable quantity of beef was usually corned at one time, especially in the late Autumn.

What piece of beef to select for corning depends on individual preference. My great-great-grandmother always used a "fancy brisket." This afforded her a good solid slice of lean beef, bordered with fat. The fat can be cut off if

---

7. Recipe in Chapter 19

232 NATURAL COOKING THE OLD-FASHIONED WAY

not wanted. She felt the "streak of lean and streak of fat" beef was unsatisfactory and uneconomical, unless you know everyone eating it likes fat. The ribs, the end of the rump, and the thin end of the sirloin make good corning pieces. But they are rather high-priced.

Even in the old days, the corned beef purchased from the butcher's cart or meat market was apt to be not corned enough. And this is true today. In great-great-grandmother's day, she could readily make arrangements with her provision store to have her favorite piece of beef put in the brine at a given time and taken out when properly corned.

GREAT-GRANDMOTHER MITCHELL'S
PICKLED CABBAGE

To prepare the cabbage, cut in quarters. Leave off the outer leaves. Put it in a kettle of boiling brine (1/2 cup salt to every gallon of water). Cook for 3 minutes. Take out, drain, and cover thickly with salt. Spread out in the sun to dry. When dry, shake off the salt and put in a stone jar. Cover with cold cider vinegar[8] in which enough tumeric has been steeped to color it well. Leave it in this for 2 full weeks. Three days before the cabbage is ready, mix all of the following ingredients in a clean stone jar:

2 gallons cider vinegar	1/4 cup tumeric
2 cups dry mustard	1/2 cup garlic, chopped
1/2 cup ginger	1/3 cup horseradish,
3/8 cup pepper	scraped
2 tablespoons allspice	8 cups sugar
1/4 cup cloves	1/4 cup celery seed
2 tablespoons mace	3 lemons, sliced very thin
2 tablespoons nutmeg	

---

8. Recipe in Chapter 19

Cover the stone jar and set this mixture in the sun for 3 days. Pack the cabbage down in it. Cover with a stoneware or wooden top. Tie a stout cloth over this. Keep in a cool, dry place. It will be ready to eat in from 6 weeks to 2 months.

PICKLED CAULIFLOWER IN THE OLDEN DAYS

Select the whitest and closest bunches of cauliflower. Cut into small sprays or clusters. Plunge into a kettle of scalding brine (1/2 cup salt to every gallon of water). Boil for 3 minutes. Then take them out. Lay on a sieve or a cloth. Sprinkle thickly with salt and brush it off when they are dry. Now put the cauliflower in a stone jar. Cover with fresh cold cider vinegar.[9] Set the jar in the sun for 2 days. Then take the cauliflower out and pack it in a clean stoneware jar. Immediately prepare some seasoned cider vinegar. For every gallon of vinegar used, the following ingredients are required:

1 cup sugar	Few bits of red pepper
12 blades of mace	pods
1 tablespoon celery seed	1 tablespoon coriander
24 peppercorns	seed
	1 tablespoon mustard seed

Blend all of the above in the vinegar and bring to a boil. Let it boil for 5 minutes. Pour, while scalding, over the cauliflower. Repeat this scalding once each week for 3 successive weeks. Put a dish on top of the cauliflower to keep it submerged in the vinegar. Cover with a stoneware or wooden top. Tie a stout cloth over this. Keep in a cool, dry place.

---

9. Recipe in Chapter 19

GREAT-GREAT-GRANDMOTHER HORTON'S SOUSE

The souse that great-great-grandmother used to make was a very fine dish. It included the pig's ears, feet, and fore part of the legs. The skin first received a thorough cleaning and scraping. The pieces were then placed in strong salt water overnight. Each piece was scraped again in the morning and given another salt water bath of about the same length of time. It was then put in a enameled kettle and covered with cold water. This was brought to a boil and allowed to simmer until the bones would easily come out. The meat was first taken out. And the gristle, bones, and superfluous fat were removed. The skin (which was the most important part) and the meat were cut up in small pieces. It was salted to taste and drenched with good cider vinegar.[10] Great-great-grandmother then packed it away in a stone jar where it would settle down into a compact mass. It could then be carved out of the mass, and served cold in slices. Or the slices were warmed up in a frying pan, or even browned, as desired.

Souse was a popular old-time breakfast dish. A batter was often made by blending 1 egg and 1 cup milk. It was salted to taste. Then 1 teaspoon butter was put in. Sufficient flour was stirred in to make a thin batter. Each piece of souse was dipped in this batter and fried in pork drippings. Some old-timers enjoyed it even more by simply dipping each piece in beaten eggs and then rolling in finely pounded crackers.[11] It was then fried until browned and served while hot.

GRANDMOTHER PELTON'S
SLICED CUCUMBER PICKLES

Take 24 large cucumbers and slice them. Put into a big

10. Recipe in Chapter 19
11. Many excellent recipes for old time homemade crackers can be found in *Natural Baking the Old-Fashioned Way*, by the same author.

enameled kettle. Add enough cider vinegar[12] to cover them. Heat slowly and then let it boil for 1 full hour. Set aside to cool. Now prepare the seasoned cider vinegar. To each gallon of cold vinegar allow the following:

2 cups sugar	1 teaspoon cloves
1 tablespoon cinnamon	1 tablespoon tumeric
1 tablespoon ginger	1 tablespoon horseradish,
1 tablespoon pepper	scraped
1 tablespoon celery seed	1 tablespoon garlic, sliced
1 teaspoon mace	1/2 teaspoon red pepper
1 teaspoon allspice	

Put the cider vinegar[12] in a large enameled kettle. Blend in all of the above ingredients. Put in the cucumbers. Stew for 2 hours. Allow to cool. The pickles will be ready for use as soon as they are cold.

CIVIL WAR PERIOD PICKLED TOMATOES

8 cups cider vinegar[13]	1 nutmeg, grated
8 cups sugar	pinch of red pepper
8 onions	8 pounds green tomatoes,
2 tablespoons salt	sliced
1 tablespoon cinnamon	1 celery stalk, cut up
1 tablespoon cloves	

Put the vinegar in a large porcelain kettle. Add the sugar and bring it to a boil. Take from the stove and skim when it has cooled a little. Then add the onions, salt, cinnamon, cloves, nutmeg, and red pepper. Lastly add the tomatoes and celery. Let it boil only 2 or 3 minutes. Put in sterilized glass jars and seal.

---

12. Recipe in Chapter 19
13. Recipe in Chapter 19

EARLY AMERICAN CORNED BEEF HEART

Get a fresh beef heart. Thoroughly wash and trim of all fat. Put it in water salty enough to float an egg. Leave it there for 2 days. Then wash the heart well and put it in cold water. Bring to a boil and simmer gently for 3 hours. Add a bay leaf, a slice of onion, 4 whole cloves and a blade of mace. Now simmer until the heart is done. Let it cool in the liquor. Cut into thin slices and serve.

21

Homemade Candy-Making
the Natural Way

Homemade candies were quite a fad in the late nineteenth century. Some time prior to this they were a necessity for the art had not yet really been commercialized. Many young women all over the country became expert "confectioners" or candy-makers. And no money-making function, for the church or any charity, was then considered complete without its homemade candy table. So fine was the product of this unique branch of home cookery that much money was netted at the candy tables. And those who purchased these homemade confections obtained delicious morsels—much tastier delicacies than those that came from professional candy-makers of the day.

In the days gone by, ingredients used in homemade candy-making were relatively unsophisticated, and the operations of manufacture were wholesome and clean. The recipes given in this chapter are those used for generations by early members of my family. Some of these old-timers gained some measure of local fame through their efforts.

GREAT-GRANDMOTHER MITCHELL'S
POINTS ON CANDY-MAKING

My great-grandmother always used porcelain-lined or agate kettles for cooking up her homemade candy mixtures.

Asbestos mats were considered indispensable when boiling sugar or candy mixtures that were not to be stirred.

If great-grandmother wanted her candy to "sugar," she simply stirred the mixture while it was cooking.

She always said to not stir candy that you intend to pull. It ruins this type of confection.

Mrs. Mitchell used a little vinegar in some of her recipes to make the candy nice and brittle.

GREAT-GRANDMOTHER SHAW'S
FRENCH CREAM CANDY

This old recipe is the foundation for all of my great-grandmother's chocolate, coconut and fruit creams. Here is how she made it: Break the white of 1 egg (more eggs if you want a larger quantity) into a wooden mixing bowl. Add an equal amount of cold water. Stir in enough confectionery sugar to mold into shape with the fingers. After molding, put on waxed paper or small plates. Set aside in a cool place to dry.

Great-Grandmother's Fruit Creams: Finely chopped raisins, figs, citron, or currants may be mixed with the above *French Cream* before all the sugar is added. Press into a cake about 1 inch thick and cut in small cubes.

Great-Grandmother's Walnut Creams: Make balls of *French Cream* (above) a little smaller than a walnut. Place a half nut-meat on either side and press them into the cream. Chopped nuts of any kind were often blended with the cream before all of the sugar was added.

Great-Grandmother's Cream Dates: Remove the pits from large dates. Roll pieces of *French Cream* (above) into long strips. Put in the dates. Press the edges of the cream strips together. Roll in granulated sugar. Set aside to harden on wax paper or a plate.

Great-Grandmother's Cream Cherries: Make a small round ball of *French Cream* (above). Cut a strip of citron to look like a cherry stem. Put the cream ball on 1 end. Put 1/2 of a candied cherry on each side of the cream ball near the stem.

Great-Grandmother's Cream Chocolates: Make small balls out of the *French Cream* (above). Put 1/2 pound of chocolate in a small saucepan and cook over boiling water until it melts. Dip in the cream balls, one at a time, until all are covered with chocolate. Place each ball on waxed paper or a dish to dry.

EARLY AMERICAN SUGAR CANDY—VINTAGE 1800

6 cups sugar	1 tablespoon butter
1 cup cider vinegar[1]	1 teaspoon baking soda
1 cup water	(dissolved in hot water)

Put the sugar, vinegar and water in a saucepan and stir until the sugar is dissolved. Bring to a boil, *without stirring,* for 20 minutes, or until it crisps when dropped from the spoon into cold water. Stir in the butter and baking soda. Add flavoring to suit taste desired. Pour on buttered plates and allow to cool. When cold, pull with the buttered tips of your fingers. *Note:* This recipe for candy was once considered the best for children's health.

---

1. Recipe in Chapter 19

GREAT-GRANDMOTHER MITCHELL'S CHOCOLATE CARAMELS

1/4 pound chocolate, grated	2 1/2 cups brown sugar
	1 tablespoon butter
1/4 cup molasses	3 tablespoons milk

Put all of the above ingredients in a saucepan and heat. Stir until the chocolate and butter have melted and the sugar has dissolved. Let it boil until the mixture begins to harden. Flavor with vanilla. Pour into a greased pan. When partly cooled, mark off into very small squares with a dull knife. Set in a cool place to harden.

ORIGINAL PLANTATION-STYLE NUT CANDY

3 cups brown sugar	1 cup cream
1 cup nuts, chopped	or
	1 cup milk

Put all of the above ingredients in a saucepan. If milk is used instead of cream, add a small piece of butter. Boil until very brittle when dropped into cold water. Pour into a buttered dish and cut in squares when cool.

GRANDPA PELTON'S FAVORITE OLD-TIME MOLASSES CANDY

1/2 cup cider vinegar[2]	1/4 cup butter
1 cup sugar	1 teaspoon baking soda,
4 cups molasses	dissolved in hot water

Put the vinegar into a saucepan and dissolve the sugar

---

2. Recipes in Chapter 19

in it. Blend in the molasses and bring to a boil. Stir frequently until it hardens when dropped from the spoon into cold water. Stir in the butter and baking soda. Pour into buttered dishes. As it cools, cut into squares, or, while soft enough to handle, pull into sticks with the buttered tips of your fingers.

OLD-FASHIONED SEA FOAM CANDY TREAT

3 cups light brown sugar
1 cup water
1 tablespoon corn vinegar[3]

2 egg whites, tsiffly beaten
1 teaspoon vanilla
1 cup nuts, chopped

Put the sugar, water, and vinegar into a saucepan and heat gradually to boiling. Stir only until the sugar has dissolved. Boil without stirring until it forms a hard ball when dropped into cold water. Take from the stove. As soon as the syrup stops bubbling, beat it gradually into the beaten egg whites. Continue beating until the mixture will hold its shape. Add the vanilla and nuts (may be walnuts, pecans, hickory nuts, etc.). Drop in small rough-shaped piles on waxed paper. *Note:* This delicious candy was popular on the plantations just before the Civil War.

GREAT-GREAT-GRANDMOTHER HORTON'S
HARD CANDIES

2 cups milk
2 1 ounce squares
   chocolate

1/2 cup butter
3 cups granulated sugar,
   heaping

Put all of the above ingredients in a saucepan. Boil together until it hardens when dropped from a spoon into

3. Recipes in Chapter 19

cold water. Pour into a buttered pan and let it cool. Then crack and eat.

GREAT-GREAT-GRANDMOTHER NORTHRUP'S NOUGATS

Grease a square, shallow pan with butter. Fill the pan with hickory nut kernels, sliced almonds, grated coconut, and a few bits of candied orange peel. Boil 4 cups sugar and 1 cup water together, without stirring, until it stiffens. Add 1 tablespoon lemon juice and stir well. Pour into the pan over the nuts. Allow to cool and then mark in narrow strips with the dull edge of a knife.

SIMPLE OLD-FASHIONED STUFFED DATES

Remove the pits from dates. Fill the dates with chopped nuts of your choice. Roll them in powdered sugar and serve.

GREAT-AUNT BEVERLY JO'S GLAZED FRUITS AND NUTS

2 cups granulated sugar   1 tablespoon lemon juice
1/2 cup water

Boil the sugar and water for 10 minutes without stirring. Test by dropping from a spoon into cold water. When brittle, remove the pan from the stove. Add the lemon juice. Set the pan containing the syrup in a large bowl of hot water. With a long pin or needle immerse sections of oranges, grapes, figs, almonds, walnuts, or pecans. Set each piece upon an oiled paper. *Note:* The fruit or nuts must be thoroughly dry before being dipped into the candy syrup.

ORIGINAL OLD-TIME POPCORN CANDY

2 cups molasses   1/4 cup butter
1 cup brown sugar   1 teaspoon cider vinegar[4]

Put all of the above ingredients into a saucepan and bring to a boil. When it becomes thick and taffy-like, stir in all the popcorn the candy will take. Mold into balls, or pour into pans, smooth over, and cut in squares.

GRANDMOTHER COLLISTER'S HOMEMADE TAFFY

3 3/4 cups confectioner's   2 tablespoons butter
        sugar   1/2 teaspoon lemon juice
1 cup water   Vanilla to suit

Put the sugar in a saucepan and wet with the water. Stir over the stove until the sugar dissolves. Boil until it thickens. Add the butter and lemon juice. Let it boil again. Flavor to taste with vanilla. Pour into a buttered pan. When cold, mark off in little squares. *Note:* Nuts or fruit give this candy a delightful taste. Sprinkle them on top before the candy hardens.

UNCLE ALBERT'S
FAVORITE OLD-TIME COCONUT CARAMELS

5 cups confectioner's   3/4 cups chocolate,
        sugar   grated
1 1/2 cups coconut,   3/4 cup cream
        grated

Blend all of the above ingredients in a saucepan. Cook slowly, stirring constantly, until thick. Pour out into a buttered shallow pan and let cool. Cut into little cakes. Set these cakes on a buttered dish to dry.

---

4. Recipe in Chapter 19

22

Old-Fashioned Miscellaneous Recipes of Importance

GREAT-GRANDMOTHER MITCHELL'S TURKEY STUFFINGS

The common foundation for simple old-fashioned turkey stuffing in early times was bread or cracker crumbs.[1] The crumbs were seasoned with sage, thyme, salt and pepper. And some people liked to add minced onions. But where an onion taste is at all offensive, it's best not to include them.

The best old-time stuffings were moistened with melted butter, or a combination of hot water and milk. And an egg was commonly added. A thin slice of finely chopped salt pork gave the stuffing both richness and flavor. If salt pork was used, then the butter wasn't required. Chestnuts, oysters, celery, and, sometimes, raisins were blended into many of the original early American stuffings. The methods of mixing a good stuffing varied extensively. Here are a few prime examples of those commonly used in the colorful past.

---

1. Many excellent recipes for old time homemade bread and crackers can be found in *Natural Baking the Old Fashioned Way*, by the same author.

Ordinary Old-Fashioned Stuffing: Blend 4 cups bread crumbs or cracker crumbs with 1 tablespoon butter. Add 1 tablespoon of mixed herbs and a pinch of mace. A tablespoon of sage may be substituted for the mixed herbs. Stuff into the turkey and it is ready to roast.

Colonial Period Chestnut Stuffing: A quart (4 cups) of fresh chestnuts should be roasted. Remove the shells and skins. Mash thoroughly and add 1 tablespoon butter, 1 teaspoon salt, and enough pepper to suit individual taste. Blend well and stuff into the turkey. *Note:* Roasted chestnuts were often served with the turkey or in the gravy when this kind of stuffing was used. It was extremely popular in the Colonies and is recommended as a gourmet treat.

Early American Oyster and Mushroom Stuffing: Make up a batch of the *Ordinary Old-Fashioned Stuffing* (above). Finely chop 12 oysters and 12 mushrooms. Blend these into the bread crumb mixture and immediately stuff the turkey.

Mrs. Horton's Finest Turkey Stuffing: This is a recipe that was regularly used in 1840 by my Great-Great-Grandmother Huldah (Radike) Horton. It was not a widely known stuffing, but in her family it was believed to be the best around. She took 15 crackers[2] and pounded them into fine crumbs. The following ingredients were then added, blended well, wet with boiling water, and stuffed into her turkey:

1 teaspoon cinnamon	1/2 teaspoon black
1/2 nutmeg, grated	pepper
1/2 teaspoon salt	1/2 cup butter

2. Many excellent recipes for old time homemade crackers can be found in *Natural Baking the Old Fashioned Way*, by the same author.

GREAT-GRANDMOTHER SHAW'S
YORKSHIRE PUDDING

3 eggs, well beaten   2 cups milk
1 teaspoon salt   2/3 cup flour

This prize old-fashioned pudding was made to be served only with roast beef[3] and it is most delicious. Beat the eggs until they are very light and fluffy. Add the salt and milk. Gradually blend in the flour, stirring all the time, to keep the mixture smooth. Butter a large pan like the one used for roasting the beef. Pour the pudding in.

Take the roast from the oven 1/2 hour before it is done cooking. Place the rack with the meat on it over, not in, the pan and pudding. Place back in the oven and allow the meat and pudding to finish cooking together. When done, take from the oven, remove the roast and rack, and cut the pudding into little squares. Serve it as a garnish for the roast. *Note:* Some old-timers poured out all the drippings from the roasting pan. They then poured the pudding batter around the meat. It was baked for 45 minutes and then served. Others liked to bake the pudding in gem pans and occasionally baste it with the meat drippings. It was then used as a garnish for the roast.

REAL OLD-FASHIONED
NEW ENGLAND BOILED DINNER

This early American recipe consists of corned beef, pork, and a variety of fresh vegetables. A fancy brisket, well corned,[4] and cooked[5] as recommended, is the foundation.

3. Recipe in Chapter 4
4. Recipe in Chapter 20
5. Recipe in Chapter 4

And a piece of salt pork or corned shoulder of pork is used for additional flavoring.

The fat must first be skimmed from the liquor in which the meat was boiled. The vegetables are put into the boiling kettle of liquor about 2 hours before dinner time. Parsnips, carrots, cabbage, turnips, potatoes, and squash were the customary vegetables used in the old days. Beets were also used but they were generally boiled alone as they tended to discolor the others. Cook until the vegetables are all tender. Take them out of the liquor and allow to cool. *Note:* This boiled dinner is better to eat when cold. The orthodox method of serving it is to put it all on one platter.

GRANDMOTHER COLLISTER'S
BEST STEW DUMPLINGS

1/2 teaspoon salt	flour to suit
1 teaspoon baking powder	1/2 cup milk

Sift the salt, baking powder, and a little flour together in a wooden mixing bowl. Slowly blend in the milk. Add flour enough to mix a dough a little softer than biscuits. Form a ball with the hands and then roll it out into a 1-inch sheet. Cut in diamond shapes. Lay them on top of the meat, which should project above the surface of the still simmering stew. Cover closely. Allow the dumplings to steam until no dough will stick to a straw when thrust into them. *Note:* These dumplings are excellent in lamb stew,[6] beef stew[7] and veal stew.[8]

---

6. Recipe in Chapter 6
7. Recipe in Chapter 4
8. Recipe in Chapter 5

OLD-TIME SALAD DRESSINGS

Various salad dressings are the foundation of most good salads. The following recipes are original old-time dressings that were highly prized in their day. Each should be made with a great deal of care.

Great-Grandmother Mitchell's Homemade Mayonnaise

1 tablespoon sugar
1 tablespoon dry mustard
1/2 teaspoon salt
pinch of red pepper
2 raw egg yolks

2 cups olive oil
2 tablespoons lemon juice
2 tablespoons cider
  vinegar[9]
1/2 cup cream, whipped[10]

Thoroughly mix the sugar, mustard, salt and pepper. Stir this carefully into the raw egg yolks. Blend in the oil gradually so the mixture will be smooth and thick, rather than oily. Before all the oil is put in, add the lemon juice, a little at a time. Alternate it with the oil. Lastly, stir in the vinegar. Set aside in a cool place until needed. Just before serving, blend in the freshly whipped cream.

Mrs. Horton's Old-Time Salad Cream Supreme: This wonderful salad dressing concoction was found in the cooking notes of my Great-Great-Grandmother Horton. It is a delightful recipe to try and it has proved to be delicious.

1 cup cream
pinch of dry mustard
pinch of pepper
pinch of sugar
3 tablespoons olive oil
3 egg yolks, hard-boiled,
  rubbed smooth

1 tablespoon cider vinegar[11]
juice of 1 lemon, strained
salt to taste
2 egg whites, hard-boiled,
  sliced in rings

9. Recipe in Chapter 19
10. Recipe included herein
11. Recipe in Chapter 19

This salad dressing is to be mixed in a "soup plate" with a "wooden or silver spoon." It is to be "rubbed smooth and gradually moistened into a smooth paste." Begin with a few drops of the cream blended with the mustard, pepper, and sugar—"each pinch the size of an English pea." Add the olive oil. Thoroughly mix it all together. To this add the yolks of the eggs. Now add the rest of the cream. Stir as little as possible. Next stir in the vinegar, then the lemon juice, and lastly the salt—"use a little more salt than seems necessary, so as to prevent having to resalt all the different articles dressed with the cream." Now drop in the rings of egg white and stir lightly. Put the mixture on ice until needed. *Note:* This dressing was often bottled for a picnic dinner in the old days. And it was invaluable to the home-maker of yesteryear because of its varied uses. It was used on chicken salad, sliced tomatoes, sardines, lettuce leaves, turkey salad, or for fresh and pickled shrimp salad.

Early American Cooked Cream Dressing:

1/2 tablespoon dry mustard   2 tablespoons sugar
4 tablespoons butter,   3 eggs
    melted   1/2 cup cider vinegar[12]
1/2 tablespoon salt   1 cup milk

Take a small mixing bowl and blend the mustard with the melted butter. Add the salt, sugar, eggs, and vinegar. Beat together thoroughly and blend in the milk. Place the bowl in a pan of boiling water. Cook in the oven (350 degrees) like a custard.

12. Recipe in Chapter 19

Old-Fashioned French Dressing:

large pinch of salt
pinch of red pepper
1 tablespoon cider vinegar[13]
   or
1 tablespoon lemon juice

3 tablespoons olive oil
1/2 teaspoon mustard[14]
   or
4 drops onion juice

Blend the salt, pepper, and vinegar or lemon juice in a small wooden mixing bowl. Slowly stir in the olive oil. Lastly add the mustard or onion juice. When finished, put in a small, tightly corked bottle and set aside until needed.

GREAT-GREAT-GRANDMOTHER HORTON'S ROAST PIG STUFFING

This is a delightful old-time recipe for making a rich and savory roast pig[15] stuffing. For a Christmas pig it is well worth while to take the trouble in preparing this. Blend the following ingredients:

1 cup bread crumbs[16]
1 tablespoon suet,
   chopped fine
bunch of parsley, minced
1 teaspoon sage
1 teaspoon salt
1 teaspoon pepper
1 teaspoon nutmeg

1/4 teaspoon thyme
2 tablespoons sherry wine
2 tablespoons butter,
   melted
juice of 1 lemon
1 cup oyster juice
2 eggs, well beaten

---

13. Recipes in Chapter 19
14. Recipes in Chapter 19
15. Recipe in Chapter 7
16. Many excellent recipes for old-time homemade bread can be found in *Natural Baking the Old-Fashioned Way*, by the same author.

OLD-FASHIONED COTTAGE CHEESE

Early New Orleans Cottage Cheese: Take a quantity of curdled milk and put it in a kettle. Heat until the curd separates. Pour into a coarse bag. Hang in a cool place to drain until the *whey*[17] ceases to run. Turn it out of the bag. Cut up with a knife. Salt each piece to taste. Add a little cream to enrich it. *Note:* Some old-timers put in a little pepper. Various seasonings such as nutmeg, sugar, or sage were used by others.

Old New England Cottage Cheese:

1 quart milk, thick and   1 tablespoon cream
    sour   dash of salt
1 teaspoon butter

Scald the milk until the curd separates. Strain through a cloth. Let it drain until quite dry. Blend with the butter, cream, and salt in a smooth paste. Make into balls and store in a cool place until ready to eat.

Plantation-Style Cottage Cheese: Take not less than 1 quart of thick sour milk. Lay a strainer cloth in the dish drainer or a colander. Pour the sour milk into it. Pour on 2 or more cups boiling water. Gather in the corners of the strainer cloth so as to work out the water and the whey. The hot water will sufficiently harden the curd. When drained, it should be salted and mixed with a little cream. Mold or press in the cloth into a round flat cake. Care must be taken not to use too much boiling water or the cheese will be tough and leathery.

---

17. The thin watery part of milk that separates from the curds.

WHIPPED CREAM IN THE GOOD OLD DAYS

Care should be taken in the choice of cream for whipping. Too thin a cream will turn to liquid rather quickly after it has been whipped. Too thick a cream will turn to butter as it is being whipped. A medium-thick cream should always be used, and it should be icy cold when whipped. Beat rapidly at first, and more slowly as the cream begins to froth. Stir the froth back into the cream as much as possible. Flavor delicately with sugar and vanilla.

GRANDMOTHER COLLISTER'S OLD-TIME GOOSE PUDDING

1/2 loaf bread,[18] shredded
cold scalded milk to suit
1 cup suet, chopped fine
3 medium onions, chopped
    fine

3 eggs, well beaten
salt to taste
pepper to taste
sage to taste
marjoram to taste

Stir the bread into enough cold scalded milk to soften it. Mix with the suet, onions, and eggs. Add the seasonings to suit. Bake on the rack of a roasting pan until browned. *Note:* This is best when served with either roast goose or roast duck.[19]

18. Many excellent recipes for old-time homemade bread can be found in *Natural Baking the Old-Fashioned Way,* by the same author.
19. Recipes in Chapter 8

Index

Abigail Adams's Hashed Steak on Toast, 79
A Colony Favorite—Eggs with Maple Syrup, 132
Adams, Abigail, 79
Adams, John, 79, 148, 149
Adams, John Quincy, 169, 172
Adams, Louisa Catherine, 169
Ageless Catsup, 224
Alberta Catherine's Old-Time Potato Recipes, 54
Albert, Uncle, 29, 128, 178, 191, 243
Almond Soup, 22, 23
Apple Cider Vinegar, 222
Apple Jelly, 214, 215
Apple Omelet, 135
Apple Pudding, Baked, 157, 158
Apricot Ice Cream, 194
Arthur, Uncle, 215
Art, Uncle, 170, 225
Asparagus Cookery, 60
Asparagus Omelet, 133

Bacon and Cabbage in the Old South, 52, 53
Baked Apple Pudding, 157, 158
Baked Beans, 62

Baked Fish Sauce, 178
Baked Potatoes, 54
Banana Fritters, 146
Banana Ice Cream, 194
Banbury Marmalade, 216
Bean and Pea Recipes, 29, 59, 60
Beans, Baked, 63
Bean Soup, 29
Beans, Shell, 60
Beef, Braised, 81
Beef Brisket, 74
Beef Cakes, 79, 80
Beef, Caring for, 69, 70
Beef Cookery, 68, 69, 70, 71, 72, 73, 74, 75, 76, 77, 78, 79, 80, 81, 82, 83
Beef, Corn, 231, 232
Beef, Corned, 74
Beef Fillet (stuffed), 75
Beef Heart (stuffed), 79
Beef Kidneys, 81, 82
Beef Liver, 80
Beef, Pressed, 75, 76
Beef Rissoles—A Favorite of Jefferson Davis, 71
Beef, Roast, 73
Beefsteak, 72, 73
Beefsteak Pie, 80

253

Beef Stew, 78

Beef Tea of Colonial Days (Bouillon), 28

Berdan's Sharpshooters, 19

Beverly Jo, Great-Aunt, 126, 166, 191, 242

Biographical Family Names: Albert, Uncle, 29, 128, 178, 191, 243; Art, Uncle, 170, 215, 225; Beverly Jo, Great-Aunt, 126, 166, 191, 242; Carol Ann, Great-Aunt, 47, 74, 109; Catherine, Alberta, 54; Collister, Grandmother, 29, 59, 78, 93, 168, 177, 196, 208, 243, 247, 252; Daniels, Great-Great-Grandmother, 31, 48, 65, 66, 88, 107, 119, 137, 144, 145, 161, 190, 216; Doris Marie, Great-Aunt, 27, 45, 55; Elias, Great-Grandfather, 41, 116, 179; Elizabeth, Cousin, 30, 42, 146, 198; Goldie, Great-Aunt, 80; Horton, David, 36, 37; Horton, Great-Great-Grandmother, 19, 23, 28, 36, 37, 40, 41, 44, 60, 62, 91, 99, 102, 104, 112, 113, 117, 122, 128, 133, 144, 150, 153, 160, 164, 176, 180, 185, 186, 187, 197, 200, 205, 207, 212, 213, 215, 216, 224, 231, 234, 241, 245, 248, 250; Marilyn, Great-Aunt, 49, 81, 100; Mary, Great-Aunt, 78, 207; Mitchell, Great-Grandfather, 199; Mitchell, Great-Grandmother, 25, 34, 35, 42, 46, 58, 69, 71, 72, 77, 82, 85, 98, 103, 110, 116, 117, 118, 124, 131, 138, 142, 151, 156, 157, 166, 177, 183, 187, 190, 195, 199, 205, 209, 219, 222, 232, 238, 240, 244, 248; Northrup, Great-Great-Grandmother, 43, 63, 95, 106, 113, 114, 126, 135, 158, 214, 242; Pelton, Frank Curtis, 94, 171; Pelton, Grandpa, 94, 240; Pelton, Grandmother, 29, 76, 83, 92, 101, 115, 147, 163, 184, 189, 195, 203, 221, 234; Ruth, Great-Aunt, 38, 188, 230; Shaw, Great-Grandmother, 24, 39, 46, 53, 73, 75, 82, 84, 85, 89, 97, 100, 108, 111, 118, 139, 164, 169, 173, 174, 182, 192, 193, 202, 210, 219, 220, 226, 227, 228, 229, 238, 239, 246; Shirley, Great-Aunt, 26, 143, 197; Vera, Cousin, 61

Biographical Historical Names: Adams, Abigail, 79; Adams, John, 79, 148, 149; Adams, John Quincy, 169, 172; Adams, Louisa Catherine, 169; Berdan's Sharpshooters, 19; Booth, Ballington, 94; Booth, General William, 94; Davis, Jefferson, 71; Dickens, Charles, 156; Grant, General, 32, 33; Grant, Julia, 32, 33; Jackson, Andrew, 154; Jefferson, Thomas, 206, 226; Johnston, Sir William, 94; Kieft, Willem, 176; Lafayette, General, 132, 133; Lee, General, 39; Lincoln, President, 48; Madison, Dolly, 201; Monroe, James, 87, 88; Polk, James, 45; Polk, Sarah, 45; Quick, Tom, 94; Taylor, Zachary, 169, 171; Thurston, Ben (Colonel), 19; Trepp, Captain, 19; Washington, George, 26, 37, 202; Washington, Martha, 22, 36, 37, 167, 201, 202

Blackberries without Sugar the Old-Fashioned Way, 210

Blackberry Cordial, 184

Blackberry Flummery (custard), 204

Blackberry Jam, 215, 216

Boiled Corn Beef in the Olden Days, 74

INDEX

255

Boiled Dinner, New England, 246, 247
Boiled Ox Tongue, 82
Boiled Potatoes, 53
Booth, Ballington, 94
Booth, General William, 94
Bouillon (Beef), 28
Brandy Catsup, 219
Brandy Sauce (Pudding), 166, 167
Breaded Eggs, 137
Bread Griddle Cakes in Early America, 140, 141
Bread Pudding, Fruit, 158, 159
Broiled Oysters in Early America, 40
Broiled Shad, 45, 46
Broiled Sweetbreads, 91
Brook Trout, 46, 47
Broth, Calf's Foot, 185
Brown Sauce, 173, 174
Buckwheat Cakes, 141
Burns, Robert, 156
Butternuts and Walnuts, Pickled, 228, 229
Butter Sauce, Drawn, 170, 171

Cabbage and Bacon, 52, 53
Cabbage Cookery, 65
Cabbage, Cream, 65
Cabbage, Pickled, 232, 233
Café Au Lait in the Colonies, 183, 184
Calf's Brains, 92
Calf's Foot Broth, 185
Calf's Foot Jelly, 1800—A Favorite of Thomas Jefferson, 206, 207
Calf's Head Pluck—A Favorite of President James Monroe (1817–1825), 87, 88
Calf's Head Soup, 23, 24
Candy Making Tips, 238
Canned Fruit Tips, 209, 210
Caper Sauce (Meat), 175

Captain Trepp, 19
Caramels, Chocolate, 240
Caramels, Coconut, 243
Carol Ann, Great-Aunt, 47, 74, 109
Carrots, Creamed, 61
Catherine, Alberta, 54
Catsup, Ageless, 224
Catsup, Brandy, 219
Catsup, Elderberry, 226
Catsup, Lemon, 223
Catsup, Oyster, 222, 223
Catsup, Tomato, 220
Catsup, Walnut, 221
Cauliflower Cooking in Early Ohio, 66
Cauliflower Omelet, 133
Cauliflower, Pickled, 233
Celery-Cheese Sandwich, 190
Celery Soup, 32, 33
Celery Vinegar of the Good Old Days, 320, 321
Cherry Cream Candy, 239
Cherry Pyramid—Martha Washington's Specialty Dessert, 201
Cheshire Pork Pie, 109
Chestnut Sauce, 176
Chestnut Stuffing, 245
Chicken, Blanquette of, 129, 130
Chicken, Broiled, 127
Chicken, Creamed, 128
Chicken, Fricassee, 126, 127
Chicken, Fried, 124
Chicken Jelly, 127
Chicken Jelly Sandwich, 190
Chicken Pilau—Old Plantation Style, 130
Chicken Potpie, 122, 123
Chicken, Pressed, 129
Chicken Pudding on the Old South Plantation, 123, 124
Chicken, Roast, 118, 119
Chicken Salad, 150, 151
Chicken Sandwich, 191

Chicken Soup, 26, 27, 32
Chicken, Stewed, 125
Chicken Terrapin, 129
Chocolate Carmels, 240
Chocolate Cream Candy, 239
Chocolate, Hot, 182
Chocolate Ice Cream, 197
Chowder, Clam, 37
Chowder, Fish, 36, 37
Chowder, Salt-fish, 50
Christmas Lamb, 101, 102
Christmas Pudding, 164
Civil War Period Cream Sauce Special, 167, 168
Civil War Period Pickled Tomatoes, 235
Civil War Period Pressed Beef, 75, 76
Clam Chowder, 37
Coconut Carmels, 243
Codfish, 48
Coffee, Boiled, 180, 181
Coffee, Buying, 181
Coffee Frappe, 198
Coffee Ice Cream, 197
Coffee Making During the Civil War Period, 179
Coffee Making Pointers from the Old-Days, 180
Cold Shrimp Salad in the Louisiana Territory, 151
Collister, Grandmother, 29, 59, 78, 93, 168, 177, 196, 208, 243, 247, 252
Colonel Ben Thurston, 19
Colonial Buckwheat Cakes, 141
Colonial Chicken Jelly Sandwiches, 190
Colonial Days Chicken Jelly, 127
Colonial Governor Willem Kieft, 176
Colonial Period Chestnut Stuffing, 245

Colonial Period Croquettes of Calf's Brains, 92
Colonial Recipes for Cooking Squash, 64
Colonial-Style Baked Squash, 64
Colonial-Style Chestnut Sauce, 176
Colonial-Style Potato Omelet, 137, 138
Colonial-Style Summer Squash, 64
Colonial-Style Winter Squash, 64
Colonial-Time Corn Fritters, 145
Common Boiled Spinach, 58
Confederacy, President of, 71
Cooked Cream (Salad Dressing), 249
Cooking Greens in Early America, 57
Cordial, Blackberry, 184
Corn and Tomatoes, 62
Corn, Baked, 62
Corn Beef, How to, 231, 232
Corn, Boiled, 62
Corned Beef, 74
Corned Beef Heart, 236
Corned Beef Soup, 30
Corn Fritters, 145
Corn, Green, 62
Cornstarch Pudding During the Civil War Period, 158
Corn, Stewed, 62
Corn Vinegar as Made in the Colonies, 218
Cottage Cheese, 251
Cousin Elizabeth's Favorite Coffee Frappe, 198
Cousin Elizabeth's Old-Time Giblet Soup, 30, 31
Cousin Elizabeth's Old-Time Lobster a la Newburg, 42
Cousin Elizabeth's Quick Banana Fritters, 146
Cousin Vera's Old-Time Parsnips, 61

Cream Cabbage in the Old Days, 65
Cream Candy, French, 238, 239
Cream Cheese-Olive Sandwich, 191
Cream Cherries Candy, 239
Cream Chocolates, 239
Cream Dates Candy, 239
Creamed Oysters, 37, 38
Creamed Rice Soup, 27, 28
Cream Sauce (Pudding), 167, 168
Creamy Hard Sauce, 164, 165
Cucumber Pickles, 234, 235
Cucumber Sandwich, 191
Cucumber Sauce, 177
Cucumber Soup, 28
Currant Jelly, 212
Currant Jelly Sauce, 174
Currant Shrub (Drink), 183
Currants, Spiced (Canning), 211
Custard, Baked, 205
Custard, Blackberry Flummery, 204
Custard, Boiled, 201
Custard Ice Cream, 195
Custard Making Rules, 200, 201

Daniels, Great-Great-Grandmother, 31, 48, 65, 66, 88, 107, 119, 137, 144, 145, 161, 190, 216
Dates, Creamed, 239
Dates, Stuffed, 242
Davis, Jefferson, 71
Delightful Old-Fashioned Veal Cutlets, 85
Delmonico Potatoes, 56
Deviled Egg Sandwich, 188
Deviled Fish (Baked), 47, 48
Dickens, Charles, 156
Dolly Madison's Boiled Custard of 1810, 201
Doris Marie, Great-Aunt, 27, 45, 55
Doughnuts, Plantation-Style, 143, 144
Doughnuts, Raised, 146

Drawn Butter Asparagus Sauce, 171
Drawn Butter Celery Sauce, 171
Drawn Butter Egg Sauce, 170, 171
Drawn Butter Lobster Sauce, 171
Drawn Butter Parsley Sauce, 171
Drawn Butter Sauces, 170, 171
Duck, Roast, 119, 120
Dumplings, Stew, 247
Dumplings, Strawberry, 203, 204

Early Alabama Fried Sweet Potatoes, 56
Early Alabama Sweetbread Salad, 154
Early American Baked Potatoes, 54
Early American Beef Mold, 76, 77
Early American Boiled Fish, 44
Early American Chicken Soup Supreme, 26, 27
Early American Coffee Ice Cream, 197
Early American Cooked Cream Dressing, 249
Early American Corned Beef Heart, 236
Early American Drawn Butter Sauce, 170, 171
Early American Lamb Stew, 99
Early American Lemon Catsup, 223
Early American Nasturtium Sandwiches, 189
Early American Oyster and Mushroom Stuffing, 245
Early American Oyster Pie, 39
Early American Poached Eggs A La Creme, 133, 134
Early American Pork Potpie, 106, 107
Early American Pressed Turkey or Chicken, 129
Early American Raisin Wine, 183
Early American Shell Beans, 60
Early American Succotash, 63, 64

Early American Sugar Candy—Vintage 1800, 239
Early American Transparent Lemon Pie, 203
Early American Turkey Scallop, 121, 122
Early American Veal Steak, 88, 89
Early American Veal Terrapin, 95
Early American White Grape Jelly, 213
Early Corn Cooking, 62
Early New England Apple Omelet, 135
Early New England Cabbage Dishes, 65
Early New England Cheshire Pork Pie, 109
Early New England Corned Beef Soup, 30
Early New England Green Gooseberry Tarts, 207, 208
Early New England Pilot Boat Fry (fish), 36
Early New England Plain Lobster, 40, 41
Early New England Potatoes in the Shell, 54
Early New Hampshire Tom Alley Sauce, 176
Early New Orleans Cottage Cheese, 251
Early North Carolina Sirloin Tips, 77, 78
Early Plantation-Style Doughnuts, 143, 144
Early South Carolina Fried Salt Pork and Milk Gravy, 113
Early South Carolina Lamb Chops, 100
Early Southern Codfish Balls, 50
Early Southern Plantation Peach Batter Pudding, 163
Early Virginia Fried Chicken, 124

Early Virginia Rice Pudding with Eggs, 159
Early Virginia Smothered Ham, 112
Eel Rack, 94
Egg and Cheese Sandwich, 188
Egg Cookery, 131, 132, 133, 134, 135, 136, 137, 138, 139
Eggnog Christmas Special, 1776, 184, 185
Eggplant, fried, 67
Eggs a la Creme, 133, 134
Egg Sandwich, Deviled, 188
Egg Sauce in Early New Orleans, 168
Eggs, Boiling, 138
Eggs, Breaded, 137
Eggs, Fricasseed, 136
Eggs with Hash, 139
Eggs with Maple Syrup, 132
Elderberry Catsup, 226
Elias, Great-Grandfather, 41, 116, 179
Elizabeth, Cousin, 30, 42, 146, 198
Escalloped Tomatoes—A Favorite During the Civil War, 58

Fig Pudding (Steamed), 163, 164
First Ladies: Adams, Abigail, 79; Adams, Louisa Catherine, 169; Grant, Julia, 32, 33; Madison, Dolly, 201; Polk, Sarah, 45; Washington, Martha, 22, 36, 37, 167, 201, 202
Fish Au Gratin, 45
Fish, Baked, 43, 44
Fish, Baked Deviled, 47, 48
Fish, Boiled, 44
Fish Chowder, 36, 37
Fish, Cod, 48
Fish Cookery, 34, 35, 36, 37, 38, 39, 40, 41, 42, 43, 44, 45, 46, 47, 48, 49, 50, 51
Fish Cooking Pointers, 34, 35, 36

Fish, Creamed, 43
Fish, Fried, 44
Fish, Planked, 48, 49
Fish, Salt, 47
Fish Sauce, 178
Fish Souffle, 49
Fish Timbales, 39, 40
Float, Strawberry, 207
Foamy Sauce (Pudding), 168
Fowl, Boiled, 120
Fowl, Braised, 124, 125
Frappe, Coffee, 198
French Cream Candy, 238, 239
French Dressing, 250
French Pancakes, 142, 143
Fried Beef Kidney, 81, 82
Fried Sweetbreads, 91
Fritters, Banana, 146
Fritters, Corn, 145
Fritters, Raised, 142
Fritters, Sponge, 144, 145
Frozen Lemons (ice cream), 196, 197
Frozen Macedoine (ice cream), 196
Frozen Pudding (ice cream), 199
Frozen Rice (ice cream), 199
Fruit Bread Pudding, 158, 159
Fruit Canning Tips, 209, 210
Fruit Cream Candy, 238
Fruit Salad in Old Tennessee, 155
Fruits, Glazed, 242

General Grant's Favorite Creamed Fish Dish, 39, 40
General Lee's Favorite Fish Timbales, 43
German Potato Salad in Early American Homes, 153
Giblet Soup, 30, 31
Glazed Fruits and Nuts, 242
Goldie, Great-Aunt, 80
Gooseberries, Spiced (canning), 211, 212

Gooseberry Fool (custard), 202, 203
Gooseberry Jelly in Old Virginia, 214
Gooseberry Tarts, 207, 208
Goose Pudding, 252
Goose, Roast, 128
Granddad's Best Oyster Sauce, 171, 172
Granddad's Favorite Boiled Onions, 59
Granddad's Favorite Stuffed Heart, 79
Grandma's Best Hamburg Steak, 83
Grandmother Collister's Bean and Pea Recipes, 59, 60
Grandmother Collister's Beef Stew with Dumplings, 78
Grandmother Collister's Best Stew Dumplings, 247
Grandmother Collister's Creamy Olden-Day Prune Whip, 208
Grandmother Collister's Frozen Lemons (ice cream), 196, 197
Grandmother Collister's Homemade Taffy, 243
Grandmother Collister's Old-Fashioned Foamy Sauce, 166
Grandmother Collister's Old-Time Goose Pudding, 252
Grandmother Collister's Special Cucumber Sauce, 177
Grandmother Collister's Veal Potpie, 93, 94
Grandmother Pelton's Best Rice Waffles, 147
Grandmother Pelton's Blackberry Cordial, 184
Grandmother Pelton's Breakfast Sausage, 115
Grandmother Pelton's Creamed Carrots, 61
Grandmother Pelton's Dainty

Steamed Fig Pudding, 163, 164

Grandmother Pelton's Favorite Old-Time Molasses Candy, 240, 241

Grandmother Pelton's Fried Pickled Tripe, 76

Grandmother Pelton's Frizzled Lamb, 101

Grandmother Pelton's Raspberry Granite (ice cream), 195, 196

Grandmother Pelton's Secret Walnut Catsup, 221

Grandmother Pelton's Sliced Cucumber Pickles, 234, 235

Grandmother Pelton's Royal Consommé Soup, 29, 30

Grandmother Pelton's Strawberry Dumplings, 203, 204

Grandmother Pelton's Veal Fricassee, 92, 93

Grandmother Pelton's Walnut Sandwiches, 189

Grandmother's Finest Lobster Cutlets, 42

Grandpa Pelton's Favorite Old-Fashioned Veal Loaf, 94

Grant, Julia, 32, 33

Grant, General, 32, 43

Grape Jelly (green), 213, 214

Grape Jelly (white), 213

Grape Salad, 154, 155

Grape Sherbet, 198

Great-Aunt Beverly Jo's Chicken Sandwiches, 191

Great-Aunt Beverly Jo's Fancy Fricassee, 126

Great-Aunt Beverly Jo's Glazed Fruits and Nuts, 242

Great-Aunt Beverly Jo's Milk Pudding Sauce, 166

Great-Aunt Carol Ann's Baked Deviled Fish, 47, 48

Great-Aunt Carol Ann's Brisket Delight, 74

Great-Aunt Carol Ann's Pork Steaks, 109

Great-Aunt Goldie's Favorite Beef Liver, 80

Great-Aunt Marilyn's Baked Leg of Lamb, 100

Great-Aunt Marilyn's Baked Salmon Balls, 49

Great-Aunt Marilyn's Braised Beef, 81

Great-Aunt Mary's Irish Stew of the Good Old Days, 78, 79

Great-Aunt Mary's Strawberry Float, 207

Great-Aunt Ruth's Fried Oysters, 38

Great-Aunt Ruth's Old-Time Deviled Egg Sandwiches, 188

Great-Aunt Ruth's Old-Time Pickled Onions, 230, 231

Great-Aunt Shirley's Chocolate Ice Cream, 197

Great-Aunt Shirley's Old-Time Waffles, 143

Great-Aunt Shirley's Puree of Green Pea Soup, 26

Great-Granddad's Favorite Potato Cakes, 53, 54

Great-Grandfather Mitchell's Favorite Frozen Rice, 199

Great-Grandmother Mitchell's Baked Apple Pudding, 157, 158

Great-Grandmother Mitchell's Braised Fowl, 124, 125

Great-Grandmother Mitchell's Brandy Catsup, 219

Great-Grandmother Mitchell's Brandy Sauce Delight, 166, 167

Great-Grandmother Mitchell's Broiled Steaks, 71, 72

Great-Grandmother Mitchell's Canned Fruit Tips, 209, 210

Great-Grandmother Mitchell's Celery-Cheese Sandwiches, 190

Great-Grandmother Mitchell's Chocolate Carmels, 240

Great-Grandmother Mitchell's Currant Shrub, 183

Great-Grandmother Mitchell's Custard Ice Cream, 195

Great-Grandmother Mitchell's Fancy Tomato Sauce, 177, 178

Great-Grandmother Mitchell's Fish Pointers, 35, 36

Great-Grandmother Mitchell's Homemade Mayonnaise, 248

Great-Grandmother Mitchell's Lamb Fricassee, 98

Great-Grandmother Mitchell's Meat Pie, 82, 83

Great-Grandmother Mitchell's Mock Turtle Soup, 25

Great-Grandmother Mitchell's Old-Fashioned Soup Stocks, 20, 21, 22

Great-Grandmother Mitchell's Old-Time Peach Trifle, 205, 206

Great-Grandmother Mitchell's Old-Time Salmon Salad, 151, 152

Great-Grandmother Mitchell's Oyster Catsup, 222, 223

Great-Grandmother Mitchell's Pickled Cabbage, 232, 233

Great-Grandmother Mitchell's Points on Candy Making, 238

Great-Grandmother Mitchell's Prize Raised Fritters, 142

Great-Grandmother Mitchell's Roast Chicken, 118, 119

Great-Grandmother Mitchell's Roast Veal, 85, 86

Great-Grandmother Mitchell's Salmon Sandwiches, 187

Great-Grandmother Mitchell's Salt-Cured Boiled Ham, 110, 111

Great-Grandmother Mitchell's Spinach Recipes, 58

Great-Grandmother Mitchell's Stuffed Round Steak, 77

Great-Grandmother Mitchell's Tips on Boiled Eggs, 138

Great-Grandmother Mitchell's Turkey Stuffings, 244, 245

Great-Grandmother's Cream Cherries, 239

Great-Grandmother's Cream Chocolates, 239

Great-Grandmother's Cream Dates, 239

Great-Grandmother's Fruit Creams, 238

Great-Grandmother's Walnut Creams, 238

Great-Grandmother Shaw's Basic Brown Sauce, 173, 174

Great-Grandmother Shaw's Best Beef Roast, 73

Great-Grandmother Shaw's Currant Jelly Sauce, 174

Great-Grandmother Shaw's Elderberry Catsup, 226

Great-Grandmother Shaw's Escalloped Oysters, 39

Great-Grandmother Shaw's Fabulous Stuffed Fillet, 75

Great-Grandmother Shaw's French Cream Candy, 238, 239

Great-Grandmother Shaw's Gooseberry Fool, 202, 203

Great-Grandmother Shaw's Ham with Eggs, 139

Great-Grandmother Shaw's Ice Cream Pointers, 193, 194

Great-Grandmother Shaw's Mushroom Sauce, 174

Great-Grandmother Shaw's Olive Sauce, 174

Great-Grandmother Shaw's Omelet Sandwiches, 192

Great-Grandmother Shaw's Old-Time Christmas Pudding, 164

Great-Grandmother Shaw's Oxtail Soup, 24, 25

Great-Grandmother Shaw's Ox Tongue Treats, 82

Great-Grandmother Shaw's Pickled Butternuts and Walnuts, 228, 229

Great-Grandmother Shaw's Potato Recipes, 53, 54

Great-Grandmother Shaw's Preserved Pears, 210, 211

Great-Grandmother Shaw's Raspberry Shrub, 182, 183

Great-Grandmother Shaw's Roast Lamb, 97, 98

Great-Grandmother Shaw's Roast Leg of Pork, 108

Great-Grandmother Shaw's Roast Turkey, 118

Great-Grandmother Shaw's Salt-Cured Ham Boiled in Cider, 111, 112

Great-Grandmother Shaw's Tips on Brook Trout, 46, 47

Great-Grandmother Shaw's Tomato Catsup, 220

Great-Grandmother Shaw's Veal Pie, 89, 90

Great-Grandmother Shaw's Yorkshire Pudding, 246

Great-Great-Grandmother Daniels' Breaded Eggs, 137

Great-Great-Grandmother Daniels' Lettuce Sandwiches, 190

Great-Great-Grandmother Daniels' Mushrooms, 65, 66

Great-Great-Grandmother Daniels' Neapolitan Pudding, 161, 162

Great-Great-Grandmother Daniels' Orange Marmalade, 216, 217

Great-Great-Grandmother Daniels' Planked Fish, 48, 49

Great-Great-Grandmother Daniels' Pork and Peas Pudding, 107

Great-Great-Grandmother Daniels'

Roast Duck, 119, 120

Great-Great-Grandmother Daniels' Split Pea Soup, 31, 32

Great-Great-Grandmother Daniels' Sponge Fritters, 144, 145

Great-Great-Grandmother Daniels' Veal Stew, 88

Great-Great-Grandmother Horton's Ageless Catsup, 224

Great-Great-Grandmother Horton's Baked Custard, 205

Great-Great-Grandmother Horton's Best Chicken Salad, 150

Great-Great-Grandmother Horton's Calf's Foot Broth, 185

Great-Great-Grandmother Horton's Calf's Head Soup, 23, 24

Great-Great-Grandmother Horton's Creamy Hard Sauce, 164, 165

Great-Great-Grandmother Horton's Cucumber Soup, 28

Great-Great-Grandmother Horton's Currant Jelly, 212

Great-Great-Grandmother Horton's Early 1800 Chicken Potpie, 122, 123

Great-Great-Grandmother Horton's 1824 Omelette Aux Fines, 132, 133

Great-Great-Grandmother Horton's Fried Drop Cakes, 144

Great-Great-Grandmother Horton's Fried Fish, 44, 45

Great-Great-Grandmother Horton's Green Corn Recipes, 62

Great-Great-Grandmother Horton's Hard Candies, 241, 242

Great-Great-Grandmother Horton's Lamb Pie, 99

Great-Great-Grandmother Horton's Milk Sherbet, 197, 198

Great-Great-Grandmother Horton's Old-Time Sweetbreads, 91, 92

Great-Great-Grandmother Horton's

Original Indian Pudding, 160
Great-Great-Grandmother Horton's Other Recipes (eggs), 133
Great-Great-Grandmother Horton's Roasted Pig, 104, 105
Great-Great-Grandmother Horton's Roast Goose, 128
Great-Great-Grandmother Horton's Roast Pig, 250
Great-Great-Grandmother Horton's Scrapple, 112, 113
Great-Great-Grandmother Horton's Souse, 234
Great-Great-Grandmother Horton's Way to Corn Beef, 231, 232
Great-Great-Grandmother Northrup's Baked Beans, 63
Great-Great-Grandmother Northrup's Baked Fish, 43, 44
Great-Great-Grandmother Northrup's Blackberry Jelly, 214
Great-Great-Grandmother Northrup's Brown Fricassee, 126, 127
Great-Great-Grandmother Northrup's Fruit Bread Pudding, 158, 159
Great-Great-Grandmother Northrup's Homemade Sausage, 113, 114
Great-Great-Grandmother Northrup's Jellied Veal, 95
Great-Great-Grandmother Northrup's Nougats (candy), 242
Great-Great-Grandmother Northrup's Roast Pig's Head, 106
Great-Great-Grandmother Northrup's Sweet Baked Omelet, 135
Green Gooseberry Tarts, 207, 208
Green Grape Jelly, 213, 214
Green Pea Soup, 26
Greens, Cooking, 57
Griddle Cakes, Bread, 140, 141

Halibut, Broiled, 38
Ham and Chicken Pie, 108
Hamburg, 83

Ham, Salt-Cured (baked), 111, 112
Ham, Salt-Cured (boiled), 110, 111
Ham, Smothered, 112
Hard Candy, 241, 242
Hard Sauce (creamy), 164, 165
Hashed Steak, 79
Hash with Eggs, 139
Heart, Corned Beef, 236
Heart, Stuffed (beef), 79
Hollandaise Potatoes in Early New York, 55
Hollandaise Sauce, 172
Homemade Mayonnaise, 248
Homemade Mustard, 219, 220
Homemade Taffy, 243
Horseradish Vinegar, 226
Horton, David, 36, 37
Horton, Great-Great-Grandmother, 19, 23, 28, 36, 37, 40, 41, 44, 60, 62, 91, 99, 102, 104, 112, 113, 117, 122, 128, 133, 144, 150, 153, 160, 164, 176, 180, 185, 186, 187, 197, 200, 205, 207, 212, 213, 215, 216, 224, 231, 234, 241, 245, 248, 250
Hot Chocolate, 182

Ice Cream Making Pointers, 193, 194
Indian Pudding, 160
Irish Stew, 78, 79

Jackson, Andrew, 154
Jam, Blackberry, 215, 216
Jam Pointers, 212
Jam, Rhubarb, 215
Jefferson's Favorite Horseradish Vinegar, 226
Jefferson, Thomas, 206, 226
Jellied Veal, 95
Jellies, Jams and Marmalades, 212, 213, 214, 215, 216, 217
Jelly, Apple, 214, 215
Jelly, Blackberry, 214

Jelly, Currant, 212
Jelly, Green Grape, 213, 214
Jelly, Gooseberry, 214
Jelly Omelet, 136
Jelly Pointers, 212
Jelly Sauce, Currant, 174
Jelly Sauce (puddings), 167
Jelly, White Grape, 213
Johnston, Sir William, 94
John Quincy Adams' Favorite Hollandaise Sauce, 172
Julia D. Grant's Cream of Celery Soup, 32

Ketchup, Tomato, 225
Kidneys, Fried, 81, 82
Kidneys, Stewed, 81
Kieft, Willem, 176

Lafayette, General, 132, 133
Lamb, Boiled, 98
Lamb, Charles, 104
Lamb Chops, 100
Lamb, Christmas, 101, 102
Lamb Cookery, 96, 97, 98, 99, 100, 101, 102
Lamb Cutlets, 100, 101
Lamb Fricassee, 98
Lamb, Frizzled, 101
Lamb, Leg (baked), 100
Lamb Pie, 99
Lamb, Roast, 97, 101, 102
Lamb Stew, 99
Lee, General, 39
Lemon Catsup, 223
Lemon Pie, Transparent, 203
Lemon Pudding, 160
Lemon Sauce, 165, 166
Lemons, Frozen (ice cream), 196, 197
Lettuce Sandwich, 190
Lincoln, President, 48
Liver, Beef, 80

Lobster Cutlets, 42
Lobster, Escalloped, 41
Lobster Newburg, 42
Lobster, Plain, 40, 41
Lobster Salad as John Adams Liked It Best, 148, 149
Lobster Soup, 33
Lyonnaise Potatoes, 54

Macaroni Pudding, 161
Macaroni with Codfish—A Lincoln Favorite, 48
Macedoine, Frozen (ice cream), 196
Madison, Dolly, 201
Making Old-Fashioned Natural Meat Stock, 21
Marilyn, Great-Aunt, 49, 81, 100
Marmalade, Banbury, 216
Marmalade, Orange, 216, 217
Marmalade Pointers, 212
Martha Washington's Best Fish Chowder, 36, 37
Martha Washington's Clam Chowder, 37
Martha Washington's Old-Fashioned Jelly Sauce, 167
Martha Washington's White Almond Soup, 22, 23
Mary, Great-Aunt, 78, 207
Mashed Potatoes, 53
Mayonnaise, Homemade, 248
Meat Pie (beef), 82, 83
Meat Sauce, 170
Meat Stock (soups), 20, 21, 22
Milk Pudding Sauce, 166
Milk Sherbet, 197, 198
Mint Sauce (roast lamb), 174, 175
Mississippi Plantation-Style Soft Fries, 57
Mitchell, Great-Grandfather, 199
Mitchell, Great-Grandmother, 25, 34, 35, 42, 46, 58, 69, 71, 72, 77, 82, 85, 98, 103, 110, 116, 117,

118, 124, 131, 138, 142, 151, 156, 157, 166, 177, 183, 187, 190, 195, 199, 205, 209, 219, 222, 232, 238, 240, 244, 248

Mock Turtle Soup, 25

Molasses Candy, 240, 241

Monroe, James, 87, 88

Mrs. Horton's Finest Turkey Stuffing, 245

Mrs. Horton's Old-Time Salad Cream Supreme, 248, 249

Mulligatawny Soup of the Civil War Period, 31

Mushroom and Oyster Stuffing, 245

Mushrooms, 65, 66

Mushroom Sauce (meat), 174

Mustard, Homemade, 219, 220

Nasturtium Sandwich, 189

Neapolitan Pudding, 161, 162

New England Boiled Dinner, 246, 247

Northrup, Great-Great-Grandmother, 43, 63, 95, 106, 113, 114, 126, 135, 158, 214, 242

Notes On Old-Time Natural Soup Stocks, 20, 21

Nougats (candy), 242

Nut Candy, 240

Nuts, Glazed, 242

Old Atlanta Simple Chicken Salad, 153

Old Boston Potato Casserole, 55, 56

Old Charleston Chicken Broth with Rice, 32

Olden-Day Asparagus Cookery, 60

Olden-Day Cucumber Sandwiches, 191

Olden-Day Lyonnaise Potatoes, 54

Olden-Day Oyster Purses, 42, 43

Olden-Day Philadelphia Peach Ice Cream, 195

Old-Fashioned Asparagus Omelet, 133

Old-Fashioned Banana Ice Cream, 194

Old-Fashioned Blackberry Flummery, 204

Old-Fashioned Cauliflower Omelet, 133

Old-Fashioned Cottage Cheese, 251

Old-Fashioned Escalloped Corn and Tomatoes, 62

Old-Fashioned Fillet of Beef, 75

Old-Fashioned French Dressing, 250

Old-Fashioned Onion Vinegar, 223, 224

Old-Fashioned Oyster Salad, 52

Old-Fashioned Peach Ice Cream, 194

Old-Fashioned Pistachio Ice Cream, 195

Old-Fashioned Pointers on Jellies, Jams and Marmalades, 212

Old-Fashioned Ragout of Turkey, 122

Old-Fashioned Raised Doughnuts, 146

Old-Fashioned Sea Foam Candy Treat, 241

Old-Fashioned Southern Broiled Chicken, 127

Old-Fashioned Southern Stewed Pork, 105, 106

Old-Fashioned String Bean Cookery, 59, 60

Old-Fashioned Tomato Omelet, 133

Old Massachusetts Baked Plum Pudding Delight, 162, 163

Old New England Apple Cider Vinegar, 222

Old New England Boiled Lamb, 98

Old New England Boiled Poultry Recipes, 120

Old New England Caper Sauce, 175

Old New England Cottage Cheese, 251
Old New England Court Bouillon, 46
Old New England Frozen Macedoine (ice cream), 196
Old New Hampshire Baked Salt Pork, 114, 115
Old New Orleans Blanquette of Chicken, 129, 130
Old New Orleans Creamed Oysters, 37, 38
Old New Orleans French Pancakes, 142, 143
Old New Orleans Plantation Chips, 57
Old New Orleans Pork Chops with Apples, 110
Old Plantation Mint Sauce, 174, 175
Old Rhode Island Oyster Stew, 50, 51
Old South Carolina Fricasseed Eggs, 136, 137
Old Southern Beefsteak with Olives or Mushrooms, 72, 73
Old Southern Oyster Fricassee, 36
Old Southern Plantation Blackberry Jam, 215, 216
Old Southern Salad Sandwiches, 190, 191
Old Southern Sweet Fried Omelet Souffle, 134
Old-Time Baked Green Corn, 62
Old-Time Beef Cooking Pointers, 70, 71
Old-Time Cabbage Cookery, 65
Old-Time Chicken Terrapin, 129
Old-Time Consommé Recipes of Grandmother Collister, 29
Old-Time Homemade Mustard, 219, 220
Old-Time Minced Spinach, 58

Old-Time New Hampshire Grape Sherbet, 198
Old-Time Notes on Caring for Beef, 69, 70
Old-Time Notes on Lamb, 96, 97
Old-Time Notes on Poultry, 117, 118
Old-Time Peas, 60
Old-Time Rhode Island Lobster Soup, 33
Old-Time Rules for Good Custard Making, 200, 201
Old-Time Salad Dressing, 248, 249, 250
Old-Time Tips on Buying Coffee, 181
Old Virginia Roast Christmas Lamb, 101, 102
Old Virginia-Style Fish Souffle, 49
Old Western Fried Beef Cakes, 79, 80
Old Western Egg and Cheese Sandwiches, 188
Olive-Cream Cheese Sandwich, 191
Olive Sandwich, 189
Olive Sauce (meat), 174
Omelet, Apple, 135
Omelet, Asparagus, 133
Omelet, Cauliflower, 133
Omelet (herbs), 132, 133
Omelet, Potato, 137
Omelet, Puff, 138, 139
Omelet Sandwich, 192
Omelet Souffle, 134
Omelet, Sweet (baked), 135
Omelet, Sweet (souffle), 134
Omelet, Tomato, 133
Omelet with Jelly, 136
Onions, Boiled, 59
Onions, Pickled, 230, 231
Onion Vinegar, 223, 224
Orange and Rhubarb Jam, 215

Orange Marmalade, 216, 217
Ordinary Old-Fashioned Stuffing, 245
Original Civil War Period Omelet with Jelly, 136
Original Olden-Day Apple Jelly, 214, 215
Original Olden-Day Veal Croquettes, 93
Original Old New England Veal with Oysters, 86, 87
Original Old-Time Green Grape Jelly, 213, 214
Original Old-Time Lemon Pudding, 166
Original Old-Time Popcorn Candy, 243
Original Old-Time Tartar Sauce, 172, 173
Original Old Vermont Delmonico Potatoes, 56
Original Plantation-Style Nut Candy, 240
Original Plantation-Style Pan Tomatoes, 59
Ox Tail Soup, 24, 25
Ox Tongue, Broiled, 82
Ox Tongue, Roasted
Oyster and Mushroom Stuffing, 245
Oyster Catsup, 222, 223
Oyster Fricassee, 36
Oyster Pie, 39
Oyster Purses, 42, 43
Oyster Salad, 152
Oyster Sauce, 171, 172
Oysters, Broiled, 40
Oysters, Creamed, 37, 38
Oysters, Escalloped, 39
Oysters, Fried, 38
Oyster Stew, 50, 51

Pancakes (bread), 140, 141

Pancakes (buckwheat), 141
Pancakes, French, 142, 143
Pancakes (fried drop), 144
Parsnips, 61
Pea and Bean Recipes, 59, 60
Peach Batter Pudding, 163
Peach Ice Cream, 194, 195
Peach Trifle (custard), 205, 206
Pears, Preserved, 210, 211
Peas, Fresh, 60
Pea Soup, 26, 31, 32
Pelton, Frank Curtis, 94, 171
Pelton, Grandmother, 29, 76, 83, 92, 101, 115, 147, 163, 184, 189, 195, 203, 221, 234
Pelton, Grandpa, 94, 240
Pepper Vinegar in Early America, 225
Pickled Butternuts and Walnuts, 228, 229
Pickled Cabbage, 232, 233
Pickled Cauliflower in the Olden Days, 233
Pickled Cucumbers, 234, 235
Pickled Onions, 230, 231
Pickled Tomatoes, 235
Pickled Tripe (fried), 76
Pickled Watermelon Rind, 229, 230
Pie, Transparent Lemon, 203
Pig, Roast, 104, 105
Pig, Roast (stuffing), 250
Pig's Head, Roast, 106
Pistachio Ice Cream, 195
Plain Lobster, 40, 41
Planked Fish, 48, 49
Plantation-Style Cottage Cheese, 251
Plum Pudding, 156, 157, 162, 163
Points on Making Old-Time Natural Soups, 19, 20
Polk, James, 45
Polk, Sarah, 45

Popcorn Candy, 243
Popular Olden-Day Pork Chops, 110
Popular Old-Time Olive Sandwiches, 189
Pork and Peas Pudding, 107
Pork Chops, 110
Pork Cookery, 103, 104, 105, 106, 107, 108, 109, 110, 111, 112, 113, 114, 115
Pork Leg (roast), 108
Pork Pie (Cheshire), 109
Pork Potpie, 106, 107
Pork, Salt, 113
Pork, Salt (baked), 114, 115
Pork Sausage, 113, 114
Pork Steak, 109
Pork, Stewed, 105, 106
Potato Casserole, 55, 56
Potato Omelet, 137, 138
Potato Pot Soup of Colonial Days, 24
Potato Recipes, 24, 53, 54, 55, 56, 57
Potato Salad (German), 153
Potatoes, Baked, 54
Potatoes, Boiled, 53
Potato Cakes, 53, 54
Potatoes, Delmonico, 56
Potatoes, Fried, 57
Potatoes, Hollandaise, 55
Potatoes, Lyonnaise, 54, 55
Potatoes, Mashed, 53
Potatoes, Sweet (fried), 56
Potato Soup, 24
Poultry, Boiled, 120, 121
Poultry Cookery, 116, 117, 118, 119, 120, 121, 122, 123, 124, 125, 126, 127, 128, 129, 130
Preserved Pears, 210, 211
President Andrew Jackson, 154
Presidential Grape Salad—A Favorite of Andrew Jackson, 154, 155
President James Monroe, 87, 88

President James Polk, 45
President John Adams, 79, 148, 149
President John Quincy Adams, 169, 172
Presidents: Adams, John, 79, 148, 149; Adams, John Quincy, 169, 172; Davis, Jefferson, 71; Grant, Ulysses, 32, 33; Jackson, Andrew, 154; Jefferson, Thomas, 206, 226; Lincoln, Abraham, 48; Monroe, James, 87, 88; Polk, James, 45; Taylor, Zachary, 169, 171; Washington, George, 26, 37, 202
President Zachary Taylor, 169, 171
Pressed Beef, 75, 76
Prized Old-Fashioned Salt-Fish Chowder, 50
Prune Whip, 208
Pudding, Frozen (ice cream), 199

Quick, Tom, 94

Raised Doughnuts, 146
Raisin Wine, 183
Raspberry Granite (ice cream), 195, 196
Raspberry Shrub (drink), 182, 183
Real Early American Kidney Recipes, 81, 82
Real Old-Fashioned Banbury Marmalade, 216
Real Old-Fashioned Creamed Rice Soup, 27, 28
Real Old-Fashioned Frozen Pudding Cream, 199
Real Old-Fashioned Ham and Chicken Pie, 108
Real Old-Fashioned Hot Chocolate, 182
Real Old-Fashioned Lamb Cutlets, 100, 101
Real Old-Fashioned Macaroni Pudding, 161

Real Old-Fashioned Mashed Potatoes, 53
Real Old-Fashioned New England Boiled Dinner, 246, 247
Real Old-Fashioned Worcestershire Sauce, 175
Real Old-Time Eggplant, 67
Real Old-Time Spiced Currants, 211
Revolutionary Period Poor Man's Soup, 25, 26
Revolutionary Period Salt-Fish Dinner, 47
Rhubarb and Orange Jam, 215
Rice, Boiled, 67
Rice Cookery the Old-Fashioned Way, 67
Rice, Frozen (ice cream), 199
Rice Pudding, 159
Rice Soup (creamed), 27, 28
Rice Waffles, 147
Roast Beef, 73
Roast Breast (veal), 86
Roasted Ox Tongue, 82
Roasted Sweetbreads, 91, 92
Roast Filet (veal), 86
Roasting a Loin (veal), 85, 86
Roast Pig Stuffing, 250
Roughnecks of the Empire, 94
Ruth, Great-Aunt, 38, 188, 230

Salad Cream (dressing), 248, 249
Salad Dressings, 248, 249, 250
Salad Sandwich, 190, 191
Salmon Balls, 49
Salmon Salad, 151, 152
Salmon Sandwich, 187
Salt-Fish Chowder, 50
Salt-Fish Dinner, 47
Salt Pork (baked), 114
Salt Pork and Gravy, 113
Salvation Army, 94
Sarah Polk's Recipe for Boiled Shad, 45, 46

Sausage (breakfast), 115
Sausage (pork), 113, 114
Scrapple (pork), 112, 113
Sea Foam Candy, 241
Seed Vinegar Sauce of 1825, 176
Shad, Broiled, 45, 46
Shaw, Great-Grandmother, 24, 39, 46, 53, 73, 75, 82, 84, 85, 89, 97, 100, 108, 111, 118, 139, 164, 169, 173, 174, 182, 192, 193, 202, 210, 219, 220, 226, 227, 228, 229, 238, 239, 246
Shell Beams, 60
Sherbet, Grape, 198
Sherbet, Milk, 197
Shirley, Great-Aunt, 26, 143, 197
Shrimp Salad, 151
Simple Old-Fashioned Stuffed Dates, 242
Sirloin Tips, 77, 78
Soup, Almond, 22, 23
Soup, Bean, 29
Soup, Beef, 28
Soup, Calf's Head, 23, 24
Soup, Celery, 32, 33
Soup, Chicken, 26, 27, 32
Soup Cooking Pointers, 19, 20, 21, 22
Soup, Corned Beef, 30
Soup, Cucumber, 28
Soup, Giblet, 30, 31
Soup, Green Pea, 26, 31, 32
Soup, Lobster, 33
Soup, Mock Turtle, 25
Soup, Multigatawny, 31
Soup, Ox Tail, 24, 25
Soup, Potato, 24
Soups, Points on Making, 19, 20, 21, 22
Soup, Rice, 27, 28, 32
Soup, Split Pea, 31, 32
Soup Stock (fowl), 22
Soup Stocks (meat), 19, 20, 21, 22

Souse, 234
Special Olden-Day Broiled Halibut, 38
Spiced Currants (canning), 211
Spiced Gooseberries in Early New England, 211, 212
Spinach, Boiled, 58
Spinach, Minced, 58
Split Pea Soup, 31, 32
Sponge Fritters, 145
Squash, 64
Squash, Baked, 64
Squash, Summer, 64
Squash, Winter, 64
Steak, Broiled, 71, 72
Steak Hashed on Toast, 79
Steak, Round, 77
Stew Dumplings, 247
Stewed Beef Kidney, 81
Stewed Chicken in the Colonies, 125
Stewed Green Corn the Old-Fashioned Way, 62
Stewed Sweetbreads, 91
Strawberry Dumplings, 203, 204
Strawberry Float, 207
Stuffed Dates, 242
Stuffing, Chestnut, 245
Stuffing, Old-Fashioned, 245
Stuffing, Oyster and Mushroom, 245
Stuffing, Roast Pig, 250
Stuffing, Turkey, 244, 245
Succotash, 63, 64
Sugar Candy, 239
Sweetbread Salad, 154
Sweetbreads, Broiled, 91
Sweetbreads, Roasted, 91
Sweetbreads, Fried, 91
Sweetbreads, Stewed, 91
Sweet Potatoes, Fried, 56

Taffy, Homemade, 243
Tartar Sauce, 172, 173
Tarts, Green Gooseberry, 207, 208

Tasty Omelet Puff in Early America, 138, 139
Taylor, Zachary, 169, 171
Tea in the Colonies, 181, 182
Thurston, Ben (Colonel), 19
Tomahawks Along the Delaware, 94
To Make Old-Fashioned Boiled Coffee, 180, 181
Tom Alley Sauce (lobster), 176
Tomato Catsup, 220
Tomatoes, Escalloped, 58
Tomatoes, Pan, 59
Tomatoes, Pickled, 235
Tomato Ketchup, 225
Tomato Omelet, 133
Tomato Sauce, 177, 178
Transparent Lemon Pie, 203
Trepp, Captain, 19
Trifle, Peach, 205, 206
Tripe, Pickled (fried), 76
Trout, Brook, 46, 47
Turkey, Boiled, 120
Turkey, Pressed, 129
Turkey, Ragout of, 122
Turkey, Roast, 118
Turkey Scallop, 121, 122
Turkey Stuffing, 244
Turnip Cooking in Early America, 61
Turtle Soup (mock), 25

Uncle Albert's Favorite Baked Fish Sauce, 178
Uncle Albert's Favorite Bean Soup, 29
Uncle Albert's Favorite Cream Cheese-Olive Sandwich, 191
Uncle Albert's Favorite Old-Time Coconut Caramels, 243
Uncle Albert's Special Creamed Chicken Delight, 128
Uncle Arthur's Favorite Orange and Rhubarb Jam, 215

Uncle Art's Basic Meat Sauce, 170
Uncle Art's Best Raw Tomato
  Ketchup, 225
Unrivaled Olden-Day Lemon Sauce,
  165, 166
Unrivaled Old-Fashioned Beefsteak
  Pie, 80
Unrivaled Old-Fashioned Escalloped
  Lobster, 41

Veal Breast, Roast, 86
Veal Cookery, 84, 85, 86, 87, 88,
  89, 90, 91, 92, 93, 94, 95
Veal Croquets, 93
Veal Cutlets, 85
Veal Filet, Roast, 86
Veal Fricassee, 92, 93
Veal, Jellied, 95
Veal Loaf, 94
Veal Pie, 89, 90
Veal Potpie, 93, 94
Veal Roast, 85, 86
Veal Scallop in Vicksburg During
  the Civil War, 90
Veal Steak, 88, 89
Veal Stew, 88
Veal Terrapin, 95
Veal with Oysters, 86, 87
Vegetable Cookery, 52, 53, 54, 55,
  56, 57, 58, 59, 60, 61, 62, 63, 64,
  65, 66, 67
Vera, Cousin, 61
Vinegar, Apple Cider, 222
Vinegar, Celery, 220, 221

Vinegar, Corn, 218
Vinegar, Horseradish, 226
Vinegar, Onion, 223, 224
Vinegar, Pepper, 225
Vinegar Sauce, 176
Vintage Pickled Watermelon Rind
  of 1820, 229, 230
Volunteers of America, 94

Waffles, Old-Time, 143
Waffles, Rice, 147
Walnut Catsup, 221
Walnut Cream Candy, 238
Walnuts and Butternuts, Pickled,
  228, 229
Walnut Sandwich, 189
Washington, George, 26, 37, 202
Washington, Martha, 22, 36, 37,
  167, 201, 202
Watermelon Rind, Pickled, 229,
  230
Whipped Cream in the Good Old
  Days, 252
White Grape Jelly, 213
White Stock (soup), 22
White Wine Sauce in the Confede-
  racy, 165
Wine, Raisin, 183
Wine Sauce (white), 165
Worcestershire Sauce, 175

Ye Olde Plum Pudding of 1820, 156,
  157
Yorkshire Pudding, 246